INTERSECTED

INTERSECTED

Kelli Kossel

Inspiring Voices®
A Service of Guideposts

Scripture taken from the HOLY BIBLE, NEW INTERNATIONAL
VERSION ®. Copyright © 1973, 1978, 1984 by International Bible
Society. Used by permission of Zondervan. All rights reserved.

Inspiring Voices books may be ordered through booksellers or by contacting:

Inspiring Voices
1663 Liberty Drive
Bloomington, IN 47403
www.inspiringvoices.com
1-(866) 697-5313

ISBN: 978-1-4624-0176-5 (sc)
ISBN: 978-1-4624-0175-8 (e)

Library of Congress Control Number: 2012940360

Printed in the United States of America

Inspiring Voices rev. date: 06/07/2012

To my forty brothers and sisters in Christ. "First, I thank my God through Jesus Christ for all of you, because your faith is being reported all over the world" (Romans 1:8). The wisdom imparted through your stories has increased my faith and brought me even closer to the Lord Jesus. Thank you for sharing your lives with the world so that God may be glorified!

"I will lead the blind by ways they have not known, along unfamiliar paths I will guide them; I will turn the darkness into light before them and make the rough places smooth. These are the things I will do; I will not forsake them" (Isaiah 42:16).

Table of Contents

Foreword

Kelli Kossel has a remarkable personal story about her life intersecting with God. That experience set her out on a quest to discover how others came to establish personal faith in Jesus Christ. Contained in *Intersected* is story after story of people who followed their own path but ended up at the same place Kelli arrived.

Reading these stories unveils what God is doing in the lives of people—all kinds of people. The beauty is that God never gives up on us ... He has given Himself for us. In Robert Frost's famous poem, "The Road Not Taken," he wrote:

> Two roads diverged in a wood, and I—
> I took the one less traveled by,
> And that has made all the difference.

Robert Frost wrote those thought provoking words in 1916, yet each of us who has come into a relationship with Christ has approached that intersection and chosen the less-traveled path. I took the one less traveled, and it has made all the difference in my life. I often think back to when my life intersected with Christ in 1972. It seems both so long ago and also like yesterday. There is no other date or decision that has impacted my life more.

Intersected is about the adventures of God's love pursuing people and inviting them to enjoy the life He has always intended for them. You will find one compelling story after another showing how the irresistible love of God, when combined with empty and broken hearts, can transform people into new creations. The result is love, passion, healing, forgiveness, and joy.

What I love, as I read the stories, is the realization that countless others will be inspired by what God has done in and through the lives of those who have shared their story. There is a warm welcome to not only read about others, but also to join the family.

Enjoy the stories and then look in the mirror and ask, "God, is there more of me I can offer? Is there more of You I can experience?"

I'll be waiting for the next book, in which I read your story. Thank you, Kelli!

Steve Johnson, pastor and cofounder of 2xGlobal

Preface

The idea for *Intersected* came to me upon awakening one morning in mid-October of 2010. I knew the instant I woke up that God wanted me to start interviewing Christians to obtain testimonials of how they came to Christ. From the beginning, I felt a sense of urgency—God's assignment would have to take precedence over my other writing projects.

Within one week, God led me to the first person—a man at church whom I knew by face only. When God put it in my heart to approach him and ask if he would share his story with me, my heart started pounding. Thinking, *I will do this for You, God, but You need to give me the right words*, I walked up to the man. Several minutes later, we had a meeting scheduled for the following week!

Over the course of a year, God guided me to various churches to meet new people. He continued leading me to people by giving me a compelling feeling to approach them. Additionally, people I told about this project often referred others to me. In many cases, the day of the interview was the first time I ever saw the person. From the beginning, I stayed out of the way and let God guide me to each person. I did not interview family and friends. In fact, most of the time I didn't even know what a person's story was prior to the meeting. Being saved was the only criterion I looked for. I relied solely on faith that God handpicked every person—only He knew whose stories needed to be included.

I obtained the stories verbally. Before writing each one, I prayed for God to guide my heart, mind, and hands to write the story exactly the way He intended in order to have the most impact. Sometimes that meant contacting a person a second time to get more details. Each person has read the final draft of their story to ensure accuracy and completeness, and each person has granted written permission to include his or her story and other items, such as song lyrics or poems.

I would like to offer sincere thanks to Carol, Erik, and Tami for editing the manuscript. And I would also like to thank Erik and Vin for help with marketing copy.

Introduction

"Come and see what God has done, how awesome his works in man's behalf!" (Psalm 66:5)

I can imagine sharing stories in heaven of the great things God has done in our lives. But ... we don't have to wait until then! The world needs to hear them now more than ever. Sharing our stories is a powerful way of revealing God's glory and power. Seeing how God has transformed others gives us hope that He will do the same for us. No one is too bad to come to God—His light outshines even the darkest past. Nor is anyone too good not to come to Him.

There is little we can be sure of in our world. Bad things will happen. People will let us down. Change is inevitable—in the world, that is. But God is a constant—He never changes. And He never goes back on a promise. God's children can be certain He will never leave them. If we feel abandoned, it is because we have momentarily walked away from Him. He is still at our side, waiting for us to reach out our hand to Him once more. Even though life is hard, God can use any circumstance for His good.

Reading the stories of people who have strong faith can help us catch the same fervor for God. Seeing how alive others are since embracing Christ makes us want the joy that comes from really knowing the Lord. Whether you have been a Christian for many years, are new to the faith, or are simply curious about how God has been at work in people just like you, *Intersected* will provide nourishing food for your hungry soul and generate excitement about how great and awesome God actually is—and how much He loves you.

No matter what your background is, I sincerely hope that *Intersected* challenges you to come closer to God. While every story is inspirational and ends on a positive note, each one is brutally honest about personal shortcomings and lessons learned from God throughout the journey. Learning from the misstep of another person can either point out an area of sin in our lives or prevent us from losing our footing.

June ~ Age 65
From Terror to Unfailing Trust

June lived in terror of her dad. The horrific fear made its home as a constant knot in her stomach; it seized her tongue, causing her to stutter. Speech class didn't help: a Band-Aid wasn't going to fix her gaping wound. Her dad drank continually, often becoming violent. He was verbally abusive as well; he frequently threw harsh insults at June and her mother. June saw him beat her mother again and again, nearly killing her. By the time June turned nine, her dad beat and slapped her upside the head just for walking past him. The police would come, after receiving a call from June's mother, but nothing changed. Because she was afraid of her dad, June spent a lot of time alone in her bedroom. June and her sister even hid in the rafters during one of his drunken rages because he wanted to kill them. Luckily, he passed out before discovering their whereabouts. A day of calm always followed the storm.

Through the mess in their lives, June's mother talked to her about God and shared her faith in Jesus. June's dad only allowed the family to attend church on Christmas Eve and maybe one other day during the year. He never knew they went to church and Sunday school on the weekends he was gone on business, which were few and far between. Hearing her mother talk about praying, and seeing how her prayers were often answered, June began to pray. She prayed for God to keep them safe and that her mother wouldn't miss the bus to work anymore—June's dad would beat her if she did. Her prayers worked: her mother no longer missed the bus!

The sexual molestation began when June was only eleven. She withdrew into herself, becoming even quieter. June had already learned to keep to herself and not talk a lot because kids made fun of her stuttering. Making friends was nearly impossible because she wasn't allowed to have friends over or go to their houses. Kids thought June was stuck up because she always said "no" when they asked her to do something. Of course, she couldn't tell them the real reason for her refusal. Around age fifteen, June mustered up the courage to tell her mother what her dad had been doing to her all those years. They went to the police station where June told her story. Her dad went to prison for five years. She was finally free from him—or was she?

Finally, June could have friends. She started going to a local youth center where the jukebox always played rock and roll and the kids laughed and danced. June had never had so much fun! She even started dating a boy she met there. In the past, when her dad was around, fun and laughter were not allowed. He wouldn't let her look at a boy, much less date one. If June even looked out the window at a boy they passed while driving, her dad reached back and slapped her.

When June was sixteen, her mother died of untreated cancer because she hadn't been allowed to go to the doctor. The house was sold. Her sister ended up in foster care; June was on her own. Homeless. Her boyfriend's kind parents invited her to stay with them. They took June to church and talked about God at home. Within a year, she quit school and got a job at the factory where her boyfriend's mom worked. A woman June befriended at work often spoke to her about God. Even though June didn't understand yet, seeds were being planted. God gently tugged at her heart by continually placing around her people who shared their faith.

Her life was in shambles. She wondered, *Why did my mother have to die? Why is my evil dad still here?* Because her new friends hung out at the bars, June began drinking too much. She liked the numbing effect of alcohol. Pent-up anger toward her dad and a distorted view of sex led her to have cold, meaningless sexual encounters with many men. June wanted to get back at her dad, but eventually realized she was only hurting herself.

Then, at age nineteen, while in a bar with some friends, June met the man she would later marry. He had just gotten out of jail. One messed-up person with another messed-up person! Although they had many ups and downs, their love and commitment has grown strong over the years because God has become an increasingly important part of their lives. God blessed them with two boys. Because neither June nor her husband had loving childhoods, they wanted to do better. She knew God needed to be in their lives because people had talked to her about Him over the years. June took her boys to Sunday school and church. Eventually, she became involved in Bible study classes—the first one focused on how to be a submissive wife. She desperately needed God's help.

In February of 1976, June asked God into her life. He forgave her sins and washed her clean with His blood. June prayed, "Fill me with Your Holy Spirit, and change me." The excitement and happiness she felt were indescribable. She felt different somehow. From then on, God convicted her when she did something wrong and helped her to change. It's been a gradual process, though, because she's needed a lot of changing! She learned to let go of the past and trust God.

After life had taken a turn for the better, more devastation came. Her youngest son, age nineteen, was killed in a car crash by a drunk driver. Heartbroken, June didn't know how she could live without him. *Why did this happen?* she wondered. June lived in a fog for the next five or six years. Although she missed her son dearly, June never felt angry toward God. She knew enough about God's Word to know He had a plan. June trusted Him. She knew God was with her and would give her strength. June started being thankful for what she did have: God, her husband, and her other son. And she was so grateful for having her youngest son for nineteen years. Even though it was a struggle, she continued going to church. Something deep inside told June she needed to be there. By God's grace, she healed and drew even closer to her husband.

About two years later their house burned to ashes, leaving them homeless. During the fire, people came from everywhere to haul furniture and anything they could get out of the burning house. Neighbors offered to store what had been saved in their garages. Although she felt depressed about losing her house so soon after her son's death, June placed her trust in God. June's sister took them in for four months while a new house was built. The house, built in the dead of winter, came together with no problems. This was fortunate because the contractor who worked on their house only built commercial buildings at the time. Clearly, God's hand was at work in every detail. God kept tugging at her heart, bringing her even closer to Himself and her husband. He has shown June there is a reason for everything. God doesn't make mistakes. And He won't give us more than we can handle.

Today, June is a new creation in Christ—off with the old self and on with the new! The Holy Spirit lives in her as a seal of salvation. God has changed the way she thinks. Gone is the "poor me" mentality. June talks to God about everything, like she talks to a friend. June and her husband are blessed with the kind of marriage neither thought they would have—all because God is in their lives. They've been married forty-four years. She offers thanks to the Lord because her mother is with Him and she'll see her again. June forgave her dad years ago. She even felt sorry for him because he was so deceived by Satan. Now she is free of him at last! And free of the hate that once burdened her heart.

June wishes only the best for everyone, including her dad. Even though Satan would love to see her resentful and disgusted with the world because of the devastating events in her life, she isn't. Thanks to God! Because God is a central part of her life, June has abundant joy, peace, contentment, and love for others—feelings she never thought she'd have. She prays, "Abba Father, thank You for loving me. I love You, too."

"May the God of hope fill you with all joy and peace as you trust in him, so that you may overflow with hope by the power of the Holy Spirit" (Romans 15:13).

June's unfailing trust in God is what carried her through the hardships. No matter what happens, she trusts God has a reason for everything. Even though she doesn't always understand why bad things happen, she knows God has a plan for good. June rests in hope, hope that God will carry her through. He always has and always will.

Don ~ Age 71
Disability Is a Small Price to Pay

As a seven-year-old boy studying the catechism, Don vividly recalls being moved by the beatitudes, especially, "Blessed are the pure in heart, for they will see God" (Matthew 5:8). Out of the blue, this Scripture would come to mind and tears would fill his eyes, often while simply walking down the street. Even though Don knew Christ came and died on the cross, he didn't really understand why Christ died for *him*. As he grew older, Don questioned many of the rules and rituals taught by his religion. Aside from going to church, Don basically went about his life giving little thought to God.

Fast forward to July of 1978. Don and his family were celebrating his dad's birthday at the lake. It was a hot summer day. Everyone sat around playing cards and drinking beer. Don's brother wanted to go swimming. Not having any swimming trunks along, Don borrowed a pair and started wading into the lake. Don didn't like getting wet slowly; he preferred to jump right in and get wet all at once. So he decided to get up on the new dock and dive in, even though the water was not very deep. After diving off the dock, his body went numb. Everything turned dark, then light—and his world kept alternating like that. Next thing he knew, his brother was pulling him out of the water. Don lay on the grass motionless. Soon, paramedics came and placed Don on a transfer board and rushed him to the hospital.

Don had broken his neck. He was paralyzed from the upper chest down. Doctors said he would be a quadriplegic for the rest of his life. No more hunting or fishing—his favorite pastimes. Don felt angry that he had to spend the rest of his life in a wheelchair. But he never felt angry toward God. After all, God didn't push him off the dock; he chose to jump.

Four pins were screwed into Don's head to hold his neck in traction while he was secured to a Stryker frame. Every four hours a nurse came in to alternate his position from face up to face down and vice versa. All Don could see was the floor or ceiling. The pins moved each time he was turned (which caused excruciating pain), so Don was afraid of being moved. Helpless and confined to the frame, night was a frightening time. He asked the nurse on duty to turn on the bathroom light at night, but she refused. Her lack of compassion made him feel even more vulnerable.

One day, while Don was face down in the frame, a friend's pastor came to visit. He crawled under the Stryker and lay on his back on the cold floor. He held Don's hand and prayed, "What a loving God whose heart is breaking because of what happened to you." In the weeks to follow, other pastors visited Don. Each one spoke of the love of God. This was the first Don and his wife, Bev, heard of God being full of love for them—previously, they had only been taught to fear punishment from the Lord if they didn't obey the law.

The wife of a Christian friend of Don's from work came to visit regularly. She talked and prayed with Don as she massaged his hands to straighten his fingers—they were starting to curl under. And she gave Don his first Bible. She placed the Bible on a TV tray under Don's head; people turned the pages for him so he could read while on his stomach. He started in the book of John, which he soon referred to as, "God's love letter to us." As Don read, he realized there was something more available to him, that the law didn't bind him. He had freedom in Christ. Finally,

Don understood why Jesus died for him on the cross: to erase his sins so he could stand before God.

After six weeks in the Stryker frame, Don was taken out of the frame around dinnertime and asked what he wanted to eat. Don said he didn't care about eating—he simply wanted to lie on his back in bed and look out the window. He hadn't been able to see outside for a long time. He took in the sunlight, sky, and trees with pure joy. How *wonderful* it felt to be unconfined!

Next, Don was placed in a full body cast with holes in the center of his chest and near each armpit. One day his youngest daughter brought some baby gerbils to the hospital. She set a tiny gerbil on his chest, and it went into the hole! It scurried across Don's chest, peeking its head out of one hole, then another. When a nurse came into the room, the family tried to act like nothing was going on, but they couldn't tell the little critter to stop poking his head out! Luckily Don's daughter was able to snatch up the gerbil when the nurse wasn't looking. This instance provided much needed laughter and relief from the serious reality of his spinal injury.

After the cast was removed, Don began four months of physical and occupational therapy. Knowing that the stronger he became, the sooner he could go home incited Don to work extra hard. He had to learn to hold up his head and chest because they tended to slump forward. His arms were only partially paralyzed, so weights were used to strengthen them.

The time came for Don to go home. He wondered how God could use him in a wheelchair. Just before the accident, Don finished building their house and garage. Interestingly, he chose to make the doorways and opening between the kitchen and living room extra wide, which now made it easy to get around in a wheelchair.

Being confined to a wheelchair meant that his way of life would change forever. Everything took more time, and there were many things Don just couldn't do anymore. Having an indwelling catheter made it impossible to have sexual relations with Bev. At first, Don had a hard time accepting this, but learned that simply holding her close was all he needed.

Don had a difficult time adjusting to his loss of independence in the prime of his life (age thirty-eight). He relied on Bev to bathe and dress him. Since he couldn't work anymore, Bev had to take over as primary breadwinner. He felt like a failure because he couldn't support his family any longer.

Shortly after the accident, Bev became involved in Aglow fellowship. Once a month, when Bev attended meetings, Don burned with anger that she left him alone. At one of the meetings Bev gave her life to Jesus. That same evening she prayed that Don wouldn't be angry when she returned home. Not only was he not angry, he asked her to tell him what she had been doing at the meetings! This opened the door for Bev to tell him how she had just accepted Jesus as her Lord and Savior.

A few years later, Don sat in the backroom listening to a tape by Don Francisco entitled *Got to Tell Somebody*. The last song, "Too Small a Price," pierced his heart that day. He thought about the two criminals who were crucified next to Jesus. How one of them said, "Jesus, remember me when you come into your kingdom." Jesus answered him, "I tell you the truth, today you will be with me in paradise" (Luke 23:42–43). The song continued, "It was still too small a price to be allowed to hear those words and to die beside the Christ." What great love Jesus had for the man! Tears rolled down Don's cheeks as he said, "Jesus, what a privilege it must have been to die beside You. I want to be with You, too." Then and there, Don gave his life to Christ. When Bev returned home from work that day, she couldn't help but notice a difference in Don. He looked happier and more at peace.

After coming to Christ, love, kindness, and mercy replaced his anger. Don's fighting spirit returned, and he thought to himself, *I'm going to be a quadriplegic, so I'm going to be the best quadriplegic I can be.* He accepted his disability, yet pushed the limits of what he could do.

His dependency shifted from Bev to Christ, which allowed Don to see her as his beloved wife rather than his caregiver. He and Bev had grown apart while raising their children. Once the kids were out of the house, Don and Bev realized they didn't have much of a relationship left. They needed to reconnect. Don and Bev's marriage grew stronger as Christ became the focal point of Don's life.

Over the years, God has always taken care of Don. Whenever he needed help, someone seemed to show up at just the right time. For instance, Don and Bev got home around midnight one evening. It was the middle of winter, bitter cold, and the wheelchair ramp was slick with ice. Bev couldn't get him up the ramp by herself. She considered going into the house to get blankets so they could sleep in the car overnight. Just then, a friend happened to come by and ask if they needed any help. Did they ever! They were able to get Don into the house with some difficulty. They both thought, *What a blessing to be in the comfort of our warm house!*

Another time, Don's fishing pole got caught under his wheelchair as he went down a ramp. He slammed into the side of the house, flipped out of the chair, and went flying onto the driveway. Before Don had time to worry, his nephew (and fishing partner) came up the driveway and helped Don back into his wheelchair. Even though his hands were bloody and he was scraped up, Don still insisted on going fishing. After all, he wasn't bleeding too badly! Then he ended up falling off the dock into the water and discovered he could swim! Needless to say, Bev wasn't too happy with him when he returned home.

He has ended up at the hospital several times with injuries that most quadriplegics wouldn't easily get. Hospital staff always questioned Bev as to how he got injured because they thought she must have abused him. They were particularly puzzled when

Don came in with a broken leg, asking, "How does a quadriplegic break his leg?" Bev pointed at Don and said, "Let him tell you." As it turned out, Don was sitting with his legs crossed doing yoga when Bev told him that his knees needed to be closer to the floor. Well Don pushed on his knees and heard a loud crack. A bone connected to his knee had broken!

Another time, Don was in the backyard trying to take down the dog pen. Using a crowbar, he pulled out staples that held the wire in place. One staple came out after he applied a great deal of force, and this action propelled Don out of his wheelchair and onto his right ankle.

In yet another instance, a large piece of wood forcefully struck him between his nose and upper lip, knocking him unconscious. And he has the "battle scar" to prove it.

Even more difficult than having to spend the rest of his life in a wheelchair was losing his son in 1993. At the age of thirty, his son went to bed on a Wednesday night and never woke up. He left behind a wife and six children. At first, Don felt completely numb; he couldn't believe his son was actually gone. Knowing his son had given his life to Jesus provided much needed comfort, though. Many people came up to Don and Bev at the funeral and told them how their son had witnessed to them about Christ. As hard as it was to lose his son, he pondered how difficult it must have been for God to give up His only Son.

Don has chosen to live life to the fullest. When challenges arise, he finds ways to overcome them. He's good at rigging up devices that increase his independence. An avid outdoorsman at heart, Don has found creative ways to go fishing and hunting, despite the fact that doctors said he'd never enjoy these activities again. For instance, he specially designed a lapboard to hold his gun. And he secured Velcro onto the pistol grips and a glove to keep the gun in his hand—he then uses his other hand to pull the trigger. A room in his house is filled with antlers of deer that Don has shot since the accident. He can drive a car using hand controls as long as someone is available to help him in and out of the car. Despite not having fine motor control, the walls in Don's house are covered with beautiful watercolor paintings of deer, fish, and other wildlife—he just holds the paintbrush with both hands. His paintings are even more amazing given the fact that he's colorblind.

Things take a lot longer to do now. For instance, Don still makes sparkly, colorful flies for fishing, but before the accident he could make one in fifteen minutes and now it takes him an hour and a half. His response? "Oh, well." Rather than getting frustrated, he accepts his "new normal."

Today, Don views the accident as the best thing that ever happened to him because it led him to the Lord. He knew about God before, but he didn't understand God's character or have any kind of relationship with Him. Don doesn't know where he'd be without Christ in his life, but doubts he would even be alive. His hope in Christ is at the forefront of his life. Love has been the biggest blessing since receiving the Lord: he has experienced firsthand the undeserved love and favor God has for His children.

Sometimes Don worries what will happen to him if Bev passes first, but then he remembers how faithful God has been over the years sending people to him whenever he needs help. Don rests in God's promise to care for him. In Don's words, "I belong to Jesus. I'm His son."

He envisions himself standing before God in heaven and being asked, "What have you done to deserve being here?" Don plans on replying in the following way: "I bring nothing. I don't deserve to be here. It's all because of what Jesus has done."

"But whatever was to my profit I now consider loss for the sake of Christ. What is more, I consider everything a loss compared to the surpassing greatness of knowing Christ Jesus my Lord, for whose sake I have lost all

things. I consider them rubbish, that I may gain Christ"
(Philippians 3:7-8).

Even though Don's life changed forever after the accident, he considers everything he lost a small price to pay for the relationship he gained with Christ.

Brenda ~ Age 44
Stepping out of the Boat

Brenda treated God like a smorgasbord: she would go to Him when she needed Him, get filled up, and then forget about Him when things were going well. She cannot remember a time when she didn't believe in God. He was always there. Church and various Christian activities had become a matter of habit over the years (rather than a matter of the heart). She had "head knowledge" about God, but she wasn't living for Him.

As a result of only allowing God to be known in her head and not surrendering her heart to Him, she became pregnant while still in college. Brenda and her boyfriend married. Her husband is a warm-hearted, generous man, but he is not a believer. Although compatible in every other way, the spiritual connection has always been absent. The spiritual chasm in their marriage has sometimes led Brenda away from the Lord.

Because she was busy being a wife and mother to her three little boys, Brenda didn't always take time out for God. Throughout an eight-year period when her boys were very young, she didn't go to church—she just couldn't get herself and the boys ready for church all by herself. Exhausted from daily life, Brenda lost her connection to God. She had no support system.

Insecurities about her kids and husband led her to become overly protective. Brenda figured that nothing bad would happen to them as long as they were with her because she knew the Lord, and He loved her.

Then she fell into a black hole of depression, fear, and anxiety. After counseling and anti-depression medication, God pulled Brenda out of the darkness. She found encouragement from God during this difficult time and started going to church again. Alone.

As her boys got older, Brenda went to work full-time. With a great job and family, life was perfect—from the outside. But Brenda was still missing the boat when it came to God. Knowing there was something absent in her life, and desperate for a deeper connection to God, she cried out, "Lord, I'm tired of this merry-go-round of finding and engaging with You and then being sucked back into the world. I need You to do something in my life that will change me forever so I will never fall backward in my walk with You again. From this day on, I choose to walk forward with You."

Several weeks later, the phone rang. Her mom called to let her know their church was organizing a mission trip. She asked Brenda to prayerfully consider going. Her head buzzed with all sorts of reasons not to go: *How can I leave my boys and husband? What about work? What if my husband doesn't approve? I'm afraid to fly!* Deep in her heart, though, she knew God wanted her to go. So she talked to her husband, and he said it was fine with him. She thought, *What? He agreed so easily! This means I'm really going!*

The trip involved a yearlong preparation. Brenda needed to save and raise a certain amount of money that would be paid in regular installments. However, one time she found herself eighty dollars short of the amount needed for the next installment. Two days before she had to send the money, though, Brenda received a letter from a couple she'd known her whole life but had grown apart from over the years. Inside the letter was a check! She could tell that the woman—who had been like a second mother to Brenda as a child—had started to write fifty on the check, but she changed her mind and made it eighty. She even wrote a note saying that she didn't know why, but God told her she was supposed to send eighty dollars. Thanks to God for her obedience!

In another instance, Brenda realized she still needed a travel alarm clock for the trip. Shortly thereafter, her office had a golf outing and a raffle at the end of the day—her gift was a travel alarm clock! One more blessing from the Lord!

While preparing for the trip, Brenda had anxiety about flying and leaving her husband and boys. *What if something happens to them while I'm gone?* While sitting in her bedroom one day, she prayed to the Lord, "I can't go 10,000 miles away carrying all of this anxiety and fear. I give it all to You, God." In that moment, Brenda totally surrendered herself to the Lord, and a feeling of absolute peace washed over her. Brenda came to experience the joy of truly knowing the Lord through complete surrender that day. God changed her and amazing things started happening. Brenda truly felt and recognized the hand of God working in her life.

Over the years, God has spoken to her in very palpable ways. One of the most enduring instances relates to a simple coin: the dime. It all started when Brenda's dad died unexpectedly at the age of forty-two from an aneurism—not long after her first son was born. While socializing with family and friends the afternoon of his funeral, a phone call came for Brenda's mom, who was a contact person for their church. Someone from church had dropped off the monthly church newsletter mailing at the post office with a check that morning. The post office was calling to let her know they were ten cents short. Of course, the person at the post office had no idea of the grief that Brenda's mom and family were going through at the time. Brenda's mom offered a quick response; she said someone would take care of it. But that matter seemed like a great obstacle in light of the funeral.

Later that day, Brenda led guests to their cars to say good-bye, and while walking back to the house, something in the lawn caught her eye: a reflection. Brenda walked over to see what was shining in the lawn—it was a dime! She knelt down in the soft grass crying, "Lord, You're in control. I just need to trust that You're in control. You know every need and will always provide." She took the dime into the house and told her mother what had happened. They knew God was speaking to them.

Ten years later, her mom's second husband was on his deathbed with cancer. Brenda's mom asked if she could come and relieve her for a while at the hospital. Brenda wasn't ready for this. *How could God take away another father figure in such a short time?* As she prayed and poured her heart out to God, Brenda emptied a craft bag and out rolled a dime! She could hear God saying, "Trust Me. I'm in control."

Brenda has learned that God has a sense of humor. At one point, Brenda and her husband decided it was time to buy a larger vehicle. So off to the car lot they went. Brenda had mentioned to her husband that she dreamed of having a navy blue vehicle with a gray interior. After looking around, a salesman insisted on showing them a trade-in vehicle that had just arrived. A dark blue Ford Expedition with a gray interior! It was exactly what they needed and wanted, so her husband went inside to start the paperwork. Brenda stayed outside with the boys. Doubts flooded her mind and she fervently prayed, "God, are You sure this is the right one? Isn't it too expensive?" Just then, one of her boys hollered, "Mom, come see this!" So she walked over to a truck where her son pointed at something near the bottom edge of the bumper. As Brenda bent over to take a look, a dime fell out of her pocket. She thought, *Okay, God. I'll trust You that this is the right vehicle.*

After three years of blessings with that vehicle, the family decided it was time for a more fuel-efficient minivan. So they went off to the car lot again. Within four hours, the Expedition was traded in and they drove home in a minivan. After a few days, a sense of doubt (or maybe buyer's remorse) came over Brenda. Raising her concerns to God she simply said, "Lord, I'm trusting You that we made the right decision!" A week later, Brenda received a check in the mail for an adjustment in the premium that the insurance company made for the new car. The amount of the check? Ten cents!

God reminded Brenda that He speaks all languages, too. She led a mission team to Sri Lanka in 2009. Even though God had prepared her for the trip, she couldn't help but feel anxious. She prayed, "Lord, I need You to take my anxiety away so I'm able to do Your work. I trust that Your Spirit will guide and lead us." As Brenda prayed and continued to pack, something rustled inside her fanny pack. She opened it up and there was a gold coin from one of her previous trips. Of course, it was a ten-cent Euro coin!

While in Sri Lanka, Brenda was asked at the last minute to speak at the church that Sunday. She thought, *Who, me? Lord, give me Your words!* While looking through her journal, Brenda came across a message she had written for her first mission trip. She hadn't used it back then, but it seemed like the right time now.

The message focused on how Peter got out of the boat and walked on the water toward Jesus in Matthew 14. Brenda had gotten in the boat with Jesus when she was just a child, but she hadn't stepped out until years later. Sure she knew God—she felt comfortable being protected—but He wanted her to have enough faith in Him to get out of the boat and walk on the water. The theme of her message posed two poignant questions: "Do you simply want to exist here on this Earth knowing who God is?" or "Are you willing to surrender everything to God and get out of the safety of the boat to experience His power in your life?" There wasn't a dry eye in the church! God used her message to impact lives.

Today, Brenda is so thankful that a day doesn't pass without God's presence in her life, and that she has faced challenges that have drawn her closer to Him. She's in a season of recovery from her last mission trip that left her physically, mentally, emotionally, and spiritually exhausted. Brenda gave everything in ways she didn't even know she could. She is waiting on the Lord, trusting He'll make known what He wants her to do next. Meanwhile, she's basking in His Word and presence, excited to see how He'll use her.

"Dear children, let us not love with words or tongue but with actions and in truth" (1 John 3:18).

Brenda lived with head knowledge of Christianity for years. Now her heart holds the truth of who God really is; her actions and daily life reflect this.

Josh ~ Age 22
A Despairing Agnostic Finds
Hope and Love

In middle school, Josh decided he didn't want much to do with God. Growing up and going to church had never actually inspired him; everything he heard just seemed like a story. Although going to church had been nice, he felt like people were polite but didn't really care about him or want to get to know him. That was the end of church.

Around seventh grade, Josh developed depression coupled with seasonal affective disorder (SAD). He didn't understand why he felt so sad and angry. As a way of expressing himself, Josh started listening to heavy metal and wearing black almost exclusively. It became an outlet for all the feelings he couldn't explain.

He didn't seem to fit in anywhere. Kids from his neighborhood and grade school all went to a private school while he attended public school. Thinking that God was always happy, he figured God wouldn't want anything to do with a depressed teenager like himself. Josh felt as if God only liked the popular kids from church who seemed happy and wore American Eagle clothing. To him, God *was* the popular kid.

In high school, Josh began building up his image on the outside. He got into the music program and became more involved with art. Josh placed a high emphasis on his group of friends—they were all he needed. Girls he dated became like God to him; Josh devoted much of his time to them. Life filled up with activities and friendships, leaving little time to think about the dark, oppressive void he felt whenever alone.

Throughout high school, Josh identified himself as an agnostic. He didn't actually deny the possibility that God existed, but questioned whether He did—and if He did exist, Josh wondered whether or not He cared about humanity. Christianity, however, was not an option worth considering. When talking to Christian friends, Josh often insulted their beliefs. He just couldn't comprehend all the "nonsense" they shared about Jesus and God.

Toward the end of high school, he and his girlfriend were quite serious and began to make plans. He decided to stay in town and work for a year until she finished school. Then they applied to the same college (plus an extra one just in case)—an ideal, picture-perfect plan. Only it didn't work out. Josh was only accepted at his second-choice college, meaning that the two would have to go their separate ways.

At first they tried to make it work, but it soon became clear that the relationship was going to end. Josh had become so dependent on the relationship, however, that he was miserable without her. Not far into the first semester, he started drinking to deal with the emptiness of being alone. He rarely went to class and his grades began to reflect that fact. The more he drank, the more his grades went down. Going to one house party after another, Josh went back to his room and crashed into bed, feeling empty.

A week before Christmas break, Josh's mom called to tell him that she had caught his dad having several affairs in the previous eight months. Not long before that, he found out one of his sisters had been diagnosed with Hodgkin's lymphoma. The world he'd created—the one free from the crutch of God—had begun to fall apart right in front of his eyes! His own situation was miserable, and now his family was broken, too. When everything else fell apart, Josh could always fall back on his family—they were his solid foundation, his rock. He thought of his father as a fine, outstanding Christian man: moral, yet accepting of his son's beliefs (or lack thereof). He wondered, *What am I to do now that my foundation has crumbled? What can I stand on for support?*

He really hadn't made any friends at college yet. Still battling depression, Josh sought out Christian friends on Facebook to ask them questions about why everything was happening. But he often blasted them for their beliefs saying, "God is ridiculous!"

Going home for Christmas was not at the top of his list that year. Unable to handle the family stressors, Josh withdrew and kept to himself. He was actually glad to go back to school after Christmas break!

While waiting for his interim class to begin, Josh began drinking heavily almost every day to cope with the pain. He didn't think, even if he conceded that God were real, that he could be saved. Josh had no hope. He didn't care if he lived anymore. One day Josh tried to commit suicide by taking a razor blade to his wrist multiple times. Though bleeding, he didn't care; he felt numb. A friend, responding to an earlier message, called back at that moment. Instead of letting it go to voicemail, Josh picked up the phone and said the only words he could think of at the time, "I'm bleeding." She immediately rushed into his room, bringing another friend with her. Seeing the injuries, she called an ambulance. Meanwhile, Josh sat on his bed bleeding, feeling completely worthless. He mused to himself, *I can't even succeed at killing myself.*

Once at the hospital, skin grafts were performed and his wrist was bandaged up. Then Josh was transported to another hospital's suicide watch program for three days. Being scared of the other people in the unit, he kept to himself and did a lot of reading. He found a book of the Psalms and the New Testament. Although not really understanding what he read, Josh found the words comforting.

He felt broken down; he had no pride left. Nobody even cared, or so he thought. On the second day of the program, the door opened and in walked his parents! They had come as soon as they'd heard what happened. As they expressed concern and love for Josh, they explained how upset his sisters were. In that moment, Josh saw a glimpse of God for the first time in his life. Not the "God" he had grown up with in church—this was different. He saw God in the love his parents and family expressed by searching him out and finding him in that place.

Josh's parents encouraged him to come home with them, but he opted to go back to school. He promised to get at least a B in his interim class, and signed a form saying that he wouldn't try to kill himself again. His mind was still a mess; he hadn't figured anything out. He continued drinking, but confined it to weekends. Josh pulled off a B in his class and went on to the next semester.

Then he met Holly, who happened to be a Christian. Thinking she was pretty cute, Josh started a conversation with her about God, saying, "How can you believe in God?" He continually tried to stump her with difficult questions like, "If God is so good, how come so many bad things happen in the world?" and, "If God is all-knowing, then how can we have free will?" She answered each question with supporting Bible verses. The most impressive thing wasn't her answers, though. Josh was most amazed that she actually seemed to want him to understand the answers to his questions. Surprised that she seemed so normal, he started spending more time talking with her. He thought, *Maybe I should learn more about God because many of the Christians I know seem to be happy and content despite having their own sets of problems.*

During a visit to his hometown, Josh ran into a friend he hadn't seen since seventh grade at the church bookstore. They wanted to catch up, but the only time she had to meet was during a Campus Crusade for Christ meeting. So Josh went along. The message didn't do much for him, but he noticed cards on the tables advertising an evangelical outreach over spring break. The card read, "Big Break, Panama Beach, One Week, $260." Even though winter was giving way to the beginning stages of spring, it was still cold. Florida sounded pretty good! Although broke, Josh was determined to round up the money in time.

After returning to school, Josh talked to Holly about Big Break and she encouraged him to go. He started going to Campus Crusade meetings for the trip. At the first meeting, Josh told the group, "I don't believe in what you believe. I don't have faith. I don't know about this God thing. Is it still okay if I come?" To his surprise the trip leader welcomed him to come, despite Josh's blatant opposition. He resolved to go strictly as an observer to see what these Christians were about, and to get a little sun in the process.

Josh went to Panama Beach with the group but made sure they knew he wouldn't be telling people about Jesus—for him it was just a vacation. After watching the other students going up and down the beach spreading the good news about Jesus, he began to listen in as they shared their faith. It was a bit surprising because so many Christians he'd seen on TV or on street corners seemed pushy and judgmental—even crazy. All he got from this group was a message he hadn't associated with the faith before—"I care about you; I care for you." That was the same message he'd gotten from Holly when he first started trying to trip her up with impossible questions.

The first day of the trip Josh met with Mark, the leader of the Campus Crusade group. They had both gotten up before anyone else: Mark had to attend a meeting, and Josh just wanted to walk and think on the beach. Mark offered to buy him a coffee. As they sat, they both shared their beliefs. Mark listened to Josh without judging or preaching to him. He didn't try to change Josh's mind; he merely listened.

Josh spent a lot of time alone walking along the beach in reflection and internal debate. *Why is Jesus so significant to people?*

He picked up a Bible and read about Paul. He could identify with him because Paul once persecuted the church of God and tried to destroy it. After receiving the Gospel by revelation from Jesus, Paul changed and went on to become one of Christianity's most influential figures. Questions flooded Josh's head: *Why did Paul change from fanatical hatred of Jesus to complete love for and acceptance of Him and His people? How could someone change so radically?*

Then came the last group meeting on Thursday night. One-by-one, students went to the front, sharing their stories from the day. Suddenly the reality of what Jesus had done began to resonate with Josh in a way he'd never felt before. *Jesus loves me so much that He suffered and died to save people like me!* More than a remembered verse from the Bible, it was a reality! He finally understood why Jesus is so important. Feeling the need to share his insight, Josh, without really knowing what he was doing, got up and suddenly found himself in the front of the room saying, "I don't want to believe what you do, but I actually think I do now!" That night, with four hundred other students from around the United States watching, he accepted Christ as his Savior.

Josh felt different right away. Yet, upon returning home, he had to deal with the reality that becoming a Christian didn't magically erase all the habits and decisions he'd made prior to leaving. Choices have consequences; old habits die hard. Josh's hurts and habits were still there. In time, he did stop drinking and sleeping around, though. The nagging suicidal thoughts and despair faded. He had real hope for the first time in his life. Josh started asking God and other people for forgiveness. He felt an overwhelming need to reconcile his differences with those he'd treated badly. Continuing his involvement in Campus Crusade, Josh had a community of people who cared about him beyond the superficial things life often glorifies. He no longer had to go through difficulties alone.

Is his life perfect? No. Far from it! Depression is still a prominent struggle. But he believes what God says is true despite how life goes or how he feels. Josh holds onto the only foundation that will never crumble beneath him: God. God deserves to be glorified in spite of Josh's depression. Some days it's hard to love others as Jesus taught because Josh becomes focused on his own pain. However, God is teaching him to take the situations where he's feeling down and turn them into love for others.

Josh is passionate about sharing what he's learned with others, letting them know that they don't have to go it alone. Care and concern for the world are of utmost importance to him. Josh is involved with *To Write Love on Her Arms*, a nonprofit movement that offers hope and finds help for people struggling with depression, addiction, self-injury, and suicide.

He feels very blessed. His parents are still together because his mom had the grace to forgive his dad. Healing a broken marriage is not an easy process, but it is possible. Many don't seek healing and leave the marriage. Seeing them hold their marriage together has been such a witness to Josh. The whole family has come closer to one another and to God.

"The man who formerly persecuted us is now preaching the faith he once tried to destroy. And they praised God because of me" (Galatians 1:23-24).

Just like Paul, Josh has now joined forces with the Christians he once ridiculed. His change of heart glorifies God because only He could have turned Josh into a Christian. Now God fills the void that used to be filled with people, drinking, and sleeping around.

Ann ~ Age 51
Brought Closer to God by a
Sacrificial Lamb

Ann's parents lived out their faith daily. A passage from 1 John reminds Ann of the godly example set by her parents: "Dear children, let us not love with words or tongue but with actions and in truth" (3:18). Even so, like her older siblings, Ann stopped going to church after high school.

Once married, she and her husband searched for a church, but they were too involved with life itself to make their search a priority. Throughout the years, Ann did have a continual relationship with God—she prayed and talked to Him frequently. However, it wasn't until holding her baby daughter, Tess, one night that Ann thought, *This is so much bigger than what my husband and I could have done; she's a miracle from God.* She wanted to raise Tess in the church so she would grow up with strong faith. Around that time a new, young priest took over at the local parish and it seemed like a good time to go back.

When Tess was just over a year old, Ann discovered she was pregnant and waited expectantly for nine months with growing hopes and dreams for her second child. Then the big day arrived and, after twelve hours of labor, Ann had her baby boy: Eric. *How beautiful he is,* she thought while holding him close.

Her husband left the room for a short time while a nurse cleaned up Eric and ran the usual tests. Ann casually asked, "So is he okay?" Not expecting or wanting anything other than a simple "yes," she was shocked by the nurse's cold reply: "The other nurses and I were talking, and we think he has Down's syndrome because of some facial features and a crease in his hands." Then the nurse abruptly left the room after saying those life-changing words.

What? How could this be? Ann thought, *I was certain my baby was completely healthy!* All alone in the room, Ann cried and cried. *Did I do something wrong during my pregnancy?* When her husband returned she blurted out the discouraging news. Afterward, Ann felt terrible for being so quick to speak words of disappointment that would shatter the dreams her husband had for his young family.

Ann just wanted to nurse and cuddle with her new baby, but the doctor wanted to run more tests on Eric to determine what might be wrong with him. So they took him away again. She and her husband were left alone in the room with no baby. They were feeling exhausted, confused, and scared.

When little Eric was brought back to the room, Ann's husband went home to get Tess. Shortly after, a very excited two-year-old, wearing a "Big Sister" t-shirt came running in with balloons—it broke Ann's heart. What should have been a happy celebration felt bittersweet. Having nine brothers and sisters herself, she worried how having a disabled brother would influence Tess; she tried to imagine the children running and playing together. *Who would Tess share such experiences with and later laugh with as they relived those moments?*

Later, Ann took a Jacuzzi and didn't want to come out. The warm water soothed her weary, sore body, and it calmed her distraught emotions. Basically, it was a temporary escape from her unsettling reality. A nurse even came to the door several times to make sure Ann was okay because she'd been in there for quite a while. She just wanted to be left alone. And she didn't want anyone to take her baby for more tests. It seemed like everything would be okay if she could just hold her son. Somehow, soaking in the water cleared her head and helped rebuild her strength. Ann came out of the Jacuzzi with a resolve to love and protect her son regardless of what others said about his potential challenges.

The next day, Ann and her husband were sent home with Eric along with an apnea monitor and directions for performing infant CPR (because he frequently stopped breathing during the night). Once at home, they wondered what to do with their fragile baby. Ann knew nothing about children with special needs.

Feedings were difficult. He nursed for a long time only to get a tiny bit of milk into his stomach; his sucking response wasn't fully developed. What milk he did take in either came back up or was aspirated into his lungs, causing repeated bouts of pneumonia. Rather than filling in with baby fat, he became nothing but skin and bones. It became clear that he just wasn't getting enough nourishment.

Finally, at the age of one and a half, fragile Eric went to Children's Hospital for a Nissan Fundoplication (gastric tube placement), a surgical procedure that would prevent him from spitting up so frequently and allow him to gain weight. The surgery took eight hours and left him with a scar running from his throat down to his navel. He had to stay in intensive care, hooked up to a respirator. Seeing her baby so helpless and limp, Ann went to the bathroom and fell to her knees sobbing. She just needed to be alone and cry for a while to release some of the devastation. Ann's sister stayed at the hospital with her that night, and her husband went home to be with Tess. Ann tried being brave, strong, and self-sufficient, but this was the first of many times she would have to learn to ask for God's help. Many complications ensued in the months that followed, and Eric nearly died several times.

For two months, either Ann or her husband stayed at the out-of-town hospital with Eric, the other stayed at home with Tess. The parent left at the hospital often felt alone and alienated from the rest of the family. However, God placed family members with Ann and her husband to support them. Additionally, the hospital staff was exceptionally compassionate. Being apart for so long left a rift in their marriage: all available energy had to go into comforting Eric.

Even after coming back home, Eric still had pain; he cried day and night until the age of four. His constant crying made Ann feel inadequate as a mom because she couldn't console him—and she became angry with him for making her feel that way. At times she had to walk away from Eric to regain her composure. Ann prayed and prayed, "Lord, please just let him be content." She needed God so much—she simply couldn't handle all this without His help. She later said, "I don't know how people can go through the struggles of life without the Lord."

The sleepless nights took their toll on Ann and her husband. Nevertheless, they had to put on a happy face for Tess. Their beautiful, cheerful little girl provided a much-needed ray of sunshine amidst the looming gray clouds of frustration and helplessness. Her smiles and laughter made everything more bearable.

Another tremendous blessing was that Ann and her husband were each granted a leave of absence from work for two years. They alternated years over a four-year period so one of them was always home with the children. Eric had to be taken to therapy twice a week—not to mention frequent doctor visits. It took four years to receive the correct diagnosis: ATRX syndrome, an extremely rare chromosome disorder.

When the kids were seven and five, the family went to church with Ann's husband's sister. After the service, Tess said she had learned so much more than at their church. Ann thought to herself, *Wow, I didn't know some of these things either; maybe it's time for a change.* After some searching, they found a new church family.

Over the next several years, Ann learned more and more about God and how He works. People came into Ann's life who brought her closer to God. She read the Bible and took classes at church. Knowing that Ann likes to read, God led her to various books. One particular book about a missionary who had forgiven people for seemingly unforgiveable trespasses really struck Ann. Reading about a real life example of a person being completely faithful to God's will opened Ann's heart to do the same.

While driving in the car one day, Ann was challenged to let go of her will and place her trust completely in the Lord. The time had come to choose between the old Ann who did things her way and a new Ann who relied upon God. She feared missing out on life by placing her trust in God; she feared that He wouldn't want her to do some of the things she enjoyed anymore, or that she would have to give up who she was. Much of her life had been spent feeling like she had to be perfect to even go to church. But she later realized that no one is perfect, except God. Salvation had been about works before, rather than God's grace. Ann had even tried bargaining with God saying, "If You only make Eric better, I'll do such and such." Finally, she was ready to take a leap of faith by letting God be God in her life—Ann fully surrendered her soul to Him.

The challenges of raising a son with special needs had become more than she could handle on her own. She simply didn't have the energy to do works. Ann was relieved to be free from doing good works to earn her salvation. In the following months, Ann recommitted her life to Christ several times just to be certain of her salvation.

By loosening her grip and letting God work, life began to flow more smoothly. Not only that, but Ann realized that God's power would be revealed to others when she allowed Him to work in her life. Seeing God working through her could help others grow closer to Him.

Even though God started changing Ann right away, she was still on shaky ground so she became selective about the people with whom she spent time. She was afraid that she might regress by being around people who didn't live a Christian lifestyle. Ann knew she would have to walk closely with God so that He could keep her on firm ground.

Eric's tenth birthday marked a turning point in Ann's faith. Whenever his birthday came around she tended to grieve and feel depressed as she recalled his birth. Ann decided Eric's tenth birthday would be different, though—God was invited that year. She realized that it was okay not to enjoy celebrating his birthday. It was perfectly natural to be reminded of how she felt the day of his birth and of all the pain he had endured in his first four years. Rather than putting on a happy face, Ann revealed her true self to others from then on. Finally, she had the courage to be honest about her painful feelings.

Eric is like a sacrificial lamb—it took his severe disability to bring Ann closer to the Lord. She feels bad he's had to suffer so much. At age seventeen, Eric is still nonverbal and unable to walk, eat, or take care of himself. He functions at the level of an infant. Eric has taught Ann what's really important in life, though. He doesn't worry about food, money, what to wear, or anything else. He lives completely in the moment. Each day he knows he'll be tube fed, bathed, dressed, and cared for in every way. Seeing Eric's unrelenting faith in his parents to care for him has encouraged Ann to trust in God, the Father, to provide for her needs.

Ann has been taught humility by the person Eric is. After all, he experiences sheer joy from simple things. He is happy playing with a rattle or car keys. And Eric loves the Lord. Whenever Christian music is played, he gets very excited. He's even tried crawling to the altar in church during worship time. God continues to teach Ann that her contentment shouldn't be so hard to come by once her physical needs are met.

Ann's relationship with God has deepened into a very personal one. She asks questions of God and talks to Him like a friend, and knows it's okay to be honest with Him about her doubts and fears. A quote from Elisabeth Elliot is close to Ann's heart: "If

God were small enough for me to understand, He wouldn't be big enough to worship."

God has been speaking to Ann through other people lately. She loves reading and music. Just when she's in need of encouragement, someone will drop by with a book or CD for her. The timing is always perfect! One time, just after starting to pray for help finding another babysitter, an acquaintance asked, "Do you guys ever get away for a weekend together?" "No, not really," Ann replied. "Oh, I would just love to take Eric for a night now and then!" responded the woman with a big smile. Ann thought, *What a blessing!*

Being a parent has tested Ann's faith. Letting her children go out into the world and trusting God to take care of them has been difficult. Imagine dropping off a nonverbal three-year-old child at school for the first time—the only way Ann got through it was to place Eric in God's loving hands. Sending Tess off to college has been another, more recent milestone. Thankfully, God is an important part of her daughter's life; she's continued going to church and has Christian roommates and friends. Today it's possible to test for ATRX syndrome and Tess wants to be tested. It's been hard for Ann to let go and not worry about the outcome; she prays that Tess doesn't have to deal with the consequences of (possibly) being a carrier. But it's in God's hands.

"As he went along, he saw a man blind from birth. His disciples asked him, 'Rabbi, who sinned, this man or his parents, that he was born blind?'" "Neither this man nor his parents sinned," said Jesus, "but this happened so that the work of God might be displayed in his life" (John 9:1-2).

God has used Eric to bring Ann to a deeper understanding of Him and His ways. Being unable to cope alone, Ann ultimately came closer to God, and He gave her the strength to deal with the challenges of having a son with special needs.

Roger ~ Age 38
Bad Boy Turns Godly

Roger played the game of going to church and being involved in his youth group, but he never got much out of church activities. He got baptized at the age of sixteen, but only to impress a cute girl and her parents. He definitely didn't understand the significance of what he'd done.

By high school, Roger was into partying, drinking, drugs, pornography, dating girls, and having sex. After high school, his drinking became more regular. He slept around and went from job to job. He continued doing whatever drugs he could get from his friends—mostly cocaine.

He got his first tattoo at the age of twenty-one, and he started working in the tattoo business by the age of twenty-three. Being somewhat shy, Roger thought having tattoos covering his entire body might scare people off, so he got one tattoo after another until he was covered from head to toe. The tattoos seemed to have the opposite effect, though: instead of keeping people away, they turned him into a bit of a celebrity. Everyone in the bars knew his name, and some nights he drank for free. Beautiful women came up to him all the time, attracted to his "bad boy" persona. He used to hang out in strip clubs more than bars, and dated a lot of strippers.

Roger drank most days from about two in the afternoon until two in the morning. He had become so mean that the guys in the tattoo shop would coax him into going to the bar just to get rid of him.

Eventually his drinking caught up with him and he lost his driver's license after too many drunk-driving episodes. Roger went for treatment in the hopes of getting his license back, but he didn't finish. Over the years he's gone through outpatient treatment for drinking four times. He has gone without a driver's license for many years and relied on friends and the city bus to get around. Sometimes he took a chance and drove himself.

At the age of thirty-three, an opportunity came up to run a tattoo shop in another state for his boss. But there was one catch: he had to get his driver's license back. This meant three hours of outpatient treatment every day for months—plus AA and NA meetings. Roger quit working at the shop and played the game, impressing the counselors with his apparent zeal to stop drinking. All the while he was thinking, *Okay, I'll stop drinking for these three months, but then I'll go back to my old lifestyle.* Roger put on his best behavior, and he even decided to go back to church. He thought, *This will really amaze the counselors!*

He opened the phonebook and randomly chose a nondenominational church. His five-year-old niece really looked up to him, so he asked her to come along. As they pulled into the church parking lot one Sunday morning, Roger said, "Maybe we could just go to McDonald's and say we went to church." His niece, all dressed up in a fancy dress and looking forward to going to church with her uncle, replied, "No. That wouldn't be right. We said we're going to church so let's go." *Great*, Roger thought, *Now I really have to go to church.* Reluctantly, Roger walked into church with his niece and found a seat by himself after taking her to a classroom.

When the worship band played Hillsong's "Mighty to Save," people raised their hands and jumped up and down. Roger had never seen such a display of praise. *Either these people love You an awful lot, God, or they're crazy!* Hearing the words "My God is mighty to save," sung over and over again, Roger felt deeply moved and decided that the people surely must love God a great deal.

Later on during the sermon, the pastor encouraged those who were not yet saved to say a prayer in which they accepted Jesus as their Savior and asked Him into their heart. *Jesus, I don't know about all this, but I'm game*, Roger thought. He said the prayer to himself along with the pastor and did feel a little different afterward. Never having prayed before, Roger wasn't sure how, but he closed his eyes and just started talking to God like he would a friend. Then he felt the warmth and brightness of a light shining on him! *Had they singled him out by putting him in the spotlight?* Knowing the lights were down low, Roger opened one eye to see what was happening; he wasn't in the spotlight after all. He kept on talking to God, and for the first time in his life, felt like he wasn't in darkness any longer.

Opening his eyes, there stood Jesus right in front of him! Jesus said, "If you walk out of this church today not knowing Me, you'll either end up in prison or dead. Or you can choose life with Me." Contemplating his drinking problem, angry demeanor, and habit of sleeping around with women he shouldn't be with in the first place, Roger figured he probably should have already been in prison. Since prison didn't sound appealing, and he was afraid to die, he chose God. He said, "I don't know how to do this, Jesus. You're going to have to come into my life and help me."

Jesus came into Roger's heart and his life took a radical turn. He found himself at church several days a week for services, and he joined the men's group. Roger sold all of his secular movies and CDs, using the money to buy Christian movies, books, music, and a new Bible. He decided that he needed to step away from the tattoo shop and his old friends and instead surround himself with people who knew Jesus. He still had urges to drink and have sex and couldn't imagine battling those desires his whole life—Jesus would have to take them away completely. All he had to do was ask and Jesus took them away. It was that simple! But were they gone for good?

Roger began having sleepless nights. If felt like someone had his hands around his neck and was trying to smother him. Frightened, he slept with a light on and Christian music playing all night. He had no idea what was happening, so he talked to the pastor's wife. She told him that demons were attacking him, which sometimes happens soon after being saved. The demons were trying to get Roger to turn away from God. She went on to say that those who come to Christ are given the power and authority of God. "When Jesus had called the Twelve together, he gave them power and authority to drive out all demons and to cure diseases, and he sent them out to preach the kingdom of God and to heal the sick" (Luke 9:1). That night, when he couldn't sleep, Roger recited Scripture out loud, and then he said with authority to the demons: "You are not welcome here. Get out and do not come back!" His sleeping troubles ended.

As a new Christian, Roger felt like he needed a sneak preview of what lay ahead, so he asked God to show him some of what He had in store for him. God revealed glimpses of His plans through dreams and visions.

During the middle of a church service one day, Roger had a vision of Johnny Appleseed walking by three different times and scattering apple seeds. At first, he wondered what in the world that meant—he didn't even like apples! He later discovered, after talking with his pastor, that God used the vision to tell him he would be an evangelist, scattering the seeds of the Gospel into fertile hearts. "This is what the kingdom of God is like. A man scatters seed on the ground. Night and day, whether he sleeps or gets up, the seed sprouts and grows, though he does not know how" (Mark 4:26–27). All Roger needed to do was share the good news of salvation through Jesus, and others would nurture the seeds he planted.

One night he dreamt of being on a battlefield fighting against demons with an army that included his pastor and two men from church. Roger remembers staying in back. His side was outnumbered and suffering many casualties. Suddenly, Roger heard God saying, "You've lost too many men. You're going to need the dead men to fight if you're to win. Go to them and raise them up. I've given you the same power and authority to do the things that Jesus did." *What? I'm supposed to raise men from the dead!* Roger went to the nearest fallen man and grabbed him under the arms while saying, "Get up and fight." Quite disturbed and confused after awakening, he pondered the dream's meaning. *Maybe God will use me to raise the spiritually dead, or those who don't know Jesus.* That fit with the idea of being an evangelist.

Roger learned a lot about God in the first year of being saved. He walked and talked with God. He prayed and read the Bible three times a day. Roger gave money to the church, even though he had little to give. He fasted, especially when needing answers from God. But he was still worshiping like people said he should and trying to do the right things on his own. Before long, Roger started going back into the shop to get more tattoos because he didn't yet know that was a sin. He thought he was honoring God by getting "Christian" tattoos! While in the shop, Roger shared his faith with the guys and told them how God was working in his life; none of them were Christians.

Meanwhile, Roger became stressed about a conflict at church regarding the woman he'd been dating. The church thought he should marry a different woman. *How dare they tell me whom to marry!* Disgusted, Roger texted a guy from the shop, "Let's party tonight!" The guy called Roger and asked why he wanted to go out drinking. Roger told him about the conflict and said, "If this is how Christians act toward one another, I don't want any part in this." His buddy said, "Dude, I'm not going to take you to the bar because you don't do that anymore. You come in the shop all excited, telling us how God has changed you. And after you leave we sit around amazed by the changes we see in you. We talk about wanting to have what you have: purpose and joy. So I can't let you throw it all away." Disappointed, Roger got off the phone and stayed in for the night.

Roger found a different church where he became very involved. He helped with the youth group and ministered to the men in the local prison on several occasions. Roger met with several pastors on a regular basis, discussing Scripture and going through theological training manuals.

Before long, Roger developed a "Super Christian" mentality—his head had gotten a little too big. Numerous people saw his transformation and told him how good he was doing, and then he began to think he could control himself on his own. So he went back to work at the tattoo shop. Everything went fine … at first. But the lyrics of the heavy metal music playing all day and night filled his head with thoughts of lust and partying—the very urges he thought were a thing of the past. And he did kind of enjoy girls giving him flirtatious looks.

Hanging out in his old surroundings rekindled some old behaviors. Roger caved a couple times, having sex with women he met in the shop. One night he even went out with the guys. He was already pretty buzzed when the shots started coming, and knew drugs would follow soon after. He had to leave. Immediately. Too drunk to reason, he got into his vehicle and drove home rather than calling a cab. Soon he saw the all too familiar flashing lights and pulled over. Standing at his window was a new cop with a veteran cop; the same cop who'd arrested him countless times in the past! The veteran cop seemed surprised to see Roger, saying he'd heard good things about him from pastors in the area—that he'd changed after coming to Jesus. Not a Christian himself, the cop seemed very impressed at Roger's transformation. Understanding that Roger had just made a poor decision that night, he decided not to take Roger to the station. Nevertheless, Roger insisted on spending the night locked up to give him time to think about what he'd done. He realized that just because he screwed up, it didn't mean life was over—God would give him a second and third chance (and so on). God's love is so great that His grace would cover Roger's mistakes.

Because of his prior drunk driving record, Roger had to see an alcohol counselor twice a month for three months. He ended up meeting with the same counselor he'd talked to years earlier. Although a Christian, the counselor's faith was weak. Each session Roger talked about God and what He'd been doing in his life, alcohol was never discussed. At the final session the counselor told Roger, "I've learned more from you than you've learned from me over these past few months. Talking with you has made me a stronger Christian. Now I get up in the morning and read a devotion to begin the day thinking about God."

Life certainly hasn't been simple as a Christian. Roger has learned that he needs to watch whom he hangs out with and where he goes. He's found it necessary to be held accountable for his actions by regularly talking to other Christian men who know him well. After all, Roger's last slipup occurred because he thought he could do it all on his own.

Today, Roger is working with pastors in the area to plant a new kind of church. He dreams of a church that would be open twenty-four hours per day, offering people a hot meal, clothing, and a safe place to hang out—in addition to praise and worship times, church services, interactive men's and women's ministries, and outreach efforts. He envisions serving brats outside of local bars and offering bar goers a free ride home. It's his hope that by reaching out to people from all walks of life and denominations that hearts will be opened to hearing about Jesus. Roger says, "We need to come together, working as one body—the body of Christ."

God continues grooming Roger for evangelism. He wants to see people plugged into churches after outreach events so they can grow in their knowledge and relationship with God within a community of believers that will offer help and express God's love. Roger hopes to see more and more Christians who are on fire for Jesus—rather than being lukewarm. The Bible says God dislikes those who are lukewarm in faith. He urges Christians, "We either need to get out of the boat and jump into the water or stay in the safety of the boat—we cannot remain half in and half out. As for me, I've jumped out of the boat in faith that God is mighty to save."

"For the grace of God that brings salvation has appeared to all men. It teaches us to say 'No' to ungodliness and worldly passions, and to live self-controlled, upright and godly lives in this present age" (Titus 2:11-12).

Roger is able to resist temptations (strip clubs, drinking, and sex before marriage, for example), because the Spirit of Christ Jesus lives in him, guiding his thoughts, emotions, and actions. Second, he knows and obeys Scripture because it's impossible to say "no" to sinful urges without knowing and doing what God expects of him.

Lauri ~ Age 51
Rejoicing in Suffering

Lauri remembers sitting on a hilltop chatting with God as a thirteen-year-old girl. Not having any friends at school, God became her "best buddy." She shared her joys and disappointments with Him. Lauri even told Him jokes, saying things like, "God, since You've been busy helping people all day, let me lighten things up for You."

By adulthood, her talks with God subsided. As the struggles of daily life took over, Lauri became very disgruntled and unhappy. She used to think, *When will I get out of financial debt? Why can't my kids be motivated like the neighbor kids? It sure would be nice to have new carpet.* Always wishing her circumstances were different or better somehow, Lauri's attitude and thoughts became quite negative. Not praying or asking God for help making decisions led to one bad choice after another.

On January 12, 2008, her benign, daily struggles fell into the background—Lauri was diagnosed with breast cancer at the age of forty-eight. From the beginning, obstacle after obstacle blocked her journey. She felt like she was on an emotional rollercoaster with an undetermined end point. Because she had several lumps, the doctors insisted on a radical mastectomy. An MRI had to be done before surgery, but the attending doctor got sick and had to postpone the scan for three weeks. There were going to be two surgeons: one general and one plastic surgeon to do reconstructive surgery. But the scheduling was complicated: the general surgeon happened to be going on a four-week vacation; and as soon as he returned, the plastic surgeon left unexpectedly for one week. Finally, the long anticipated day arrived: April 2. A scan taken the day prior showed no lymph involvement but, after surgery, Lauri was told that twelve lymph nodes tested positive! She wondered, *How could this have happened overnight?*

She needed to have a PET scan before seeing the oncologist, and that revealed cancer had spread throughout her whole body! The oncologist looked Lauri squarely in the eyes and said, "You're going to die in two years or less. There is nothing we can do for you because the cancer is stage 4-D." The only thing the oncologist offered her was pain medication to keep her comfortable. "But I don't have any pain," Lauri replied. The doctor found this hard to believe, considering the advanced stage and severity of her cancer.

After leaving the oncologist's office, Lauri and her husband immediately went to church and prayed. Her husband prayed, "Lord, please give me the strength to give up my wife when you take her." Realizing she had no control over her life or death, Lauri pleaded, "May I be obedient to Your will."

One day, Lauri received a call from the oncologist's office. He wanted to do one more test. "No," she immediately said. After all, every test she'd had turned up something worse. She questioned, *What good will another test do at this point? They can't do anything anyway.* After some thought, however, she agreed to have a full-body MRI. The report came back clean—nothing showed up! The oncologist was baffled, but Lauri and her husband praised the Lord.

Shortly thereafter, chemotherapy and radiation treatments began to ensure the destruction of stray cancer cells left behind. Because her cancer was in the last stage, chemo treatments were strong—harsh enough to wipe out all the bacteria (good and bad) in her intestines. Lauri had emergency surgery on Mother's Day to remove a dead section of her colon—yet another obstacle.

Her last radiation treatment was on December 24, 2008, just in time for Christmas.

Lauri prayed fervently every day that year, even keeping a prayer journal of her deepest feelings. She longed for a relationship with God again—like the one she had as a teenager.

One seemingly ordinary day, God did something extraordinary for Lauri. While praying, she felt His Spirit come into her heart. His spiritual fire ignited the glowing embers in her heart, creating a glorious, blazing fire that refined her faith. Cradling her in His bountiful love, God said, "I am here by your side. There is no need for you to be afraid." She fully surrendered to God. Lauri stopped fighting Him. Her fear turned into trust in the Lord.

She never wrote in her journal after that day because she had found what she'd been seeking: a close relationship with God that went from her head to her heart. She'd come full circle back to being best friends with Him again. Lauri began serving God because she wanted to, not out of an obligation to do so.

Her thought process changed quite dramatically. Lauri quit worrying about mundane matters, like not having new carpet. Gone was her desire to have more than what she had. She no longer tried changing things she couldn't control anyway. Lauri was just happy to be alive.

Today, Lauri is thankful for her trial with cancer. It has been a true blessing, bringing her close to God. Lauri loves the Lord totally from the deepest reaches of her heart. She feels at peace with God and her life. She no longer questions anything; she trusts Him fully. Lauri likens her walk with God to a path with a ladder that allows her to jump three steps at a time. Now that He's taken her through the fire, God tells her, "Let's walk together and see what we can accomplish." Even though she doesn't know how many steps she has left before becoming a perfect reflection of Christ, she's miles ahead of where she was several years ago. God is in her life 24/7.

Lauri feels strongly about sharing her story with others to let them know what God has done for her. And she wants others to know what He will do for them if they surrender to His power. She urges, "Submit to God and pray. Chat with Him like a friend. Surrender your control. You'll come closer to God, and He'll do more for you than you can imagine."

"In this you greatly rejoice, though now for a little while you may have had to suffer grief in all kinds of trials" (1 Peter 1:6).

Lauri's story shows how God uses our suffering to bring us closer to Him. She cannot picture how life would be if she hadn't gotten cancer, but she knows it wouldn't have been half as good as it is now. Being stubborn, it took something that would leave her feeling helpless and out of control to make her realize just how much she needed God.

Kirk ~ Age 45
Living Completely Surrendered

Every night, after eating dinner together, Kirk's dad read a devotion to the family. This planted the seed that it's okay to be open about one's faith in God. Kirk's family ritualistically attended church on Sundays and holidays, but he had nothing other than head knowledge about God.

In 1977, Kirk's oldest brother was seriously injured in a motocross race and ended up dying. His mom had a very hard time dealing with the loss of her son. She became overprotective of her three younger sons, suggesting that everything outside of the norm was dangerous. The death of Kirk's brother created much tension in his parent's marriage, but Kirk's dad stayed strong. He remained committed to his marriage and kept his family together. The godly example set by his dad during this grievous time taught Kirk not to walk away when times got tough, but to persevere.

As soon as Kirk got his driver's license he started taking flying lessons. He did this on his own because it took his mom some time to warm up to the idea. One particular flight instructor, Gene, laid a foundation for Kirk that went well beyond simply how to fly an airplane. Gene invested the time to mentor Kirk by sharing his life experiences. By the end of high school, Kirk had completed his flight training and obtained the necessary certifications. Skipping college, he went right into flying, working as a pilot for many large corporations.

Then Kirk started working for a local airline and dating one of the flight attendants. The relationship was on and off. During one of the "off" times, Kirk and his girlfriend were working on the same flight. She sat in the back of the plane when not attending to the passengers. In the seat in front of her sat a man writing. Curious, she looked over his shoulder and discovered he was working on a sermon. The two ended up talking, and Pastor Dan invited her to his church. She mentioned this to Kirk and they decided to go to the church one Sunday in 1993. There, Kirk heard the Gospel preached for the first time.

In the months to follow, he and his girlfriend decided to get married. Shortly thereafter, both lost their jobs, so they moved up to the northern part of their state by Kirk's family, and he went into the real estate appraisal business with his father and brothers. Kirk never enjoyed this line of work, however, and he really missed flying. For him, it was nothing more than a job to pay the bills and support his family. He pondered, *Is this all that life holds for me?*

Between two and three in the morning on a clear, crisp night in February of 1995, Kirk sat in a rocking chair in the nursery holding his newborn girl. The moonlight shone through the window. He could see shadows of trees in the yard. It was a perfect winter night in the North Woods. As Kirk looked at his daughter, he thought to himself how beautiful she was and how blessed he and his wife were to have this precious baby. While rocking her, he felt the most warm he'd ever felt—emotionally, physically, and spiritually. The feeling was incredible and indescribable. Then the Gospel began bouncing around in his head. It made perfect sense to him and he prayed to receive Christ into his heart. Kirk would never forget the intense warmth of God's presence on that chilly February night. He immediately developed a passion for God and dove into the Bible, wanting to learn more about God's ways.

Kirk and his family decided to move back to the central part of their state. They liked the church there, and Kirk had recently been hired by a major airline. They joined a small group at church, and Kirk became one of the overseers. In time, Pastor Dan and Kirk became close friends.

Everything about his life was great. His marriage was going well. Kirk and his family lived in a beautiful "Captain's house"— the kind of home that airline captains customarily acquire due to their large income. They had expensive cars and "toys," and frequently vacationed in Hawaii. Kirk had all the things that money could buy.

Then came September 11, 2001. Kirk was doing some things around the house when he received a phone call from a friend who told him to turn on the television. He couldn't believe his eyes as he watched the second plane crash into the World Trade Center. Kirk thought, *How could this be happening?* His heart sank to the floor when he found out that his personal friend, Jason Dahl, was the captain of Flight 93—the one that went down in Pennsylvania. In one morning, Kirk lost sixteen fellow coworkers.

The entire aviation system shut down for one week. Kirk didn't fly for the next three months because so few flights went out. He stayed at home grieving and trying to understand why the attacks happened. People were still on edge at the time of Kirk's first flight after 9-11. Walking into the cockpit felt surreal because there were added security measures and orders to perform certain maneuvers with the plane if someone entered the cockpit.

After losing two airplanes and experiencing a significant decrease in ticket sales, the airline filed for bankruptcy. This resulted in a forced 60 percent pay cut and a total loss of all pensions and stocks. Because everything Kirk owned was mortgaged, the sudden drop in income caused intense financial stress. He had to sell the house and cars and downsize everything. Kirk wondered if he should even continue working as a pilot. But, at the same time, he knew that finding other work would be difficult without a college degree.

His marriage dissolved very rapidly as their lucrative financial situation turned into loss. Kirk viewed his financial circumstance as a challenge to be conquered. He knew God would always provide—he just didn't know what that would look like. His wife, on the other hand, didn't handle the struggle well and was very disappointed. This definitely wasn't what she had signed up for. The divorce process lasted two long years, during which time Kirk had to resign as an overseer at his church because of all the discord in his life. He received partial custody of his girls and would have them fifteen days every month.

Kirk went through a time of darkness and extreme stress in the midst of his divorce and financial struggle. His ex-wife repeatedly suggested that Kirk was messed up because of his friend, Dan. Eventually he came to believe she might be right and began to persecute Dan. Kirk said things to his dear friend that a person should never say to anyone. His tirades cost him his friendship—yet another great loss. After a year had passed, Kirk invited Dan over to the house and they talked for three hours. Kirk got down on his knees and asked Dan for forgiveness. Dan forgave Kirk. But it took one year to reconcile and rebuild their relationship.

Kirk never walked away from his faith. In fact, he ran toward God at full speed. He prayed, read, and studied the Bible, and he started keeping a journal to express his deepest feelings and concerns with God. As a tool to discern what God wanted him to learn, Kirk developed twenty questions that led him deep into the Bible for answers. He not only learned more about who God is, but more about the things God wanted to nurture in him. Kirk grew more in love with God than he ever thought possible.

He chose to rebuild God's way. Kirk redefined his entire life from God's perspective to achieve spiritual health in every area of his life. It made sense to begin with finances. His priorities completely changed; Kirk realized there were a multitude of things more important than money. Years earlier, Kirk enjoyed listening to Dave Ramsey on the radio while commuting to and from the airport. Dave shared practical financial advice. Kirk started listening to Dave's shows regularly, and he enrolled in Financial Peace University. Later, he went on to lead Financial Peace at his church for two years. He appreciated that Dave's advice was based on the biblical principles of giving first, saving second, and living on the rest.

In 2009, Kirk decided to fully surrender to God's will. He was drawn to Romans 12, and the idea of submission clearly stood out. Kirk went on a search for his spiritual gifts. In addition to reading the Bible, Kirk considered the results of personality and aptitude tests and the Strengths Finder Inventory. His top five strengths and personality traits lined up very well with his primary spiritual gift of giving. After prayerful consideration, he came to a crystal-clear understanding of how God wanted him to manage what he'd been blessed with. Now Kirk immensely enjoys giving far above and beyond his normal tithing to the church.

Kirk ultimately came up with a life statement inspired by Romans 12: "Today I choose to live surrendered, separate from the world with a sober self-assessment, serving God for His glory, overcoming evil with His supernatural good." This statement has helped Kirk live God's way every day.

Although Kirk desired to live every part of his life God's way, he fell short in the area of dating. Every one of Kirk's relationships had started in the wrong manner: based on lust and physical intimacy. And they all ended. It was time to enter into relationships how God intended. His next relationship would be based on friendship and love. Kirk decided to stop dating and remain pure until he married again. Rather than trying to find a girlfriend on his terms, he would wait for God's guidance. Little did he know that God would bring the love of his life to him in just a few short months.

The date was July 3, 2010. Kirk and a friend were at a street dance in his hometown. A beautiful woman down the street caught Kirk's eye, and he asked his friend, "Who is that woman?" "Oh, that's Becky. Don't you remember her from high school?" his friend replied. God told Kirk that she was the one for him, so he made his way over to her. They went out to dinner the following week. Kirk learned that she had accepted Christ the previous year. And she, too, had recently made a decision to remain pure until getting married. They courted and developed a strong friendship that blossomed into deep-seated love.

Kirk and Becky married on October 1, 2011. Their vows were especially sweet because they courted as God intended, staying sexually pure. Another blessing on their wedding day was having Dan as Kirk's best man.

"Never be lacking in zeal, but keep your spiritual fervor, serving the Lord" (Romans 12:11).

Kirk has been more fulfilled, happy, and satisfied since he radically submitted his life to serving God and carrying out His will.

Dianne Marie ~ Age 70
Overcoming Mental Illness

Spirituality played a central role in Dianne's life. She went to a Catholic grade school and high school. Her father often brought the family together for prayers and devotions, and he encouraged them to attend Sunday Mass. Christmas and Easter were joyous occasions that led to a profound spiritual experience. As a young girl, Dianne deeply loved Jesus and understood she was a sinner and that He died on the cross so her sins could be forgiven.

During her senior year in high school, Dianne and her best friend met under a lamppost every night to discuss their future. Both felt called by God to be nuns. After spending so much time with nuns at school and hearing about religious vocations, Dianne became intrigued by the idea of entering a convent after high school.

Dianne entered a convent the year she graduated, at age seventeen. She had fallen in love with God to the point that nothing else mattered anymore. Life seemed comparable to heaven. Sure, she had to work hard, but she completed her tasks with a cheerful heart. Everything came easy to her, from keeping general silence to meditating at six each morning and praying at night in the dark, little chapel.

Rather than socializing with the others during free time, Dianne loved to pray in the chapel. Painfully aware of her many faults, she confessed her sins with sadness and repentance. Nothing meant more to Dianne than pleasing God and being in

His favor. Having a passion for prayer, she wished to become a Contemplative—a nun who prays from morning to night.

Things quickly went downhill once Dianne made her desire known to her mistress. The mistress believed it was the devil's doing to entice Dianne out of the Active Order. Dianne grew anxious over the possibility that what she considered a blessing might actually be a temptation. Her arms and legs ached, and she tired more easily. She lost a lot of weight over a three-week period. Dianne even lost the ability to concentrate on her lessons. She isolated herself, spending all of her free time in church. Her prayers became pleas; she wanted to suffer for Christ in any way He chose, even if it meant giving up her treasured vocation. Increasingly more aware of sin, Dianne started making a list of her sins that she read to the priest during weekly confession. Obsessed with perfection, Dianne became so pious that she stopped talking with the other young women, keeping general silence at all times. Soon, Dianne overflowed with pride; she was no longer at peace with God or herself.

Noticing a change in Dianne's behavior, Sister Lucretia made an appointment for her to see a psychiatrist. Dianne spent about an hour with the psychiatrist and cried nearly the whole time while talking about her parents and how upset she was that her father never tried to end her mother's affair. (Her mother ran around town with another man during Dianne's teenage years.) She never understood why her parents wouldn't discuss the affair with her. For years, confusion whirled around under the surface of her mind. She couldn't cope with the thought that her parents, whom she deeply loved, strayed far from God's path.

The psychiatrist spoke with Sister Lucretia and Dianne was told, "You're not cut out to be a nun. It was a mistake for you to come here. You are to leave the convent—and don't ever try to enter the religious life again." She couldn't believe it! Completely unprepared for such a shock, Dianne cried uncontrollably.

Anguished by what she perceived as total rejection from God, Dianne felt even more isolated and alone.

Her physical condition deteriorated to the point of extreme exhaustion. Unable to even walk down the hall, Dianne stayed in the infirmary for three weeks until the day after Christmas when she went home.

At the age of twenty, after two and a half years in the convent, Dianne had to start over with her life, not knowing what to do. Deep depression hit. She didn't have the energy or motivation to do anything other than lay in bed despondently all day while her mind reeled with dark, obsessive thoughts. Feelings of inadequacy pervaded Dianne's entire being; she spent much of the day crying. She thought, *Why is God treating me this way? I thought He wanted me to be a nun.*

Dianne's depression lifted the following year when she enrolled in college to finish her education. It helped having something to live for again. Weekly meetings with the college psychologist helped Dianne cope with her problems. The psychologist's support and faith in Dianne to succeed gave her the incentive to graduate.

Although hired for the first teaching job she applied for, Dianne ended up being in way over her head. In the morning, Dianne taught art at the grade school, and in the afternoon, she drove to the high school to teach three levels of English. By the end of her first year, insecurities crept in—even though the high school principal insisted she was doing a great job. He even offered her a substantial raise for the next year. Feeling the need to try harder, Dianne started working throughout the entire weekend. There was no time for socializing or entertainment. She isolated herself—just like in the convent.

Strange things began to happen. Everything went smoothly in the classroom, but when she went out into the halls, the noise of students talking and passing by became unbearable. On the way home at night, Dianne thought about how easy it would be to drive her car off the road. Other self-injurious thoughts, such as punching her fist through a window or bashing her head against a wall, grew more intense.

When Dianne shared her problems with a priest who knew her well, he suggested she see a medical doctor. That doctor then referred her to a psychiatrist. The doctor asked her to admit herself to the psychiatric ward in the hospital if she felt like she couldn't handle things.

Dianne reached the point of not being able to control her thoughts anymore, so she drove to the hospital. Dianne lay awake all night. She felt alone and frightened, not knowing what to expect. To make matters worse, she heard someone screaming, "Please help me! Help ... God, help me!" from another wing.

First thing in the morning, an aide gave Dianne liquid Thorazine. Breakfast was silent, reminding her of the general silence observed at the convent. Then everyone wandered into a huge recreation room. Doctors and nurses watched the patients through a window wall, making Dianne feel like an animal at a zoo.

For the first couple of days in the psychiatric ward, she didn't even feel alive; she'd lost contact with reality. But after two days, Dianne felt like a human being again. Slowly she felt a little better each day.

While putting together the pieces of a large puzzle, she reflected back on her life. Dianne realized she didn't know herself or what she wanted. Her focus had been on making her parents proud. They had always expected perfection in everything, rewarding her for good behavior and punishing her for not doing her best. Everything she had ever done was done to please them. Thinking that her parents would see her as a failure if they knew she was mentally ill, Dianne refused to give the staff their names. Her parents could never know about her hospitalization.

After being released from the hospital, Dianne went back to work. Her self-confidence deteriorated. She couldn't focus while preparing for class or teaching, noises were amplified, and it seemed as though students were talking about her behind her back. Incapable of controlling her strange thoughts and emotions, teaching turned into a frightening experience. After one week, Dianne ended up quitting because she just couldn't cope with the stress of working anymore.

Dianne attended recovery meetings every night to prevent another hospitalization. She still had challenging symptoms and a strong, lingering, deep depression. Several times, Dianne nearly jumped off the bridge she crossed on the way to her meetings.

At the age of twenty-five, Dianne married Joe, a man she met at a dance the previous year. Things went well for the first several years, but after having her second baby girl, Dianne became overwhelmed. Feelings of boredom and anger festered deep inside her. A noisy man who lived above them often disturbed her sleep. She talked less to her husband and grew dissatisfied with their relationship to the point that she wanted a divorce.

Her inability to cope with daily stressors led to a prolonged stay in a mental hospital. Dianne took a psychological test that seemed to open up a new means of expressing her mental illness. Suddenly, she became exceedingly fearful of everything and everyone—including God. Dianne even had the crucifix in her room taken down.

After some reflection, Dianne realized that the problems with her marriage stemmed from her illness. She had imagined many faults in her husband that were not real. When he visited her in the hospital, they had many heartfelt discussions. Soon the marriage was back on track, which provided much-needed relief for Dianne. At least something in her life was solid and genuine. As the weeks passed, she slowly improved to the point of being released.

Back at home with no medication, her thoughts quickly turned to suicide. She couldn't cope with the noise upstairs, the hormonal fluctuations of a recently confirmed pregnancy, and the care that she was required to provide for her daughters. Dianne lost all motivation to do anything. Her mood became so black that it seemed as though she would be depressed forever. She blamed God for even creating her. The world seemed too impossible to live in any longer; suicide consumed her every thought.

The extreme nature of her depression and suicidal thoughts led to a swift return to the mental hospital. This time she had no interest in anything, not even art projects—and she deemed that lack of interest another "failure to fit into God's world." After washing up one day, Dianne noticed that she had taken her deodorant bottle back to her room. Without a second thought, she broke the bottle and used a sharp edge to cut her wrists. Blood poured out. She walked out into the hall and was quickly rushed to surgery. From that point on, a nurse's aide stayed with Dianne every moment of the day and night. Dianne sought confession from a priest on her ward to receive God's forgiveness for having attempted suicide.

Slowly, she began to participate in activities again—but with great effort. There was nothing she wanted to do and no place she wanted to be. She didn't want to exist. Dianne repeatedly tried to escape from the hospital, but without success. Even though people were all around, she avoided them. She was too focused on thoughts of how to end everything.

One day, Dianne knocked down the light fixture in her room. After finding a razor sharp piece of glass, she pushed it deeply into her armpit. Blood gushed out and shot up and over her clothing, going everywhere. A nun happened to be passing by and went into her room when she heard the loud crash. Once again, Dianne was rushed to surgery. It never occurred to her at the time that, if she had killed herself, she would also have killed her baby.

Dianne's husband got her out of the hospital near the end of her pregnancy. The first three weeks after delivering her baby girl, Dianne stayed on the couch, too depressed to feed, change, or bathe the baby. Watching this happy, smiling baby day after day slowly brought Dianne out of her depression. She came to realize that the girls needed a mother, and the baby depended on her care to survive. Although still tempted to commit suicide, turning her thoughts to the reality of hell kept her alive. Even though life was horrid, it would eventually end—but hell would last forever.

Each week, Dianne met with a priest and a psychiatrist. She called both men to talk almost daily in between visits. In time, she became dependent on them in an unhealthy way. Dianne had a pattern of developing crushes on her doctors because they expressed concern and kindness. She even interpreted a simple smile as a flirtatious gesture. After realizing her feelings, her psychiatrist told her that she needed to come with her husband from then on. Completely devastated by his apparent rejection, Dianne deteriorated to the point of being hospitalized the following week.

Fear consumed every moment of every day. To make the days shorter, Dianne went to bed early and slept late each morning. When she returned home, many days were spent lying on the couch with the TV on as a distraction while she attempted to watch the girls play. She only got up to do necessary tasks, like making meals and changing the baby's diapers. Dianne felt worthless and ashamed of her laziness.

Very gradually, Dianne came out of her depression. She took an interest in her family and the outside world once again. While the girls were at school, she filled her leisure time with activities so she wouldn't have time to think. She baked bread and went to rummage sales and house parties with her new friends. Suddenly, Dianne had the enthusiasm of a newborn baby, as if experiencing everything for the first time.

Dianne began to think about God more and more, and she came to rely on Him as she had in the convent. Life became more meaningful as she realized that God had given her life for a reason and would use each new experience to refine her in some way. Teaching religion to first graders allowed Dianne to see the wonders of the God-given world through the eyes of children.

Her newfound excitement increased to an extreme level—a full-blown manic episode. In the middle of the night, Dianne woke and knew she had to leave. It was time for a road trip. She left a letter sitting in the typewriter that read, "I will come back only after I've proven that I'm not ill." After her husband and girls left the next morning, she packed up the car and started out on her journey.

She pondered, *Where should I go?* As Dianne reached a large city in another state, it seemed like a good idea to go to a hospital because of her familiarity with them. She talked to the chaplain who encouraged her to stay at the YMCA for the night.

Dianne sought one new experience after another. For a time, she moved in with a young woman she met on a subway train. Dianne met with psychiatrists at several different mental hospitals. She slept in her car many nights as she continued on her journey. One night, Dianne found herself sitting at a bar in the Playboy Club with no money. Two men talked with her and bought her drinks, all the while thinking she was a prostitute (even though she said she wasn't). The men paid for a hotel room for her and gave her gas money. That night, in her luxurious room, Dianne called her husband. He came to get her the next morning. On the drive home, he talked about how sick Dianne was, but she thought she was perfectly fine.

Immediately after arriving back home, Dianne's husband admitted her to a mental hospital. She had been off all her medication since the day she'd left home. The doctor medicated Dianne to the point that her laughter and extreme happiness gave way to deep depression. She could barely get out of bed.

Not liking how it felt being so heavily medicated, Dianne escaped from the hospital one night. She took a taxi out of town and stayed at a women's shelter. Her husband was so concerned about her whereabouts that he hired a private detective.

She had gone off her medication again because she didn't consider herself mentally ill. The time had come to prove she was well, so she went to a psychologist for testing. After talking with him, she realized that she really did have a mental illness—a severe one! That night, Dianne went out and drank until she fell off the barstool.

After a while, Dianne got a job and rented an apartment. Most evenings were spent in bars and nightclubs. The men she met saw her as an easy target, and Dianne slept with a few of them.

Realizing that she was frantically manic one night, Dianne admitted herself to a mental hospital. She decorated her hospital room by using pictures from the hallway. In no time at all, Dianne had moved all the furniture and turned the room into a chaotic scene. Her extreme manic behavior led to her being moved to a locked ward. Her hands and feet were strapped to the bed. A lawyer came in to talk with Dianne about being restrained and ended up getting her out of the hospital.

It wasn't long before Dianne went back to the hospital—this time for an eight-month stay. After being released, she found work at a bank and moved into the YMCA. As her mood stabilized, she thought about her girls and longed to be with them. Dianne called her husband every night and begged him to let her come home. Night after night he refused, until one night when he unexpectedly said, "Yes."

For the next seven years, Dianne controlled her depression by staying busy. Still, she grew more and more dissatisfied with her marriage, and eventually asked for a divorce. Her husband replied, "Don't ever, ever change your mind!" They never discussed the matter again.

In the spring of 1985, Dianne left her husband and daughters—then aged fifteen, sixteen, and eighteen—and moved to a different town. She had a hard time adjusting to living alone. Each day she came home from work to an empty house with bare walls. Alcohol became her rescuer. On most days, Dianne walked to the liquor store and purchased as much alcohol as she could carry home. She had regular appointments with a counselor who, after becoming aware of Dianne's drinking problem, advised her to go into outpatient rehabilitation. After falling asleep at the wheel one night and driving into a telephone pole, Dianne quit drinking alcohol.

Life wasn't easy. Within a few years, she moved five times and held several different jobs. She had to quit her last job after becoming paranoid that someone at work was going to kill her. A full-scale nervous breakdown ensued. A late evening walk to the police station led to yet another psychiatric hospitalization.

Dianne was frightened. She vacillated between being "out of her mind" and clear-headed. Rather than being pleasant, Dianne acted distant and paranoid; she was convinced that the staff did everything they could to keep the patients sick. The staff feared her because they never knew what stunt she would pull next. She often barricaded herself in her room. Noncompliant behavior led to her being placed in leather restraints on many occasions. In these instances, Dianne was often left alone all night where she had to lie in her urine until an aide came to let her out the next day.

In the midst of the terror came a beautiful blessing. Early in her stay, Dianne received an oil painting of Jesus from a missionary friend. The picture reminded her that the Lord would be with her through everything. She had forgotten that He was always there, especially when she lost contact with reality all together.

Nothing ever lasted—the good times or the bad times. Over the years, Dianne cycled between depressive and manic episodes, sometimes having a lull in between. An inability to sleep plagued Dianne much of her adult life, especially during manic episodes. It wasn't uncommon for her to walk the downtown streets from midnight until four o'clock in the morning. Over a forty-year period, Dianne had been hospitalized over twenty-five times and attempted suicide six times. She had been under the care of more than fifteen psychiatrists and several different counselors.

About twenty years ago, Dianne started going to a Spirit and Fire Prayer Group. She learned about the power that's available to her through the Holy Spirit. Refusing to submit to her illness any longer, Dianne began to live by the motto, "I shall overcome." Her mental illness was largely healed after many years of prayer and placing her trust in God. Dianne gives God all the credit for her current state of mental health. Today, Dianne is relatively free of psychotic symptoms, but she is still aided by a spiritual director, psychiatrist, counselor, and very low dose of Zyprexa. She is so grateful that the extreme highs and lows of her mental illness are a thing of the past.

Because she has a lot to share as a result of overcoming her mental illness, Dianne recently helped develop an ecumenical support group called "Faith in Recovery." The group is for people dealing with mental illness, and it seeks to help them find health and healing through faith in God.

Today, Dianne has close relationships with her daughters and seven beautiful grandchildren, whom she has babysat a lot over the years. Dianne feels honored to be an important part of their lives. She is blessed by her daughters' support.

Even though God has been present throughout her life, it has only been in the last few years that Dianne has developed an intimate relationship with Him. She has surrendered everything to God and passionately loves Him above all else. Dianne is at last fully receiving the grace and love that God offers freely. Her early years in the convent were about pleasing God. Dianne felt like she had to be perfect, which led to her obsessions. She became so devout in her religious practices that pride reared its ugly head. Before long, she completely lost her peace. Today she knows that losing her peace is a sign that she's falling away from God's will.

Placing God in the center of her life has made all the difference. She lives a simple life with very few possessions, and that allows her to focus more clearly on God. Most mornings, Dianne goes to Mass. She spends an hour of meditation getting to know God more intimately. Prayer is intricately woven into the fabric of her life. The closer Dianne comes to God, the nearer He comes to her. Spending significant time with God every day has awakened the fire of the Holy Spirit inside her; she feels His presence most of the time. God has finally brought her to a place of total love and peace. Dianne trusts Him with her whole heart and soul.

The following prayer, written under the guidance of the Holy Spirit, paints a beautiful picture of Dianne's current relationship with the Lord:

Love without Measure
By Dianne (May 2011)

You truly are my everything.
Every thought, every word, every act
Is performed with You in mind.
My desire is to love You beyond measure …
To love You to distraction,
So that nothing might ever interfere
With my relationship to You.
You above all, You in all, You beyond all.
I want to be so near to You
That nothing else has meaning …
To be wholly within You,
And wholly without.
All my deeds will be with You in mind.
All my thoughts will be of You alone.
All my love granted without measure.
Oh my eternal treasure!

Please be ever near my heart,
Within and without, with nothing interfering,
With no one else taking that space …
No one even coming close to that space
I have reserved for You alone.
Please grant me all the grace You have set for me,
The grace You have portioned out for me,
And let me assume that grace now and always,
So that I will not only be within You, but that
I will be nothing without You.
Let me never allow another to take the spot
You have reserved for me alone.
If I can be so near to You, without
Letting anything or anyone enter my heart but You,
I will be happier than the mighty wind,
Happier than the rolling sea,
Happier than the sun and moon.
I will be one with You as my center,
You as my greatest desire,
You as my sole companion on this Earth,
And hopefully, in the next world.
I will be able to snuggle next to You
As a child with her mother, or a woman her lover.
Oh, my God, please grant my only and great desire,
To live for You alone,
To be with You now and for all eternity
In that blissful marriage that follows life,
That completes my every wish and prayer,
That calms my every fear.
My only fear is losing You—
All that You are to me.
Please God,
Let this never happen.
Be my lover forever!

"To him who overcomes, I will give the right to sit with me on my throne, just as I overcame and sat down with my Father on his throne" (Revelation 3:21).

With the Lord's help, Dianne overcame her mental illness and now has a peaceful, happy life with God residing in the center.

Jen ~ Age 25
An Orphan Who Found Home

Jen thought her family was normal. That is, until the fifth grade. Then she realized she'd been abused emotionally, mentally, and physically. It started with her mom but, before long, her dad and three brothers joined in, too. She was constantly being blamed for things she didn't do. Jen remembers her mom tearing all the pages in one of her schoolbooks to get her in trouble with the teacher. Her mom cut her hair in the backyard, chopping it off even shorter than her brothers'. She thought it was funny that Jen looked like a boy. By the time she was ten, Jen had to live in the basement, completely isolated from the rest of the family. Although sad and alone, she felt safer being by herself. At least they couldn't hurt her if she wasn't around them. Her family never called Jen by her proper name, instead using the terms "it," "the thing that lives in the basement," and "numbnutz." Although her parents expressed love to her brothers, she received none. At family gatherings, her mom told everyone Jen was a bad person and that they shouldn't like her.

Though she was feeling alone, ridiculed, and dehumanized on the inside, everything appeared fine on the outside. Jen made friends easily and spent as much time away from home as possible. Being the class clown brought her happiness; she loved making others laugh.

On her thirteenth birthday, Jen was told she needed to be out of the house by midnight the day she turned eighteen. The locks would be changed and she would no longer be welcome. They said she had never been part of the family—that they had made a mistake adopting her. (Jen had been adopted from an orphanage in India where she spent the first year of her life.)

When she was around thirteen, teachers began questioning whether something was wrong at home because Jen's behavior changed and they noticed scratches on her body. A social worker even took her out of class in the eighth grade to determine whether she was being abused. Jen lied and said that everything was okay because her parents had threatened to place her in foster care if anyone found out. The social worker believed her story and never went to her home or looked any further.

By high school, Jen immersed herself in sports, joining the basketball and track teams. Lacking any connection to her own family, being a team member quenched her deep need to belong. When it came time to apply for college, her parents refused to give Jen money to send along with her applications, or to fill out financial aid forms. Jen waited and waited for acceptance letters, but none came. Her parents hid them from her! They were continually taking privileges away.

After graduating from high school, a teacher she assisted her senior year invited Jen to live at her home in exchange for babysitting her kids. Jen stayed with them during her first semester of college. She got her driver's license, which her parents never allowed. After completing a mountain of paperwork, Jen was declared independent, making it unnecessary to provide information about her parents on financial aid forms. This led to her getting a full-ride scholarship for her first semester of school.

Jen kept busy so she wouldn't have time to think about the bad things that had happened. Her happiness increased the more she was involved in activities. But, for three and a half years of college, she drank and had unhealthy relationships with men.

Crowned homecoming queen at the university, Jen asked if she could speak at a Campus Crusade for Christ meeting. Unaware of the mission of the organization, Jen thought the point was to tell a story of something bad that had gotten better. So she shared how her parents had abused and rejected her and how she made it to college against all odds.

During the Crusade meeting, Jen heard about a trip to Florida they were organizing for spring break. Thinking it was going to be like a Habitat for Humanity trip, Jen agreed. Soon after arriving in Florida, she couldn't help but notice that everyone was talking about Jesus. She wondered, *What kind of trip is this? What is it about this Jesus guy that people love so much?*

Now very curious, Jen talked with Kyle, one of the group's leaders. She had compiled a list of questions about God, Jesus, and the difference between believing, accepting, and knowing Him. Kyle responded to each question by opening his Bible and reading a passage to Jen, followed by an explanation she could understand. Still, something kept her from accepting Jesus. Trust was a big issue for Jen because both her biological and adoptive parents had rejected her. "How can I trust in a God I can't even see when my own parents don't love me?" Jen asked. Kyle replied, "God loves each of us more than any parent loves their child." Then he quoted John 3:16, "For God so loved the world that he gave his one and only Son, that whoever believes in him shall not perish but have eternal life." Jen paused to think about how lovingly her friends were treated by their parents and couldn't fathom how God could love her even more!

Later that night, Jen gave her life to Christ; Jesus freely offered His love to her. How wonderful to finally be loved! There wasn't a doubt in her mind that she had fully accepted Jesus.

Returning home from the trip, everything seemed new. Jen heard things she hadn't heard before, such as Christian songs on the radio, and saw things she hadn't noticed before: colors appeared brighter and more intense.

Jen started going to a nondenominational church close to college. At the first service she attended, "Amazing Grace" was sung, and she finally understood what it meant! She spent quiet time alone with God each day. Within one month of accepting Christ, Jen was publicly baptized at church. Her relationship with God rapidly grew.

Only one week after being back, Jen led her roommate, two sorority sisters, and another girl on her dorm floor to Christ. She continued to see more and more people coming to know Christ, and she almost immediately developed a passion for evangelizing. Thus began her discipleship with a mentor at Campus Crusade for Christ. Jen read and studied the Bible along with other books that taught her how to bring others to Christ.

Because Jen never had loving, nurturing parents, it was a true blessing that God gave her several spiritual parents. They are people she feels comfortable enough with to open her heart. Jen's spiritual parents have shown her Christ's love, and they have helped her develop a deep, passionate love for her Savior.

After many counseling sessions and prayers, Jen has forgiven her parents. During one of her quiet times with God, He asked her to write down two positive qualities of each parent. At first she thought this would be impossible. But she persisted. Then the lesson unfolded: even though her parents were not God's children yet, He created them and loves them anyway. God expected her to love her parents just as He loves them. Jen wrote a letter to her parents saying that she forgave them, which she later burned. Finally free of the bitterness and pain, Jen prays they will come to God someday. It's been over seven years since she's seen or heard from her family.

Today, Jen is passionate about God, people, evangelism, and adoption. She openly shares her story to help bring others to Christ. Jen uses her special gifts for the benefit of the church and for mission work. She allows herself to continue growing in God. Recently, God revealed 1 Peter 5:10 as her life verse:

"And the God of all grace, who called you to his eternal glory in Christ, after you have suffered a little while, will himself restore you and make you strong, firm and steadfast." This verse holds so much hope and power. It reminds Jen that there is redemption in Christ, and her suffering will only be a short season compared to the eternal glory of being made whole. When Jen let God in, He redeemed her and set her free from the burden of her painful past.

"I will not leave you as orphans; I will come to you" (John 14:18).

Jen cannot imagine her life being any different. God brought good from her painful experiences: she has a heart for adoption and deep compassion for children who suffer neglect and abuse. God loves her so much that He brought Jen to Himself. Now she has a heavenly Father who loves her more than any earthly dad ever could.

Jim ~ Age 64
Giving in to God's Sovereignty

Although raised in the church, Jim made it through college only knowing *of* Christ, rather than actually knowing Him personally. Praying was the extent of his relationship with Christ. Jim only occasionally went to church, mostly on holidays.

In college he met and married Paula, his best friend. Religion wasn't important to either of them. Besides going to school, they both worked, which left little time for anything else. After college, Jim and Paula had two children.

They moved when the kids were quite young, and they were befriended by a couple living down the street. The couple offered to take Jim and Paula to church, but they weren't very interested. Instead, their friends took the kids to Sunday school while Jim and Paula enjoyed having the opportunity to sleep late. With the year's end approaching, Jim decided they had better go to church a few times before the Christmas program. After all, it would be a bit embarrassing to show up for the first time on Christmas and have the congregation wonder who they were. The family continued going to church on a regular basis the following year.

One weekend in November of 1978, the relatively conservative church hosted a lay witness mission—people from within two hundred miles came to share their faith, testimonies that encouraged attendees to seek a relationship with Christ. They were taught how to pray and that authentic prayer reaches far beyond reciting the Lord's Prayer and the creeds. Actually talking to God like a friend and expecting an answer was a radical concept to Jim. He had been taught that God was very busy listening to everyone's prayers and would eventually hear his prayer and might answer it sometime—he didn't realize that God desired to engage in a continual dialogue with him throughout the day.

A month later, the pastor gave a sermon on tithing. Because he didn't make much money at the time, Jim figured he'd hold back on giving until he had a bit of a financial cushion. He thought, *Ten percent of my meager salary doesn't seem like much to offer, anyway.* Within a week, Jim was laid off—just at Christmas time, too! Upset with God, Jim expressed thanks for all the gifts he'd received until now, but he sarcastically asked, "How are You going to fix this?"

The first unemployment check arrived: $178.00. That wasn't even enough to cover the mortgage and bills, much less food. He and Paula discussed what they could cut. Not alcohol. Every night after work, Jim had some cream sherry and Paula had some beer. Then Paula suggested they try tithing because the Lord rewards those who are obedient. Jim didn't like the idea at all, thinking it was ridiculous to give money they didn't have. But there was only one way to find out how God would respond: to faithfully tithe. Jim thought, *If He wants one tenth of my check, He'll get $17.80 but not a penny more!* That winter they couldn't afford to heat the house, so Jim chopped enough wood to burn in the fireplace. The house was so cold that even their shampoo froze in the bathtub! Jim didn't have money to feed his family. But he continued tithing anyway. They decided to cut out alcohol, realizing they were using it as a crutch to fill their need for something else.

God amply provided. Bags of groceries regularly appeared at the back door; they never did find out who brought the food. Then, one Sunday after church, an elderly lady came over and invited the family out to dinner. It was an offer they couldn't refuse! While eating together, the lady mentioned that her aunt had just passed away and left her some money. She went on to say, "I heard you're having a hard time making ends meet lately. I'd like to share my inheritance with you." Jim's pride got the better of him and he said, "No. We don't need any help. Thanks again." After dinner, the car doors were not even closed when Paula asked, "What were you thinking? You know we need the money. What are we going to eat tomorrow night?" He knew Paula was right.

Three days later, Jim humbly called and asked if the offer remained open. The lady responded, "Yes, under one condition." *Great,* Jim thought, *here comes the hitch.* She continued, "I don't want the money back. When you can afford it, pass it on to someone else in need." What a wonderful idea! Jim accepted her offer. Needless to say, he's been tithing ever since—God really had provided abundantly for his family.

Jim didn't stop there. The Bible says to freely give your tithes *and* offerings. In one instance of this, Jim's family sponsored a young man in the Dominican Republic for one dollar per day as an offering to God. They've served as missionaries with IHOP (International House of Prayer), YWAM (Youth With A Mission), and Campus Crusade for Christ. And they have kept their promise to bless many other families in need.

Jim and Paula started a sharing group with four other couples deeply touched by the witness mission. Meeting three to five nights per week, they often prayed late into the night. Miracles happened: a girl's curved spine straightened; a child's short leg grew out. The group learned firsthand about the healing power of prayer.

Around this time, Keith Green, a Christian music artist, came on the scene. His song lyrics pierced Jim's heart. Some lyrics, "My eyes are dry, my heart is cold, and my prayers are old," spoke to where Jim was in his relationship with the Lord at the time—and he didn't want to be there any longer. Listening to "So You Wanna Go Back to Egypt" nudged Jim even more.

God offered to set him free of everything holding him back from having an intimate relationship with his Creator, only Jim hadn't yet let go of the illusion of security that came from remaining in control of his own life. Stubbornness prevented him from accepting the promise of new life in Christ.

Jim and Paula's daughter, now in high school, belonged to a youth group of three hundred teens. They went with her one night and saw all those kids with hearts on fire for the Lord. That sight lit a spark in their hearts to seek the same fervency of faith and dependence on God. They began attending the church that hosted the youth group. Not long after, Jim and Paula started and led a group called "Jesus Christ Power Outlet" for middle school students. They ended up with one hundred and fifty kids! Church politics and money eventually got in the way, however—taking precedence over Jesus—so they moved on to a new church and hosted a movie night for middle school kids.

Paula and her close friend attended a worship conference at a Vineyard church in Toronto, Canada—a worldwide movement birthed after a revival in Toronto in 1994. She came home on fire for the Lord! After going a second time, the fire burned hotter still! Jim wanted what Paula had. He thought, *That's it. I need to go and see what this place is all about.*

So Jim and Paula took a trip to Toronto for the next worship conference. He started out cautiously, not quite knowing what to make of the whole experience. But he slowly built up the courage to stand in the prayer line. Although most people had their eyes closed, Jim stood with one eye open. Suddenly, he found himself flat on his back, not knowing how he got there. He remembers fighting to get up, not wanting to lie on the floor. It was like being glued to the floor! Not only could he not move a muscle, it felt as if someone was sitting on his chest, making it hard for him to breathe. Then Jim's legs slowly began to lift off the ground until they were straight up in the air! *How did that happen?* A quiet voice said, "Give in." Jim stubbornly replied, "No!" Unable to breathe at all, a few moments later he heard, "You ready?" "Yeah, yeah. I give in," Jim muttered in desperation. He was immediately able to breathe again. Even though he was able to move, it took twenty minutes or so to recover from the spiritual battle. A lady came and stood over him playing the violin as he pondered the incredible experience—God delivered Jim from his stubbornness! Now that Jim had given his heart to the Lord, their relationship could move to a deeper level.

Another day at the conference, Jim was convicted of a judgmental spirit. One of the men on the worship team happened to be overweight and wearing a t-shirt three sizes too small with a huge coffee stain right on the front. *Oh come on, now!* Jim thought—until the man started playing his instrument. Could he ever play sweet music! The next day Jim had a similar reaction when a group of men in their forties who went by the name "Delirious," came on stage to play light Christian rock. Again, he was pleasantly surprised once they started playing—the lyrics ripped his heart out.

Jim and Paula became "God chasers." They traveled to several revivals around the country. After being prompted to visit IHOP in Kansas City, they made several trips there over the years. Continuous worship and prayer around the clock was really something to experience. Both grew closer and closer to the Lord.

When Paula developed cancer, Jim's ongoing struggle with finances came to the forefront again. Cancer treatments were so expensive that he was afraid of losing their cushion for retirement. Then he realized that it was only money—it did you no good once you left the world behind. Just when he gave up trying to control the finances, God provided. The health insurance provider called and said, "You don't have to do this yourself. Send us the receipts for Paula's pain patches and all medical bills and expenses." Well a $30,000 per month treatment bill cost them $400 a month! And a $21,000 hospital bill ended up being lowered to $7,000! When their provider suggested hospice care, Jim hesitated. Not only did he not want to give up on Paula, but he also figured it would be very expensive and wondered how they would manage to pay for it. As it turned out, hospice care actually saved money for them and the insurance provider. When she passed away, the funeral expenses were covered.

After witnessing many healings over the years, Jim wonders why Paula wasn't healed. Although he enjoys times of worship and refreshment from the Lord, he isn't particularly happy—he still dearly misses his wife and best friend. Jim has learned to trust God even though he does not always agree with His decisions. He knows it isn't necessary to understand why God does what He does. Jim has realized that we're all here for a purpose: to love and serve God and others, and to praise and worship God.

Paula's suffering and cancer progression taught Jim a valuable spiritual lesson that he likely wouldn't have thought about until much later in life. When the Bible talks about being the bride of Christ, it's more than just symbolism. Faced with having to let Paula go, Jim realized that "love isn't about what she could do for me, but what I could do for her." In the same way, it's not about what we can do for God, but what He wants to do for us. He's looking to give us more than we could ever fathom, if only we would receive His gifts. Jim feels that too many people are sitting around and waiting for others to help them. They are not giving of themselves even though everyone has something special to offer. Now Jim frequently asks, "What can I do for you?" The more he trusts God, not expecting anything from Him, the more he receives.

"The Spirit and the bride say, 'Come!' And let him who hears say, 'Come!' Whoever is thirsty, let him come; and whoever wishes, let him take the free gift of the water of life" (Revelation 22:17).

Everyone is invited to come to Jesus and experience the joys of God's free gift of salvation in Christ. When Jim gave in to God's sovereignty he opened the door for God to give him countless blessings as a follower of Jesus.

Tricia ~ Age 36
A New Attitude

Her parents brimmed with pride the first time Tricia got drunk—at the age of twelve. You were not part of the family if you didn't drink. Alcohol was central to every activity. Tricia's parents drank every day except Wednesday—grocery night. Verbal insults flew around the house like an untamed bird. Tricia would lie awake some nights listening to her parents argue.

Her parents often inflicted emotional and physical abuse in their drunken state. While playing one day, Tricia and her brother accidentally pulled the button off their push button television set. When her dad found out, he picked her up and forcefully threw her from the living room into the dining room. She was actually airborne! Another time, Tricia was beaten so badly that she couldn't even sit; she had to lie on her side. She remembers her mom sitting beside her on the couch throughout the night.

Not knowing how to cope, Tricia cut and burned herself to release some of the pain. Hurting on the outside distracted her from the gaping wounds deep inside.

Tricia had to think twice before doing or saying anything, for fear it might set her parents off. Everything had to be done their way or no way at all. Tricia felt like she could never do anything right. Coming home late from her first sporting event in high school, Tricia was chewed out. Her parents complained how much it inconvenienced them that they had to wait up for her. Feeling like her sports activities interfered with their lifestyle, the next day Tricia talked to the coach and quit the team. She thought, *Surely this will make my parents happy.* But when she told them, they called her a quitter.

Feeling like nothing mattered anymore, Tricia fell in with the "bad group" at school. Although her friends smoked, drank, and used drugs, at least they didn't judge her. She felt accepted.

Despite the pervading negativity at home, God started planting seeds in her as a little girl. While playing Barbie with her cousin one day, Tricia thought, *Someone up there is playing with us like this.* Some of Tricia's fondest memories are of spending time with her grandparents; they were the only ones she could trust. Their love was unconditional. She remembers being in awe when they took her to church; she liked being there.

Tricia and her husband met when she was fourteen. They dated on and off throughout high school. The proposal came on New Year's Eve of 1991. In April of 1994 they decided to get married in July. Having only three short months to prepare, everything fell into place quickly and easily for her dream wedding. God made the impossible happen. Without Him, there was no way a caterer or a hall would have been available for a summer wedding on such short notice!

Tricia's husband developed a rare form of skin cancer in 2006. Not knowing how to handle the news, she drank all day until passing out around midnight. She also got several intricate tattoos of lizards on her arms because the pain temporarily numbed her fear, giving her something else to focus on for a while.

Unable to care for herself, much less her kids, Tricia's oldest daughter stepped up. This little ten-year-old girl suddenly became mom. She made sure her younger sister and brother were bathed, dressed, and fed—and Tricia, too. Wiser than her years, she asked if the family could go to church. But Tricia didn't listen … not yet.

Faced with the possibility of losing her husband, Tricia cried out, "God, why is this happening? I need Your help." After some soul searching, she realized life is about people, not things. Her kids tried to teach her this lesson years earlier by showing her they could be happy with nothing; all they really wanted was her love. But Tricia didn't listen—not then. Now she got it, though. Nothing in the world could have replaced her husband. Shortly after this revelation, Tricia cleaned the house and got rid of the clutter. Out went assorted knickknacks and other items they had collected over the years, such as toy racecars. She began drinking less and less. In time, her husband experienced a complete recovery from his cancer.

Her younger daughter had deep emotional scars from the traumatic family dynamics of the previous years, and she tried to kill herself with scissors in 2008. Luckily, her big sister came to the rescue. Seeing her daughter in such emotional anguish made Tricia feel like a failure as a mom. She took to drinking again. For a month or so, she needed a drink the moment she got out of bed to make it through the day. Finding herself at rock bottom one morning, Tricia prayed to God, "If I need a drink to make it through this life, it isn't worth it. I need help." By the grace of God, she stopped drinking and threw all the alcohol out of the house.

What didn't change was her negative attitude. She only thought about the bad stuff, too lost in her selfishness, insecurities, and fears to notice the good. Life was hellish. Tricia never smiled. She walked looking down at the ground to avoid eye contact, figuring she had enough of her own stuff to deal with to worry about other people. Still unhappy, Tricia snapped at her husband and yelled at the kids over petty things.

Her husband's boss gave him a Bible for Christmas in 2009. He had been brought up in the church, but never read the Bible. This special gift broke the ice—it gave his family the stepping-stone they'd been waiting for. Her husband had wanted them to go to church for years, but something always got in the way. Having a Bible in their home steered them all in the same direction, though—toward knowing God in a way they couldn't have imagined before.

Tricia and her husband were invited to his boss's home one Friday night the following March. They discussed some problems in their life with the couple—one being Tricia's emotional ups and downs. Her husband knew she needed God in her life. His boss opened a Bible and asked Tricia, "Are you ready?" Knowing exactly what he meant, she exclaimed, "Yes!" He read a Bible passage and she accepted Jesus into her life. Immediately, Tricia felt God's presence come into her being. It was even better than a high, and without chemicals! She felt unimaginable peace and joy.

Tricia experienced a radical attitude change. While running errands one day, God nudged her to make eye contact and smile at people. What a concept! Everyone responded like she used to: they ignored her or turned their head away! On the way out to her car, she noticed a license plate that read "SOURPUS." "Okay, God, I get the message," Tricia said with a smile. Now people can see the joy of the Lord pouring out of her. Little things that once upset her don't anymore. Tricia looks for the good in all situations and focuses on positive things.

Her new attitude has brought with it a new philosophy on life. If something piques her interest, she tries it. Before, she had been afraid to try new things. God has replaced her insecurities with confidence. Some big lessons learned include: keep it simple; be childlike; don't over think; and take in what your kids say!

Tricia is learning to trust God. Every time she tries to quit smoking on her own, she ends up smoking more. When she gives it over to God and doesn't think about it, she barely smokes at all.

Today, Tricia goes to church regularly with her family, belongs to several church groups, takes Bible study classes, and goes on mission trips. Tricia desires to believe in God more deeply, and is excited to see where He'll take her as she continues walking with

Him. When life gets hard, she seeks God's will. Tricia gets upset with herself when she fails to listen to God. Although she still has a tendency to fall back into negative thinking when stressed, she catches herself before spiraling downward too far. Instead, Tricia prays for God's help and reads His Word. Since giving her life to Jesus, she's experienced a kind of peace she had never known—the kind of peace that reaches into every circumstance, no matter how trying, and washes her anxieties away. She feels that as long as God is in her life, she'll experience a "little taste of heaven on earth."

"Whatever is true, whatever is noble, whatever is right, whatever is pure, whatever is lovely, whatever is admirable—if anything is excellent or praiseworthy—think about such things" (Philippians 4:8).

Tricia learned the hard way that her thoughts determine what is expressed by her words and actions. Pounded into her from childhood, negative thinking was all she knew. The more she thought about all the bad stuff, the more depressed and anxious she felt and the more irritable she became. God has given her a new attitude: one that is positive and allows her to focus on good things.

Carol ~ Age 65
From Fear to Faith

Carol's parents were good Christians and their love for God poured out into each other and their nine children; they had the kind of marriage every couple longs for. Even so, Carol became very rebellious as a teenager and looked for love in all the wrong places. She became pregnant at the age of seventeen. Her parents sent her away to a house for pregnant teens about one and a half hours from home. Carol was alone, frightened, and angry with her parents. When she went into labor, the housemother dropped her off at the hospital door, saying she was too busy to stay. After only fifteen minutes of holding her baby girl, a nurse came and took her away. Forever.

Carol's parents made sure her baby was adopted into a Christian home, which comforted Carol. She hoped her daughter would have loving parents, but she still felt an overwhelming emptiness. Filled with grief and anger, she became even more rebellious after returning home. Before long, Carol moved out.

She found herself pregnant again at the age of eighteen. Since Carol couldn't bear to lose another child, she kept her baby boy and married a year later. A weekend drinker, her husband soon turned emotionally abusive. They had another son—along with three miscarriages.

Carol had another baby, this time a girl. The baby was taken to intensive care immediately upon being born. She died within an hour, before Carol even had a chance to see her. A nurse came to ask if she wanted to see her baby before the coroner came. Grief stricken and in shock, Carol said, "No. I don't want to see her dead." After it was too late, she had second thoughts: *Maybe I should have let the nurse bring her. If only I could see my baby just once.*

That night, something miraculous happened. Carol woke up and looked at the clock—it was 3:00 a.m. She lit up a cigarette and closed her weary eyes. A man in a flowing, white robe walked toward her, carrying a baby. The robe covered his face, but she knew it was Jesus. As he came near to her, Carol realized God had answered her prayer: Jesus was carrying her baby girl! She was beautiful and perfect in every way. It seemed as if about twenty minutes had passed, but when Carol opened her eyes and looked at the clock, it was still 3:00 a.m.! The peace of God washed over her, melting the bitterness she had felt moments before.

The peace lasted for a while, but it was soon overshadowed by anger and fear. She was mad at her husband and at God. *Why has this happened to me? Why have I lost another baby?*

Her marriage quickly deteriorated, and Carol met a flirtatious man at work. Before having an affair, she told her husband about the man. They decided to get a divorce, thinking their marriage was beyond repair. After a brief affair with the man from work, Carol realized the grass was not greener on the other side of the fence. It, too, was full of weeds.

Shortly thereafter, both of Carol's parents fell ill and had to be moved into a nursing home. Carol was very close to her dad—he was her best friend. He asked her to promise him she would remarry so he knew she and the boys would be cared for. To honor the promise made to her dad, Carol married the man she was dating at the time. The marriage ended in divorce not long after her dad's death because her new husband was a chronic liar. She decided to give her first husband another chance, but she ended the relationship for good after he refused to give up drinking.

Carol ended up dating the owner of a bar she and her friends frequented. The relationship lasted eight years. She found herself with another alcoholic who became very physically abusive. He was very controlling: Carol was not allowed to attend church anymore. Instead, she was expected to help clean the bar on Sunday mornings. Carol desperately missed going to church, but she never stopped praying. God was always there to listen when nobody else would. After being badly beaten one day, Carol knew she had to leave to protect herself and the boys. One of her sisters helped pack up her things, and they passed her boyfriend on his way home—only a block or two away. What a close call! God surely had His hand in that situation.

Carol had faithfully gone to church every week throughout the years (with the exception of the eight-year relationship she eventually ended), but hadn't learned anything. She often found her attention drifting away from the pastor's message. By the late 1970s, Carol really enjoyed going to church because of a new minister. He had a way of explaining biblical concepts in a way she could understand. Around this time, Carol became involved in Bible study classes. But even then, something still seemed to be missing.

Although Carol thought of herself as a good person at heart, she had picked up some bad behaviors in her late teens that stuck like glue. Going out to the bars had become a way to drown her anxieties and fears. Her friends saw drinking as a way out—an escape from the pressures of life.

By this time, Carol had had enough of abusive, alcoholic men. She decided to give her full attention to the boys. They went to church each week as a family, and her sons attended Sunday school. Carol became a very independent and arrogant woman, though. She was proud of being able to take care of everything on her own. Looking back, Carol realizes she really hadn't been on her own after all. God was by her side.

Carol

Her oldest son was diagnosed with a brain tumor in 1994, when he was in his late twenties. The fear and anxiety that rose up after receiving the news were more than Carol could handle. She could not bear to lose yet another child. Carol turned to God in prayer. God told her that she was not strong enough to deal with everything on her own. She needed His help. Carol fell to her knees weeping, giving it all over to God. Her old ways were forever washed away. No more going to bars. No more prideful reliance on her own strength to get through tough times. God made her into the woman she was born to be—she experienced a complete personality change.

From that day on, Carol has relied on God, rather than herself. She began reading the Bible again, but had difficulty understanding what it all meant. Reading Max Lucado's books helped her understand the Bible stories and parables she had read many times before. At last, Carol knew who God was and that He desired to have a close relationship with her.

Carol prayed without ceasing for her son during the time he suffered with the brain tumor and underwent brain surgery. Her son healed quickly from the surgery with no complications other than some hearing damage and slight impairments to his right side. God had worked a miracle!

Today, Carol is a woman of strong faith, and she has made God central in her life. Involvement in Bible study classes has brought her even deeper into God's Word, which she now reads for two hours per day. Carol reads only a few passages at a time, asks God what He's trying to tell her, and then sits quietly waiting for an answer. Meditations on God's Word and conversations with God have allowed her to build an intimate relationship with Him.

"The Lord is with me; I will not be afraid ..." (Psalm 118:6).

Carol dealt with so much loss that fear became her ruler. Knowing that God will remain in her life forever, she is no longer afraid of losing earthly things. Today, Carol relies completely on God to carry her through every difficulty.

Vin ~ Age 41
Pursued by God and Satan

As a little boy, Vin remembers seeing his dad spend a lot of time with the Lord. Vin and his younger brother would run into their parent's bedroom, jump onto the bed, and climb onto their dad's back as he prayed. But he kept on praying. His dad wanted to show them he was a man of prayer and had strong faith in the Lord Jesus. Vin's dad accepted Jesus at a Billy Graham crusade within the first few years of marriage, and he dreamed of becoming a pastor or Bible teacher. The issue of his dad being a Christian and his mom being a nonbeliever led to many arguments.

By the time Vin was five years old, his mom sought a divorce because his dad had developed schizophrenia; she couldn't deal with his strange behavior. Within two years, his dad was locked up in a mental institution and his mom remarried.

Vin's grandparents took him and his brother to visit their dad. Vin dreaded going because his dad always talked about Jesus. Even though he had lost his mind, wife, two boys, job, and all of his belongings, his dad never lost his faith in God. Relatives cautioned Vin, "If you don't want to become schizophrenic like your dad, don't become born-again." Comments like this led Vin to associate Jesus with mental illness. He was too young to understand what happened to his dad. He wondered, *What is schizophrenia? Why does my dad have it? Why does he have to live in a mental hospital?* Confusion overcame him like a plague.

At the age of seven, music became the center of Vin's world—a way of expressing creativity and escaping from his confusion. Cousins turned him on to heavy metal music, with KISS being his earliest band of choice. By fifth grade, Vin started playing the drums. His mom always supported his drumming and bought Vin his first set of drums at the age of twelve. Deciding he would be an entrepreneur, Vin got a paper route to save up enough money to buy a better drum set.

In the sixth grade, Vin met Lee, and they became inseparable. Lee's mom allowed the kids to smoke and drink in her house, and soon Vin took up these habits. Vin wanted to be one of the "bad boys." He pierced his own ears without even freezing them, and he let his blond hair grow long. His pursuit of the rock and roll lifestyle left little time for school—he and Lee failed the sixth grade. They were excited about being held back because it would be easier to dominate the other kids now that they would be bigger than the other boys. Vin and Lee planned on being the leaders of a gang. Everyone came to know Vin as "Crash" when he started fighting for the position of "alpha dog" at his school.

Vin and Lee were completely driven by entertainment. Life became all about heavy metal music, smoking, drinking, watching R-rated movies, and going from one girl to the next. The two even chose girlfriends who were friends so they could all hang out together. Their behavior in school was crude enough that they were able to manipulate teachers to let them attend class together—that is, when they didn't skip.

As Vin's behavior became more and more vulgar, his mom decided that he should attend confirmation classes at church, even though they weren't Christians. Vin played the game of going to church and signing in, and then he would sneak out and walk over to his girlfriend's house a block away. It turned out that his science teacher taught the confirmation class. Hearing the same man preach about evolution and God took Vin over the edge.

He decided to take an anti-Christ and anarchist stance. Vin was against God, the family, church, and education. Chaos became his worldview. At the time, he knew his beliefs and behavior were sinful, but he didn't care. In his mind, he realized that if there were a God, he would definitely go to hell. Angry over what happened to his dad, Vin chose to be God's number one enemy.

The summer before seventh grade, Lee's mom and sister became born-again Christians. Because Vin spent so much time at their house, he couldn't help but notice their transformation. Soon the household went from immoral to godly. A pastor visited often and invited the guys to church. They had no interest.

For some reason, they did accept an invitation to a Billy Graham affiliated crusade, maybe because they saw the pastor as a cool guy. Even though Vin heard the Gospel, he didn't really *hear* it. The crusade actually fueled the fire of his anti-Christ stance, and his rebellion escalated. Living on animal drive alone, Vin took the path of self-fulfillment. Most days he skipped school in search of a party.

Vin ran away from home for weeks at a time. The police would find him and place him in shelter care. When he returned home, his crass behavior created an atmosphere of tension that disrupted his mom, younger brother, and half brother and half sister. Vin didn't believe in following any rules, and he started pushing his mom around when she tried to set boundaries. He hoped to treat her so badly that she would shove him out of the house so he wouldn't have to run away anymore.

Finally at the age of fifteen, Vin had enough of running away and keeping track of all the lies. One day he sat down with the school counselor and said that he had a problem with drugs and alcohol. Secretly, though, Vin knew he could control these behaviors. They were only a symptom of the real problem—anarchy. His attitude of chaos, domination, anger, and bitterness was the culprit. Within one month Vin was pulled out of school for thirty-eight days of inpatient drug and alcohol rehabilitation.

In rehab, Vin went through severe withdrawal. A blood test was ordered to find out what he had been taking. It revealed PCP (angel dust). The pot his uncle brought along on a hunting trip several weeks earlier had been laced with PCP! Having such severe withdrawal symptoms scared Vin enough to swear he'd never touch alcohol or drugs again.

Finding a higher power was part of the twelve-step program in rehab. Vin sure didn't want to become a Christian. A girl came up to him after group one afternoon and said, "Have you considered worshiping Satan?" At first it seemed like a viable option. Then he realized that if he didn't believe in God, he couldn't believe in Satan either (because he would be admitting that God exists).

The school system placed Vin in the ninth grade when he got out of rehab. Being more of a hands-on learner, Vin couldn't stand sitting in a classroom all day; it was boring. He had fallen so far behind in school that he didn't even try. Many days he ditched school to play the drums. All of his energy went into music. Vin stopped using drugs and alcohol for nearly a whole year following rehab. Not surprisingly, however, he still failed that year of school. By the end of the first month of his second year of ninth grade, the principal called Vin's mom and said, "You have to sign Vin out of school. He skips so often, and when he comes to class he is very disruptive. Although intelligent, he's just too undisciplined for school."

So he was forced to drop out of school at the age of sixteen. He now had the freedom to play drums all day long. Instead, he decided to work and save money for his music career. His days became structured: mornings were spent practicing the drums, afternoons were spent at the technical college to catch up in school, and evenings were spent cleaning carpets and working third shift at a restaurant on the weekends. Vin even placed an advertisement in the newspaper to put together a heavy metal band. Before long, he found a group of talented musicians.

By this time, Vin had moved in with a cousin because he refused to live by his mom's rules. His cousin was going through a divorce and had custody of three children. Vin could live there rent-free under the stipulation that he would watch the kids when not working. When his cousin came home from work, the two drank and did drugs.

Vin's girlfriend at the time was a Satanist. She read tarot cards and used a Ouija board. All of this seemed pretty strange to Vin, but he put up with it because she was a good artist. He liked how she played the role of a heavy metal girlfriend—wild black hair and cool threads. She lived fifteen miles out of town, so Vin rode his bicycle over an hour to get to her house. One day she came to Vin and told him the devil wanted them to have a baby to offer as a sacrifice. That about did it for Vin! Not only did he not want to have a child, he certainly did not want to kill one. He broke off the relationship soon after.

He went back to partying with a group of teens from his hometown. Mary happened to be one of the girls in that circle. Vin had known Mary and her two sisters for a few years. Mary had a baby several months after Vin had gotten out of rehab. Somehow, Vin ended up being the only one with her at the hospital, and he even helped name the baby after a rock star. After going to a Boston concert over the summer, he and Mary started hanging out more often. Then Vin's cousin told him that a woman only a block away was getting divorced and was looking for a roommate. Mary and the baby moved in with her. Of course, Vin ended up moving in, too. When his mom found out that sixteen-year-old Vin was living with a nineteen-year-old woman, she threatened to have Mary locked up for statutory rape. Vin denied sleeping with Mary, but his mom knew better.

Vin's metal band practiced in the attic space. The musicians were very good, and the band thrived ... until the middle of winter. One day, John, the lead guitar player, walked into a jam session as the others sat around drinking and doing drugs. He looked them square in the eyes and said, "Okay guys, I'll tell you what. I can't do this anymore. I'm following Jesus—I'm born-again." That got everyone's attention pretty quickly! Then John encouraged the others to join him. Vin said, "Whatever, John. Good for you, but I'm not following you. I'm not following Jesus. Maybe someday when I have kids." Vin overlooked the fact he was already helping Mary raise her baby. That same afternoon, the bass player called Vin and said, "I'm leaving the band. I'm born-again." Vin replied, "I can't believe that Jesus Christ is ruining my life!" Thus began a serious battle between himself and God, and the band fell apart after losing two key members.

Within six months, Vin joined another heavy metal band. The guys were mostly in their mid-twenties, much older than Vin. They practiced in an old barn out in the country—the ultimate space to play as loud as they wanted—and to do drugs without anyone knowing. One day, the lead guitarist took Vin out of town to buy some cocaine. Knowing that his motor was already too revved up, Vin refused to do the drug. While sitting at a table in a café, Vin's buddy said, "If you want to understand this band, you have to understand the occult—the secrets of Satan." Without hesitation Vin replied, "I can't."

That winter, an old friend encouraged Vin to check out his new band. They had the heavy metal music and the hair, and they were talented musicians. But they were all born-again Christians! While reading their lyrics during practice sessions, Vin discovered they sang about deep spiritual truths. He wondered, *How could they play that kind of music and worship God at the same time?* He had always seen metal music as secular and antiestablishment. Vin would say to Mary, "I can't believe these guys are so good *and* Christians." Vin was drawn to their music like a bug to a flame, and he slowly became friends with them. During this time, he fell away from drugs and alcohol because the guys were clean. They invited Vin to Bible studies and prayer meetings. When they encouraged him to pray during their meetings, Vin dropped the "f-bomb" in his prayers. He was testing their faith. If the guys truly were Christians, they would accept him for who he was. They never forced their views on Vin; they only befriended him.

Vin experienced a change of heart and wanted to seek God. For some reason, Vin thought he had to move to another state to start over—away from family and friends, away from his past. He was ready to embark on his journey when Mary came to him and said, "Vin, why don't we give Jesus a try? Why don't we become Christians? I want to stay with you. I love you." Something about the way she approached him and the way she made this request felt right to Vin. After thinking about it for a while, he went back to Mary and told her, "I've made a decision to believe in Jesus." It was August of 1988. Coming full circle from his anti-Christ stance, Vin made the radical choice to place his faith in Christ.

Then the father of Mary's baby suddenly wanted visitation rights with his two-year-old daughter who he'd never even seen. Seeing how upset Mary felt about this, Vin suggested making an appointment with her family's lawyer. Vin said to the lawyer, "The father has never been there. What would it take for me to adopt her daughter?" Shocked, the lawyer replied, "Adopt? First of all, you're not even eighteen yet. You haven't finished high school, and the two of you aren't married." What the lawyer thought were reasons to dissuade Vin from pursuing adoption were to Vin a list of things he could accomplish to make it happen. After all, he would turn eighteen in only two months. Meanwhile, he completed the coursework and received his HSED. After turning eighteen, Vin got a full-time manufacturing job. Then, only one month after his birthday, he married Mary. He wanted to save her little girl from growing up without a dad around (like he had). In a very short time, Vin's perspective on family changed from chaos to unity and peace.

The following February, long-haired Vin found himself standing before a judge in court. After asking Vin if he understood the serious responsibility of being a parent, the judge looked Vin in the eyes and said, "I wouldn't normally do this. But something in my heart says I need to give you this adoption." The next day the Lord led Vin to Proverbs 8:15, "By me kings reign and rulers make laws that are just." This Scripture confirmed to Vin that God had worked through the judge, that he was meant to adopt this little girl.

Several years later, Vin crashed into a deep depression because Mary had asked him to give up the opportunity to go on the road with a Christian metal band that had recently won a three-record contract in a battle of the bands. Consumed by self-pity over the death of his dream, God seemed very far away.

Then, one day, at the age of twenty-three, the silence from God ended—God spoke and revealed to Vin that he was to become a pastor. In his heart, he knew this message came from God. But in his mind, he made one excuse after another. He thought, *After all, I don't even have a good education. And I still have long hair; how many pastors have long hair?* Vin didn't tell Mary out of fear she would ask him to turn away from yet another dream.

He kept coming back to a conversation he had with one of the guys in a former band. His friend asked what it meant to love Jesus. Vin couldn't answer. His friend replied, "To love Jesus is to obey His commands," as the Bible says in 1 John 5:3. Although not ready to start Bible College, Vin couldn't stop himself from sharing the Gospel. He became heavily involved in ministry outreach and evangelized to anyone who would listen. God told Vin that his voice would be heard all over the state—and this happened through a morning radio ministry program.

At the age of twenty-eight, Vin fell into another depressive state, this time over a conflict at a church he helped plant. At a loss for what to do, Vin prayed for the church, "Lord, what is it You want me to do about this?" The Scripture, "honor thy father," flashed into his mind. Vin questioned God, "How can I honor my dad if I can't even forgive him?" He was angry with his dad for not being there for him. The struggle lasted less than a week, though—Vin quickly acted in obedience.

He decided to meet with his dad, who had been transitioned to a halfway house years earlier. As Vin sat across the table from his dad, he noticed his dad's eyes brighten and posture straighten in the chair. Then his dad spoke coherently, leading to the first and only normal adult conversation they ever had. He began, "Son, do you know why you became a Christian?" Vin said, "I want to know." His dad went on, "When you and your brother were little, before I got very sick, I took you to church and walked up to the altar. I dedicated both of you to serve in ministry." Vin knew right then that the way to honor his dad was to go into ministry.

Five years after receiving God's call to become a pastor, Vin finally told Mary. She discouraged him by saying that she didn't feel prepared to be a pastor's wife. They had been through a lot (they had three miscarriages over the past five years). Vin was being tested to see if he would follow God anywhere, through any circumstances—even without the support of his wife.

Little did Vin know that a blessing was right around the corner. One Monday morning, Mary told him, "I'm pregnant, but I don't want you to tell anyone." She was afraid of having another miscarriage. Early the next morning, Vin had a vision of sitting on a park bench with a little girl who had curly blond hair. She wore purple jogging pants and a purple shirt. He watched her walk away from him and fall backward. Just then he called out the name *Joelle*. Hearing Vin cry out in his sleep, Mary asked what was wrong. After Vin shared what he'd seen, Mary looked up the name Joelle in a book of baby names. She discovered it is the Hebrew name for "Yahweh is Lord." Vin said to Mary, "God is revealing His character to us. We're having a girl." Later, an ultrasound confirmed his conviction. Within the next four years, they had two more precious daughters.

God began doing unusual things in Vin's life he hadn't seen before. These little miracles helped reveal more of God's character. The most dramatic instance was being healed after a three-year bout with Crohn's disease. When Vin began to chase after miracles, however, God stopped producing them. Vin entered into a season of trials, during which time terrible things happened. He lost his job approximately every six months, for example. But no matter what, Vin didn't fall away from God.

Vin seriously considered going to school for ministry at the age of thirty-three. The day after talking with a friend about this, he woke up at five o'clock in the morning. Even though dark outside, bright light permeated his mind and a voice said, "Vin, I want you to go check your email." At first, Vin tried reasoning with God: *Surely it could wait a couple of hours.* No. Between the light and an overwhelming feeling to check his email, there was no way he could fall back to sleep. So he dragged himself out of bed and stumbled to the computer. Sure enough! There was a new email: "Your application has been accepted at The Sure Foundation Theological Institute." Under normal circumstances he would have been very excited, but the strange thing was, he hadn't applied to that school! There must have been some mistake!

That morning Vin called and asked to speak with the administrator. He said he had received an email from the school, but had never sent in an application. The man on the other end of the line said that he had Vin's application sitting on the desk right in front of him. They just needed some more financial information and ministry background, and then everything would be in order. The school ended up giving Vin a full-ride scholarship. Over the years, circumstances made it necessary for him to take time off, but the school always encouraged him to continue because they believed in him.

The year Vin turned thirty-eight, Mary lost her job, Vin's dad died, two businesses he started collapsed, and the family lost everything (including their house). While preparing the eulogy for his dad's funeral, Vin remembered that the one thing his dad never lost was his faith. All Vin had left was his faith in God and family—the only things that really mattered. If his dad was able to stay strong in faith, so could he. Vin completely depended on God to meet his most basic needs. His relationship with God deepened as it became more about believing God's truths than seeing miracles.

In November of 2008, Vin and his family moved across the country to start an organic farm. For several years leading up to that move, God had been revealing to Vin that he would be heading out west. They lived with their oldest daughter and her husband on farmland owned by the son-in-law's parents.

Early February of the following year, Vin prayed for God to supply two hundred dollars for seed. At 7:25 a.m. he told Mary that he fully expected God to meet their needs. They didn't even have money for the gas to drive into town, but then came a knock at the door. The time was 7:30 a.m. It was Loyal, a cowboy who lived thirty-five miles away. "Brother Vin, God sent me here. He wants me to give you this money," Loyal proclaimed. Vin opened the envelope to find two hundred dollars cash!

In the following month it was time to break ground. But Vin couldn't afford any equipment. One day his grandma called to say that his dad had an insurance policy that the state dictated would be divided between Vin and his brother. They each received three thousand dollars—more than enough money to buy farming machinery and tools!

On July 3, 2009, a storm came rolling in after lunchtime at a speed of about eighty miles per hour. Vin's family was indoors during the heat of the day while Vin worked in the field alone. The storm stopped over the valley. Vin ran to herd the chickens to the pen when he noticed the windows of his in-law's RV were open. He hurried to close the windows; but, just as he went to open the door with his right hand, lightning struck—it took out the electricity in the whole valley. He saw a bright flash and felt a surge go through his body. At that moment—frightened and awestruck—Vin knew the storm was meant for him. It reminded him of the time when Jesus calmed the wind and waves as He and His disciples crossed to the other side of the lake in a boat. The disciples were afraid of drowning, and Jesus said to them (in Mark 4:40), "Why are you so afraid? Do you still have no faith?" Vin realized that the lightning could have killed him, but that God, in His power and majesty, had chosen to use the lightning strike to test Vin's faith.

That fall, the farm animals were wiped out by pestilence, and Vin couldn't afford to replace them. He looked for work but couldn't find anything. On Thanksgiving Day, the son-in-law's parents sent him a proposal. They asked him to pay a certain amount of money per month or else he would have to move off of their land. Vin had no cash or savings. All of their money was invested in the farm. Everything had been lost for the second time. Vin prayed, "God, I don't know what to do, but I trust You." God whispered, "Go back home." "What?" Vin replied, "I just left fourteen months ago and You want me to go back?"

By December 31, much tension had developed in Vin's family over what to do. By this time, Mary felt prompted by God to move back home, too. Vin called a pastor friend and mentor. After explaining their desperate situation and God's answer, the pastor exclaimed, "Go for it!" So on January 1, 2010, the family got in the car with their dog, Bibles, a laptop, and five hundred dollars Vin had just earned. They made it back home with one hundred and forty dollars to spare—relatives helped provide money for hotels and some food along the way.

Their marriage was crumbling, though; Mary considered divorce. She still loved Vin, but she was tired of the drama and the need to start over from nothing. Vin and Mary met with the pastor who had encouraged them to come back. He said to Mary, "I know this is one of the worst trials yet, but Vin is one of the most gifted men I've met in all my years of ministry. If you divorce him now, the devil wins." Vin and Mary have since worked hard to save their marriage.

God blessed Vin for being obedient. Within one month of getting back, the pastor found Vin's family a fully furnished, rent-free house. In less than three months, Vin got a job. He resumed his schooling and is currently working on a doctorate in theology.

Today, writing and preaching have replaced Vin's passion for music. He quit music five years ago and never looked back. God continues to polish his spiritual gifts related to ministry. Because he has been without money, belongings, and a house, Vin knows full well what it is to lose everything. God's love is all he will ever need. Above all, Vin hopes to be used for honorable purposes in the house of God.

"Put on the full armor of God so that you can take your stand against the devil's schemes" (Philippians 6:11).

Vin's life has vacillated between being tempted by Satan and being pursued by God. In the end, God won Vin's heart. As Vin studies the Bible in preparation for ministry, he is becoming better equipped for battle against Satan.

Trudy ~ Age 24
Big or Small, Sin Is Sin

In second grade, Trudy accepted Jesus one Wednesday night at church after some clowns shared the Gospel in a kid-friendly way. Trudy belonged to a group called AWANA (Approved Workmen Are Not Ashamed) based on 2 Timothy 2:15, "Do your best to present yourself to God as one approved, a workman who does not need to be ashamed and who correctly handles the word of truth." One particular night, clowns came in and talked about God; they explained that He is love. They went on to say that we all do wrong and sin against God, but Jesus forgives our sins if we ask Him to. Being aware that she sinned, Trudy gave her life to Jesus right then and there. As small and young as she was, Trudy trusted God and started reading the Bible. Since she'd decided to live for God, she needed to read His Word to learn how to live for Him and serve Him.

By the fifth grade, she began telling her friends and other kids about Jesus. One of her friends didn't want to hear about it, which was hard for Trudy, so she prayed that her friend, as well as others, would come to know God. Because she openly shared her faith, many kids didn't like her.

In the sixth grade, Trudy went to a new school where many kids liked and befriended her. Faced with the choice of being friends with the popular kids, Trudy opted out. Part of being popular meant putting other kids down, and Trudy wasn't comfortable with that; she wanted to be friends with everyone.

God blessed her with real friends who liked her without placing stipulations on the friendship.

Both of her parents worked and were gone most of the time, which left Trudy home alone a lot. Aside from a couple close friends, it seemed like nobody was invested in her or cared for her. Trudy thought about suicide in seventh grade, even though, deep in her heart, she didn't want to end her life. Knowing it wasn't right in God's eyes, she called her two closest friends. Although nonbelievers themselves, her friends shattered the lie that no one loved her. They pointed to what was real and said, "We love you, and your parents love you." After talking with them for a while, Trudy's thoughts of suicide ended.

High school was a mix of growth in God and temptation. Trudy continued reading the Bible and became involved with a group called "Reaching Our Campus for Christ" that met over the lunch hour. The students worshiped, talked, prayed, and listened to mini-sermons. By her sophomore year, Trudy stepped up into a leadership role. Around this time, she started dating a guy at school. Before that relationship, Trudy had been oblivious to the fact that people her age drank. Her boyfriend and his friends were interested in drinking and having sex, even though he didn't drink around her. Trudy could see how empty they felt—and how empty their homes were. Their parents didn't seem to know how to be a family and love one another. Without God, they were just chasing after the things they thought mattered. But these things weren't filling them up. The relationship didn't last long once Trudy realized they had little in common.

In her senior year, Trudy dated a guy two years older than her. She placed her self-worth, wants, and desires in him—she was just looking to be happy without the struggle of fighting temptation. Trudy wanted him to see how much he needed God, but, at the same time, she was walking away from God. Her boyfriend lusted after her, and although they didn't have sex, Trudy behaved in ways that were mentally, emotionally, and physically impure. He cheated on her three times; she forgave him every time. She showed him unconditional love—the same kind of love God has for us. Troubled about the relationship, Trudy prayed, "God, this isn't right. I need You to take him away because I can't let him go." Shortly after her prayer, he broke up with her. Before parting ways, he told Trudy that she'd loved him more than anyone else he'd ever dated.

Troubled that she'd sinned with her impure thoughts, feelings, and behavior, Trudy learned that all sin has consequences. She pondered, *Why do I want someone else there for me? Why isn't God my all?* Being so thankful for God's forgiveness, Trudy felt blessed that she had made sinful choices because they helped her better understand sin and God's redemption. She learned, "It's often the big things people see as being unforgiveable, yet the little things, such as white lies and thinking sinfully about someone else, are just as wrong. God's forgiveness covers all sins, regardless of whether they are big or little in our eyes. What's more, He uses all sin for His glory." God worked in all things so Trudy could learn this lesson without destroying the plans He had for her.

After high school, Trudy spent a few summers as a counselor at Bible camp. She shared her story with girls who longed for a boyfriend (just as she had). "Our society makes it seem like everyone needs to get married, have children, and live in a nice house—even though God calls some of us to be single. It comes down to having Jesus be your all, your everything—finding deep intimacy and satisfaction in God. He knows and loves you more than anyone else ever could. It's good to rest in God and the plans He has for you. His plans are always best, even if you don't see it at the time."

The learning process that ensued after she broke up with her boyfriend helped Trudy in her marriage. Without that experience, she wouldn't have known how to help her husband with an issue of his own. He had been exposed to pornography in the seventh grade and became addicted to it for a while. God used this addiction in his life to point out that we are all sinful at our core. Like Trudy, he learned that it's not about us being good enough. The fact that God forgives us shows it's about how deep God's love for us goes. We cannot overcome sin on our own. Only by God's grace can we do the right thing. Being able to talk about his struggle with pornography has allowed a common place for Trudy and her husband to help and better understand one another, but, even more so, it has helped the two of them build trust in their relationship. Openly sharing their weaknesses in sin has drawn them closer together.

Today, Trudy continues to learn about and grow in God. Whatever she faces, she knows God is with her. He is pruning and cutting off aspects of her that are not bearing fruit. She's working on letting go of herself and the things she wants in order to let God shine in her. Trudy knows she can't always do things her way and carry out God's plans.

She's trying to perceive exactly what God wants her to do now, knowing that she'll have to work exceptionally hard to carry out His plans. She wants to bring Him glory and receive blessings, both in this lifetime and when she sees Jesus face to face. Deep in her heart, Trudy is confident that God will work everything out for His good, but she also needs to be faithful by doing her part. The great hopes and ambitions God is revealing to her will require that she go out of her comfort zone, and reach far beyond what she thinks is possible. Only faith and hope in God will make her dreams—what she calls "God's inspired ideas"—come true. She'll also need to rely on other people to help her. Trudy is walking out on a limb to pursue the dream God has placed in her heart, waiting in faith to know exactly what it is, when to do it, and who needs to be part of it.

"All praise be to Him for not letting go of me," she says. Trudy wants the world to know that God has the same love for everyone that He has for her. All they must do is receive it. She firmly believes God is real and cares about every little thing we do. Trudy emphasizes, "There's only one way to God: believing what Jesus says about Himself, that it's true, and living your life in faith that it's true." In a way, her story is believing His story.

"Everything is possible for him who believes" (Mark 9:23).

Trudy knows that anything is possible for the believer because nothing is too difficult for God. In faith, He'll provide everything she needs to serve Him.

Chris ~ Age 51
The Power of God's
Unconditional Love

After eighth grade, Chris decided she didn't want anything to do with church anymore. She was sick and tired of not getting anything out of it, even after attending parochial school for eight years. A negative encounter with her pastor near the end of confirmation class was the last straw. Chris raised her hand and asked, "In Genesis, when it says God created the heavens and Earth and everything in them by the seventh day, could it really have been seven years or seventy years? Is it possible that evolution took place?" Rather than answering Chris's questions, the pastor hollered and kicked her out of the class. These hadn't been her first unanswered questions. She wondered, *How am I to learn about God without asking questions?*

As a sophomore, Chris joined the Jesus movement of the 1970s—for a summer. Her friends made fun of her for being a Jesus freak, and she didn't have an adult to answer her questions. Because Chris had no one to nurture her faith, she fell away again.

After this, Chris turned into an "awful kid." She started drinking and using drugs, and she even ran away several times. Being a headstrong teenager who didn't like rules, she constantly argued with her mother, saying many things she later regretted. Chris got pregnant at the age of sixteen, and she was persuaded to give up her daughter for adoption against her wishes.

In 1994, Chris, married to her third husband, had another daughter. She took her daughter to church only because it seemed like the right thing to do. Chris stopped taking communion when her daughter got too heavy to hold because she didn't want her to take up a space where someone else could kneel. After a time, the pastor said that she was no longer welcome at church if she didn't take communion. She thought, *Whether I take communion or not is between the Lord and me. How could the pastor make such a request?* So Chris stopped going to church.

Then in 2003, a kid t-boned Chris as she drove through an intersection. It left her with two herniated discs in her neck and constant pain. She went to doctor after doctor, but all of them said they couldn't help. One doctor even said that it was all in her head, that she really didn't have any pain! After hearing so many doctors say, "There's nothing wrong with you," Chris began to doubt herself and her sanity. The pain became intolerable. What made it even worse was that nobody, including her family, seemed to understand. That's when she started cutting and burning herself. She thought, *Maybe people will believe I'm in pain if there is something physical they can see.*

Hit with terrible depression, Chris woke up every day only to stay in bed and fall back asleep—for the whole day. She had no ambition and didn't want anything to do with anybody. Chris felt like an observer, not being able to engage with life. After reaching her lowest point, she checked herself into a hospital for treatment of depression and self-injury. A doctor put Chris on an antidepressant. Gradually, her mood lifted enough to get out of bed and carry on with life.

Around that same time, Chris ran into a girlfriend who suggested that she should visit her church. She decided to give it a try. From the beginning, people were friendly and took Chris under their wing to nurture her relationship with God. They answered her questions. Pastor Bob even befriended her. Wow! The pastor actually wanted to be her friend, and he didn't act as though he was superior to her. Chris felt welcomed and accepted at church for the first time.

After attending services for a while and talking with other parishioners and Pastor Bob, she learned more and more about God. All of a sudden, Chris woke up one day knowing God loved her and wanted her to be with Him—she knew she was one of God's children! The people at church showed her what God's love was all about. They loved her for who she was rather than judging her for who she had been.

Chris's husband only goes to church on Christmas and Easter to please her. Having to attend church alone is difficult. She'd like to share the most important part of her life—her faith in Jesus—with her husband. He doesn't say anything to discourage her from going to church or participating in activities, but he doesn't say anything to encourage or support her either. When she has tried talking to him about God, he doesn't show any interest. So life goes on, day after day, in silence about a matter that is dear to Chris's heart. It's hard for Chris—knowing he doesn't believe in God—but she loves her husband and prays that he comes to know the Lord before it's too late. She wonders, *What if he died tomorrow?* Chris is comforted knowing she'll meet her mother again in heaven, and would like to feel confident that her husband will be there, too.

Chris cannot imagine the guilt she'd feel today for how she treated her mother as a teenager (or for all of the things she has done), if she hadn't received the forgiveness of Jesus. He wiped her guilt and sin away, allowing her to go forward without the weight of the past on her shoulders.

Some days are harder than others. She's still taking antidepressants and probably always will. What's changed is that her down days aren't quite as down. Now Chris can go to God for help. Before, she had nowhere to go. Her pain hasn't gone away, though. There's always at least a nagging pain in her neck; on bad days, the pain radiates down her back and legs. Chris has lost her sense of balance as well. Falling is commonplace, and she even broke her knee one time.

Today, Chris is a deacon at her church, a position she never would have anticipated. She's gone from not knowing where to go with her life, and not knowing how to listen to God, to knowing how to listen to Him and allowing Him to lead her in the right direction. He's been teaching her patience—even though she wants to know God's plans now. She is finding it difficult to wait.

God is leading Chris to work with American Indians—in particular, First Nations men and women. She's discovered from several mission trips that they have a lot of unmet needs. Many American Indians have a poor view of Christianity that's been passed down through generations since the times when missionaries came to "civilize" them. They also have a hard time with trust because of how they've been treated over the years. While Chris recovered from the car accident, God gave her the gift of making jewelry. The money she makes from selling jewelry helps fund her mission trips.

"Dear friends, let us love one another, for love comes from God. Everyone who loves has been born of God and knows God" (1 John 4:7).

It wasn't until experiencing God's love through others at church that Chris finally understood His unconditional love. Since love comes from God, it opened her heart to receiving Him.

Mike ~ Age 58
Surrendering Sexuality to God

In high school, Mike felt called to be a pastor. Church had been a safe haven from a discordant home life. He immersed himself in church activities—choir, ushering, and youth group—just to get away. His dad was an alcoholic, and he abused Mike's two older brothers. But Mike was spoiled because he was the baby of the family. Being quite a bit younger than his brothers, Mike never spent much time with them. Mike's mom had a simple kind of faith, and she raised him strictly. She didn't even let him read Mighty Mouse comics for fear he would be exposed to improper material. Something kept him from seriously considering becoming a pastor: same-sex attraction. Knowing how God felt about homosexuality, Mike didn't think himself worthy of going to seminary, so he went to college where he had his first same-sex encounter.

Longing to get involved in a church, Mike talked to a local pastor who said, "Oh you'll be so busy with your studies that you won't have time for church activities. Just focus on school for now." Mike left discouraged. He wondered, *What will fill the emptiness, isolation, and shame of having same-sex attractions?*

He joined a fraternity and got into the drug scene. Mike did pot and acid, but not to get high. Rather, he did drugs because he was seeking a (potential) spiritual experience. He thought, *If only the hunger in my soul could be satisfied.* Not finding the intimacy he desired with God, Mike sought intimacy through the dark underbelly of perverse sexuality. He dove into pornography and anonymous same-sex encounters. These activities so consumed him that he never graduated from college.

Between the ages of twenty and twenty-six, Mike broke away from God and sought to quench his soul's hunger through other means. Besides sexual activity, Mike developed a sense of purpose by playing foosball. He became quite skilled and earned shelves full of trophies from playing in semi-professional tournaments.

Mike worked second shift at an out-of-town factory. During his commute one evening, he tuned into *Nightsounds* with Bill Pearce on WEMI, Christian Family Radio. This thirty-minute radio broadcast of beautiful, mellow music and biblical commentary provided Mike with soul-satisfying inspiration and hope. *Nightsounds* tugged at Mike's heart and whetted his appetite for the things of God again.

Before long, Mike visited WEMI and asked if there were any local Christian groups. They suggested he check out Singles Together for Christ, an interdenominational group that met weekly for Bible study and social outings. Mike enjoyed the group and got plugged into a church. So happy to have found a church, he went on Sunday mornings and evenings—as well as Wednesday nights. The singles Bible study group met in a building adjacent to an adult bookstore. Mike got in the habit of spending Friday afternoons at the bookstore before going to the meeting. Every Friday night he sought forgiveness for viewing pornography.

Mike started dating a girl he met in the group, and she moved into the family house with him. This worked because his mom had been placed in an Alzheimer's unit, leaving him alone. Even though he was engaged, Mike still acted out on his homosexual urges. One month before the wedding, his fiancée left him for another woman! A mixture of shock and hurt whirled in his mind and heart.

One Sunday, Mike's church hosted a play, *Heaven's Gates and Hell's Flames*, featuring different vignettes. People who had a personal relationship with God went to heaven, and those without went to hell. Even though he'd been going to church several days a week, Mike had been deceiving himself by thinking he could change his sinful behaviors on his own. He needed God's help—desperately. In a quiet voice, God said, "You've been trying to come to Me on your terms. You need to come on My terms." Mike felt compelled to go up to the altar and receive Christ as his Savior that night. Immediately, he had a sense of relief, knowing God would satisfy his famished soul.

Despite praying for God to change his behavior, Mike still found himself going to the adult bookstore and having same-sex encounters. Feelings of total shame and isolation still weighed heavily on his heart. After six months or so, Mike had to sell the house because his mom moved into a nursing home. He needed a place to live. Steve, the pastor in charge of the singles group, let Mike live in a trailer on his property. Mike felt comfortable discussing his same-sex attraction for the first time. Steve suggested a book—*Beyond Rejection: The Church, Homosexuality, and Hope*—that detailed one man's restoration process. God used the book to teach Mike that his problem was relational—God would use relationships to heal his brokenness. Around this time, he and Kathy, a woman in the singles group, started meeting as prayer partners. They became really great friends, and Mike shared his struggle with same-sex attraction.

Having a distorted self-image, Mike knew he was a male, but he didn't feel like a man. He had never been taught what it meant to be a man—much less a Christian man. Mike likened himself to a dirty toilet bowl; he needed Jesus to wash him clean. If only God would break through his self-contempt and hatred so that he could see himself as a man who has value. But it didn't happen. Not yet. After developing some close relationships with godly men in the singles group, Mike learned to feel more comfortable with his masculinity.

Feeling the need to talk to others facing the same kinds of issues, Mike attempted to join Christward Bound, a ministry for people dealing with homosexuality. Unfortunately, they had just begun a closed group so he was unable to get help there. Mike then connected with Solid Rock Ministries, a Para-church ministry, where he met a counselor named Don.

Over time, Mike saw how alive and vibrant Don's relationship was with God. He wanted that spark. When Don asked how Mike's week had been, Mike replied, "I'm struggling." Don thought he meant more of an internal struggle; but, in reality, Mike was still acting on his urges. The cold truth came out one day when Mike mentioned wanting to be tested for HIV. He said that he'd have to wait six months for an accurate reading. Don raised his voice, "You liar! All of this time I thought you were clean!" Mike realized how deceptive his life really was, and decided to end his sexual encounters.

He continued meeting with Don and another pastor. Whenever they pointed something out about Mike's behavior or thoughts, Mike deflected the comment. But, after being confronted one day, Mike looked up and said, "I don't think that's right." Both pastors' eyes filled with tears as they said, "You know, that's the first time you stood up for yourself." Understanding that self-contempt was actually a strategy to avoid dealing with his unhealthy behaviors, Mike was ready to move into the dignity of his God-given longings—and out of his perverse desires.

On a short-term mission trip in Mexico, Mike thought of Kathy when he spotted a beautiful turquoise and silver bracelet. He came home excited to give Kathy her gift. What Mike didn't know was that she had started dating a guy during his trip. Kathy met Mike to receive her gift but brought her new boyfriend along! Not expecting this, Mike awkwardly handed her the bracelet without saying that he would like to be more than friends. Kathy just thought it was a thank you for watching his cat. When Mike did tell her that he would like to start dating her, she dropped her boyfriend then and there. Within six months the two were married.

Five years into the marriage, Mike still viewed pornography and made sexually explicit phone calls. He shared his struggle with Kathy who expressed love for and acceptance of him. At the same time, though, she did not condone his behavior. It couldn't have been easy for her because Mike was grouchy and not very pleasant to be around.

He sought help from a Christian counselor. In counseling, Mike realized that although some of his behavior had changed, his heart hadn't. That was why he continued to struggle with unhealthy urges and act on them. Without a change of heart, everything was still about him, not God. Starting to understand his brokenness, Mike experienced a softening and deepening of his relationship with God and Kathy.

God put on Mike's heart that he needed to share his experience to help others. He and Kathy started a ministry for those dealing with same-sex attractions and their loved ones. The local newspaper happened to be featuring articles on gay and lesbian issues for a week, so the paper contacted Mike and requested an interview. A week later, a couple called after reading the article about their ministry. They were looking for support to cope with their son's same-sex attractions. Mike and Kathy's ministry is really Christianity 101; they seize every opportunity to share the Gospel. The goal is to help others grow in Christ and be encouraged in the process. They have since partnered with Exodus International, the world's largest ministry to individuals and families impacted by homosexuality. Mike feels so blessed to be sharing the Gospel and seeing broken families and marriages restored.

Mike knows firsthand that people with same-sex attractions cannot just "play church." It won't work. God requires total surrender of every aspect of our life to Him, including sexuality. Many people dealing with sexual brokenness have never heard this before. When Mike's same-sex attraction emerged in high school, he just figured he was born that way. Not until he developed a close relationship with God and fully surrendered to Him did Mike realize that his sexual perversion was no different than any other sin. Each of us has tendencies to sin in various ways. We may not be able to choose what our inclination to sin is, but we all have to decide what we will do with our sin. "Death unto life," Mike says, "is the rhythm of the cross and of the Christian life. The only way we can change for good is if Christ changes our hearts. Christ changes us from the inside out. Heart change is a continual process whereby we die to our sinful nature and allow Christ to live in us. Will we play a victim or live triumphantly with the help of God? It's our choice."

Although Mike still has a vulnerability to his old temptations, God gives him the power not to act on them. When an urge to sin arises, it is much like the "idiot lights" on the dashboard of a car—an indicator that something is about to go wrong. This signals the need for Mike to talk to God to deal with the temptation before he sins.

Today, Mike is hungrier than ever for the Word of God and seeks to deepen his relationship with Him. Mike encourages the body of Christ to realize that there is so much more to being a true Christian than simply going to church and doing good works. He has given talks on Christian Family Radio and at local colleges where he has shared the Gospel and the power of God's love and grace to help others overcome sinful tendencies.

"The heart is deceitful above all things and beyond cure, who can understand it?" (Jeremiah 17:9).

Even though Mike's heart was inclined to same-sex attraction, he chose to discontinue in sin by asking God to help him resist sinful urges. Mike lives an abundant life in Christ today because he surrendered his life and sexuality to God and allowed Christ to change his heart.

Kristen ~ Age 37
Sacrificing Fertility Led to Adoption

As a girl, Kristen listened intently in Sunday school and church services. After church one Sunday at the age of five, she came home knowing she was a sinner and that Jesus died so her sins would be forgiven. Kristen went off by herself to the playroom and accepted Christ. At the age of eight, she confidently walked up to the altar and told the pastor she needed to be baptized—he seemed surprised that such a young girl was so determined to honor God in that way. Kristen loved God with her whole heart, and she remained close to Him as she grew older.

Kristen married Steve in 2001. They planned to start a family the following year, but she didn't become pregnant in 2002, 2003, or 2004. During those years, they went to several ob-gyn doctors, and Kristen took various medications that gave her horrible mood swings. She felt like a failure because all she had ever wanted her whole life was to be a mom. Not being able to have children made her feel like less of a woman. She wondered, *Why am I not able to get pregnant?* Kristen remembers playing with dolls in a pink bedroom at her grandma's house when she was eight and thinking, *What if I can't have babies someday?* God planted a tiny seed way back then to help prepare her for her struggle with infertility.

Trying so hard to conceive for all those years left her emotionally drained, not to mention isolated. Going to church on Mother's Day and watching little children buying roses for their moms was a heart-wrenching sight. Her friends didn't know what to say to comfort her, and they especially felt guilty when they told her they had gotten pregnant. Of course, Kristen wanted to share in their joy even though she wept privately for several hours after hearing the news, reminded of her repeated failures. Sadness and confusion lay deep in her heart, but they never turned into anger toward God. Kristen knew that God had a good plan in store; she just didn't know what yet.

Kristen and Steve went to their "last hope" appointment with a reproductive endocrinologist in 2004. After a painful medical exam, the doctor shared his diagnosis and her likelihood of getting pregnant. The odds weren't good. She and Steve walked away from the medical community and placed the matter in God's hands. Before even leaving the doctor's parking lot, they decided to adopt internationally—both felt peace about this.

Kristen and Steve researched three adoption agencies and went with the first responder to their paperwork. Then came time to decide what country. China appealed to them because of the plight of females there—many were not loved, wanted, or needed. Although Kristen knew adopting a baby girl from China was God's plan for her family, she still had fears and doubts. God used the lyrics, "I choose to listen and believe the voice of Truth," from the song "Voice of Truth" by Casting Crowns to give Kristen the faith to jump into the adoption process for God's glory, leaving her fears behind.

A surprise came in January of 2005—Kristen became pregnant! They were shocked and excited. She and Steve were definitely not expecting such news since she was off the fertility drugs. Since a couple cannot proceed with an adoption if they become pregnant, she and Steve planned to put the process on hold for three months. Because she firmly believed God wanted them to adopt, Kristen was puzzled about the timing of the pregnancy. At her two-month check-up, however, a red flag went up when the technician quietly called in the doctor after doing an ultrasound. Their baby had died.

Kristen took one month off work to spend time with God. She studied 1 Peter and learned how to honor God through trials. Knowing the trials with infertility and losing her baby would end up leading to something much better, she was able to look ahead with expectation. Even though her baby died, Kristen considered her pregnancy a gift from God. She was thankful she actually had the chance to see two lines on the pregnancy test and experience morning sickness like other women.

In April of 2006, Kristen and Steve received paperwork and pictures from China for six-month-old Adeline. Her birthday was October 28, only ten days later than Kristen's expected due date! What a gift! They went to China in June to bring home their daughter. Kristen was not an adventurous person; only by the grace of God was she able to fly to China—halfway around the world! Her love of children and deep, lifelong desire to be a mom overrode her fear of travel.

They flew to Adeline's province their third day in China, but they had to wait in the airplane for several hours in 100-degree temperatures due to mechanical problems. The hours crept by as they waited in anticipation. On the bus ride to the hotel, Kristen read an information sheet she'd been given about Adeline's likes, dislikes, and personality. Suddenly it hit—*this is my baby!*

Adeline was sleeping when she was handed over to Kristen. After she woke up and saw Kristen, she cried for the next five hours. It was very hard to see Adeline so unhappy, but the fact that she grieved leaving her nannies meant that she had formed a close bond and could do so again. Although Kristen was ready to love Adeline, she had to accept that Adeline wasn't yet ready to love her. By the fourth day, Kristen could tell Adeline liked her, and it felt like she loved her by the seventh day.

When Adeline turned two, God began tugging at them to adopt another baby from China. One night, Kristen prayed quietly in the corner of Adeline's room while waiting for her to fall asleep, "God, I feel like you want us to adopt again, but how are we going to do this financially? You know I quit my job to stay at home with Adeline and that we depleted our savings to adopt her. Please guide us." The next day, a summary of Kristen's retirement account came in the mail—there was enough money in it to fund half the adoption! Then Steve was blessed with a small inheritance. It turns out the check was made out for the amount they needed to pay their next installment to the adoption agency! Checks continued arriving in the mail from friends—not a typical occurrence! Kristen and Steve were amazed at the way God very clearly made the adoption possible.

At a Bible study class one morning, Kristen heard God telling her to go with a special needs adoption. She talked it over with Steve that night and he suggested they pray while requesting the special needs paperwork. Then they researched possible disabilities and made a list of those they thought they could handle. Even though the paperwork was completed, something kept Kristen from sending it in until a friend asked, "What are you waiting for? Send it in!" It was just the confirmation Kristen needed. Off the paperwork went! She knew in her heart that God wouldn't give them more than they could handle.

Four weeks later, Kristen got a call at eleven o'clock in the morning about a baby girl, Ruby, born prematurely with some irregularities in her genetic testing reports. She and Steve only had until the next morning to decide if they wanted to adopt! The pressure was on! At two o'clock, Kristen met with a pediatrician filling in for their regular doctor. As it turned out, she just happened to have adopted two boys through the same adoption agency. The pediatrician suggested Kristen talk to a specialist at Children's Hospital. By four o'clock, Kristen connected with a doctor at the hospital who then had several geneticists review the baby's medical information. An hour later, the doctor called back and said that her irregularities were nothing to worry about.

Kristen and Steve prayed and felt pretty confident that this was their baby but didn't know what to expect. They really liked that she was only two years younger than Adeline because the typical wait time for an international adoption from China was lengthy—this was another gift from God!

They went ahead with the adoption and continued filling out paperwork, but they ran into several snags. Kristen and Steve relied on faith alone that God would work everything out. They didn't even know Ruby's exit visa paperwork was ready until one half hour before boarding the plane to China! It was a close call, but God came through for them once again.

Walking into a room inside a large government office full of babies, children, and couples from many different countries waiting to meet their adopted children, Kristen was touched by the bravery of the children—many of whom were between one and eight years old. The children had to leave the nannies who had cared for them and go home with strangers. Most of the children had very obvious physical abnormalities such as cleft palates, clubfeet, and missing arms or legs. Then Kristen saw sweet Ruby's face across the room. She thought, *There is my beautiful, precious baby!* When their name was called, a woman handed Ruby to Steve; this was a very special moment because Kristen had been the first to hold Adeline.

Ruby, then fifteen months old, was very quiet and shy. Steve put her down and she walked and ran. She looked completely healthy. Praise the Lord! They didn't know she could walk yet, much less run! Back at the hotel, Kristen commented, "I don't think there's anything wrong with her at all!" Even the doctor who gave Ruby a medical exam before they left China said she was just fine. Back at home, their pediatrician said not to bother taking Ruby to a specialist for an extensive exam. She said, "There is nothing wrong with her other than being a bit behind developmentally." How amazing that God had gotten them to think about special needs adoption, then blessed them with a perfectly healthy baby!

It took a while for Ruby to warm up to Kristen. Ruby would not let Kristen comfort her for several months. Kristen understood that was because Ruby had a rough start and did not receive the love and nurturing that a baby needs. But, by the time she turned three years old, little Ruby became affectionate and talked nonstop.

Today, Kristen and Steve work for the adoption agency they went through. They give several adoption seminars in churches across the state each year. God has given Kristen a huge burden for the adoption crisis around the world—and a heart for people living in China. She hopes God will allow her to return to China at some point to help out with the orphans. Her heart goes out to all of the children who never get adopted and are eventually timed out of the system—never knowing the love of family. Kristen is saddened by the Christians in China who are not able to worship the Lord publicly and do not have Bibles. Kristen prays that the girls' families come to the Lord so they can be reunited in heaven because it is unlikely they will meet here on Earth.

Kristen is happy to have sacrificed her fertility to open her heart to adoption. Even though she experienced sadness during her trials with infertility, Kristen counts it all joy now. Her beautiful girls are such a blessing. She has learned to always trust that God knows what is best even though it may not be what a person thinks he or she wants; He always has a plan for good.

"Rejoice that you participate in the sufferings of Christ, so that you may be overjoyed when his glory is revealed" (1 Peter 4:13).

Kristen is glad God caused her to sacrifice her fertility so she could experience the joys of adoption. Her inability to have a biological baby made it possible for God to bless her, Steve, and their two daughters as well.

Andrew ~ Age 20
Deep Depression and Fear
Dissolved by the Truth

At the age of five or six, Andrew awakened from a weird dream and felt depressed. He told his dad how he felt, and his parents scheduled an appointment with a psychiatrist. The doctor diagnosed Andrew with depression and ADD, and then he prescribed several medications. His parents said he should expect to take medication for the rest of his life because they were taking medication for depression, too. Being labeled with depression gave Andrew little hope of ever having a normal life—he figured he would feel that way forever.

A conference on autism spectrum disorders that his mom attended led her to believe that Andrew had Asperger's syndrome. His psychiatrist confirmed the diagnosis and added yet another medication. By this time, at the age of eight, therapy was part of everyday life.

Andrew behaved quite differently than most young boys. He spoke in a monotone and acted very distant. He generally chose to play alone. His thought pattern was negative all of the time. If a story started with something bad happening to a character and had a happy ending, Andrew fixated on the beginning. The fact that the story ended well didn't even register.

Kids made fun of Andrew because he wasn't very sociable and didn't stand up for himself. The bullying made him feel even more self-conscious and fearful.

Around the sixth grade, Andrew got more into God. He thought, *If God is all-powerful, I want to know Him.* He took church more seriously. Before, he'd considered church a nuisance because it caused him to miss his favorite television show, *Transformers.* Andrew spent time reading the Bible. He started with Exodus and Numbers and then jumped to Daniel, Ezekiel, and Revelation. The more he learned about God, the more he became interested in a career in theology. Kids made fun of Andrew because of his faith—they saw him as a religious freak. They laughed because he wouldn't swear.

Thinking it might help if he went to a Christian school, Andrew asked to transfer in seventh grade. Nothing changed. Kids still made fun of him and treated him poorly. Because those so-called Christians were just as abusive as anyone else, Andrew gave up—he saw no point in being a Christian if they didn't behave differently than other people. Andrew grew so tired of being bullied at school that he decided to stand up for himself by throwing harsh verbal threats at the kids who made fun of him. He thought, *I'll show them!* In time, Andrew became arrogant and prideful; he believed he was better than the other kids.

Wildly depressed, Andrew lived in fear of "flipping out" at any time. Every few months, all of his medications were changed due to a lack of effectiveness, and he went through therapists just as quickly—nobody seemed capable of establishing a rapport with him.

Two incidents threw him over the edge. First, he asked a girl at school out on a date and she told him she was grounded. Andrew found out that she lied, and the next day he walked up to her and proclaimed, "Liars go to hell!" Her mouth fell open, and she didn't even have a response. The second incident was in art class. All of a sudden, a guy yelled across the room, "Hey, Andrew, do you have a hit list?" Andrew said that he didn't, but before long a rumor spread around school that he did! Kids teased him by asking what number they were on the list. He started playing along by saying that everyone was on the list and making up imaginary numbers. Eventually, the hit list prank landed Andrew in the principal's office, even though he wasn't at fault.

He was sent to a psychiatric center for eight days. His behavior was just as rebellious there as anywhere else. By the seventh day, Andrew realized that he was being punished for telling the truth about how he felt, so he decided to tell the nurses and doctors what they wanted to hear. They released him the following day.

Knowing the kids at school were unceasingly bullying Andrew, his mom stood up for him by going to the principal and demanding a solution. They agreed that Andrew could stop by after school twice per week to pick up his homework assignments and study at home. That's how he completed the remainder of middle school. Andrew entered high school with a D average, but not because he wasn't intelligent—he simply didn't apply himself.

His depression sunk even deeper; Andrew had no motivation to do anything. He started stealing money from his parents, somehow thinking he was better than everyone else and deserving of an easier life. Yet, at the same time, he felt worthless. Every day after school, Andrew looked for a rope to hang himself, but he never found one. Halfway through the year, he started cutting himself. At least the physical pain temporarily masked his emotional turmoil. Although he continued therapy, it did no good—the therapists didn't know how to talk to him, and he closed up. This led to a change in therapists every few months.

In a desperate attempt to find meaning outside of himself, Andrew tried atheism. That lasted about one month. Atheism didn't work because he had an indescribable feeling that there was something more. He spent nearly two hours per day researching different religions, and he decided to try Wicca—an earth-centered, pagan religion. Wiccans practice magic and have eight annual celebrations of seasonally based festivals. The focus is on worshiping creation itself rather than the Creator. Even though all reality is considered divine to them, Wiccans worship a god and goddess. It seemed to him like they just crammed all sorts of beliefs into one religion.

Andrew found a group of Wiccans to hang out with. Before long, he realized they didn't seem to know what they believed. He was supposed to study for initiation into Wicca, but never got any straightforward answers to his questions. There didn't seem to be a clear purpose—only rituals and ceremonies. They had him study things like astrology, tarot cards, divination, and the powers of gemstones.

Andrew always thought the dynamics of the group were dysfunctional. The group's leader sat back and made everyone else do his work, and he scolded the others for not doing what they should. Only one guy was nice to Andrew; everyone else yelled at him and bickered with one another.

Early during sophomore year, Andrew brought a razor to school. He went into the bathroom and tried to cut his left wrist down the center. As hard as he pushed the razor along his skin, though, it didn't leave any more than a scratch! This seemed preposterous! Getting frustrated, Andrew tried cutting on the outside of his wrist—the razor cut deep into his flesh. When he tried on the inner side again, however, nothing happened! Disappointed at his failure, Andrew sheepishly walked into the nurse's office, ashamed of having to face anyone. The nurse called his parents; when they arrived at school, his dad was furious and his mom was crying.

Needless to say, this incident resulted in another hospitalization. All the psychiatric hospitals nearby were full, meaning that Andrew had to stay in an out-of-town facility for really troubled kids. They even locked the doors. Luckily, he only had to stay for seventy-two hours before being moved to the same hospital he'd been admitted to before. Andrew was released after one week.

Before being hospitalized, Andrew had started dating a girl. Shortly after he returned to school, she ended up moving out of state with her mom. They corresponded for a short time before she broke up with him to date someone else. By that time, Andrew felt stoic; he was not fazed by anything—he simply didn't care.

While his ex-girlfriend dated another guy, she and Andrew communicated on the Internet. She mentioned that she would like to see him, so Andrew ran away from home and took a bus to visit her. He expected someone to pick him up at the bus depot, but no one came. Because he was a good sixty miles away from where she lived (without food or money), Andrew started walking. He walked about five miles with his thumb out to the road. Even though he didn't have any particular belief in God at the time, he stopped and looked up to the sky and said, "God, if You're there, get me a ride. Let someone stop and pick me up, and I will never deny Your existence again." The very next car to pass stopped! It turned out to be a hippie who had done his share of hitchhiking. The man took Andrew as far as he could. This happened two more times until he arrived at his ex-girlfriend's house. After he traveled all the way there, she acted like she didn't want to talk. Not knowing where else to go, Andrew went to the police station, and they called his parents. They came to take him home the following day.

Toward the end of sophomore year, Andrew tried to kill himself again—this time at home. He went into the bathroom and selected a new razor. Once again, he tried to cut the inside of his left wrist but something prevented the blade from cutting his skin. Andrew stood by the sink crying and feeling completely worthless—*I can't even kill myself!* Figuring it didn't pay to try anymore, Andrew gave up.

He focused all of his energy on getting through high school. Even though his grades were poor, Andrew wanted to take physics—he really enjoyed science and math. Part of him simply wanted to prove he could do it because physics is such a difficult subject. Figuring he had nothing to lose, Andrew asked the physics teacher whether he could take the class without meeting the prerequisites. To his amazement, the teacher agreed. Life got a little better once he started the physics class. Andrew has always thought in images, and physics meshed with the way his brain worked. He earned a B in physics—his highest grade ever!

Andrew barely passed high school—he only had earned a D average. Even though he really wanted to study physics, his grades were too poor to get into a university. First, he would have to prove himself by getting a degree from a technical college. Sometimes he went to school, sometimes he didn't. It seemed like a waste of gas to drive there. Having no motivation to succeed, Andrew withdrew from every class.

On a heavy cocktail of medications, including sleeping pills, Andrew couldn't take it anymore. One day, late in the spring of 2010, Andrew took a heaping handful of sleeping pills—enough to kill a horse. Typically, after taking only one pill, he would fall asleep within a half hour. But he didn't feel tired at all this time. Andrew took a forty-five-minute walk, and then called a friend to come over. She called his parents, who took him to the hospital to get his stomach pumped. On the way to the hospital, Andrew started feeling a little tired, but he never fell asleep!

Life continued going downhill quickly. Another hospitalization ensued. After getting out of the hospital, Andrew stole over two thousand dollars from his parents in one and a half months by charging their credit cards. That, together with what he'd stolen during high school, amounted to over four thousand dollars! Because they were no longer able to trust Andrew, his parents kicked him out.

Andrew moved in with a Wiccan couple he knew from the group he had joined earlier. Much of his time was spent taking care of their little boy, whom they basically ignored. As summer approached, the couple said he would need sixty-five dollars to go camping for the Summer Solstice celebration. Because he didn't have any money, Andrew couldn't go; the members of the group yelled at him for not going on the trip. He later found out that he wouldn't have needed to pay for the trip after all—the couple had lied to him. That was the last straw: Andrew decided to leave the Wiccan group.

Late in August of 2010, he decided to give Christianity another try. This was his last chance at life. If it didn't work, he planned to find a way to kill himself. Andrew just couldn't face living every day for the rest of his life feeling hopeless and worthless.

A few months earlier, a friend had mentioned something about a home church ministry. Andrew started to hang out with the members of the ministry group. They answered any questions he had about God, the Bible, or life in general, and they genuinely wanted to get to know him! At first, when one of the guys came over and asked Andrew about himself, he talked and talked, figuring the guy would tire of hearing his stories. But he didn't! The guy actually listened to every word, and he even asked Andrew questions to get to know him even better. He thought, *Wow! These people are interested in actually knowing me!*

In January of 2011, Andrew talked to his doctor about stopping all medications. Now that he'd come back to God, he had hope that his depression would lift in time. The doctor worked with Andrew and helped him gradually get off the medications.

Meanwhile, the ministry group helped Andrew identify and change his negative thought patterns. They asked why he did certain things. When he seemed upset, they asked him why. It always came back to the following phrase: "Because I'm terrified of being alone!" Andrew's friends helped him discover why he felt that way, and they used cognitive therapy techniques to reprogram his brain. The most effective approach for processing his thoughts and feelings was journaling. It helped stop negative thought loops and got him right back on track with God. Because Andrew's thinking tended to go on and on, he wrote in his journal an average of five times per day. The group filled him to the brim with doctrine, love, and fellowship. He pursued God and placed the spiritual over the physical and mental. The more his eyes opened to the spiritual, the more he could see how being alone would be impossible. Eventually, he learned that the feeling of being alone was a lie from Satan.

One day, late in the summer of 2011, a pastor in the group gave a lesson on what it meant to be saved. The lesson really spoke to Andrew, and he felt an overwhelming need to be saved—to know for sure that he would spend eternity with God. In that moment, it was the only thing he really wanted. Andrew pondered Titus 1:2: "a faith and knowledge resting on the hope of eternal life, which God, who does not lie, promised before the beginning of time." The fact that God cannot lie struck him; it meant that the Bible was completely true! Because Andrew had been lied to so many times over the years, it meant so much to know that God's Word is the absolute truth.

By the end of the message, Andrew cowered a bit, slowly raised his hand and asked, "Can I be saved?" They all exclaimed, "Yes—and you didn't have to raise your hand!" One of the pastors walked to the front yard with Andrew and read a few Bible verses (such as Romans 10:9) that explained the statement of a person's will to be saved. Openly crying, Andrew felt vulnerable, self-conscious, and completely broken. He prayed out loud for God to save him. He confessed his attempts to kill himself, running away to see his ex-girlfriend, and worshiping another god as examples of the sins that needed to be forgiven. Andrew said, "God, I owe You so much for all You've done—You've already saved me from death six times. And You sent Your Son to die, even for me. I give You my entire life." Still weeping, Andrew knew he had just made the most important decision of his life.

Today, life is getting better and better. He's back in school. The depression is gone, and Andrew is not taking any medications. This is the first time in his life he remembers not feeling depressed, and it's all because of God. He describes his newfound relationship with God as being "better than winning a million dollars." Now Andrew knows that he, and every single person, has great value in God's eyes. Andrew is happy and joyful—he can still hardly believe how good he feels! He offers this advice, "You can't wait for happiness to find you, you have to pursue it by jumping right into it." Noticing a radical change in his behavior and attitude, Andrew's parents have repeatedly said, "We just can't fathom how much faith you have!"

Since fully surrendering to the Lord, Andrew's greatest desire is Jesus—to know Him, be with Him, and stand beside Him one day. Andrew enjoys mental health today in large part because Jesus has shown how deeply and unconditionally He loves him. He's pursuing God with every fiber of his being. On a daily basis, Andrew receives some sort of revelation about God.

"Have I not commanded you? Be strong and courageous. Do not be terrified; do not be discouraged, for the Lord your God will be with you wherever you go" (Joshua 1:9).

Andrew overcame major depression with a combination of pursuing God, studying the Bible, changing his thought processes, placing the spiritual over the physical, and writing in a journal. He is no longer terrified of being alone because he knows God is always by his side.

Darlene ~ Age 68
Trust Is the Key

One Sunday, the pastor read Ephesians 2:8–9, "For it is by grace you have been saved, through faith—and this not from yourselves, it is the gift of God—not by works, so that no one can boast." Even though very young, Darlene immediately knew Jesus was her Savior and had forgiven all her sins. She understood how deeply He loved her. When she said her nighttime prayer, "Now I lay me down to sleep..." Darlene felt a sense of security in Christ. She knew that, no matter what, Jesus would be with her.

Growing up with four brothers, Darlene longed for a sister, but whining and feeling sorry for herself got her nowhere. God made her strong. After all, she needed help surviving in a house full of rambunctious boys! Over the years, God nurtured her strength in Him, grooming her for leadership roles in the church.

After being married and having three children, a hunger for the Lord grew in Darlene's heart. Even though she wasn't a reader, Darlene found herself in a Christian bookstore one day. She bought a book on marriage that she really enjoyed. Darlene read other books by the same author. One book, on the empowerment that comes from fullness of the Spirit, fed her hunger. It was exactly what she wanted! Darlene learned that Jesus desired to be her Lord, not only her Savior. As her Lord, He would satisfy her every need because of His faithfulness and rich love; she only needed to call on Him.

Darlene prayed for God to fill her with the Holy Spirit, and she felt His Spirit come into her being in great power and majesty. Shortly after, God convicted her of being too busy working at church rather than spending time bowing at His feet. So Darlene began cutting back on activities, leaving more time for the Holy Spirit to work in her life. Around this time, she joined a women's group that focused on empowerment to live for God via the indwelling fire of Christ's Spirit. God spoke to her through Romans 12:11: "Never be lacking in zeal, but keep your spiritual fervor, serving the Lord." Darlene's security in Christ grew stronger still; she learned she could do all things through His strength.

Her oldest son became seriously ill with a joint disease during his middle school years. His health deteriorated to the point that he couldn't even attend school anymore. It broke Darlene's heart to hear her son crying out in pain as he lay in bed. Early on, she prayed for God's help—she didn't know what was going to happen to him. God answered, "Your son will be healed." Standing on His Word made it easier to hear heaps of discouraging news from doctors. Her trust in God grew stronger as she grasped tightly to His promise in the darkest moments of pain and sadness. God led Darlene to a nutritionist who put her son on a body-cleansing program. His health gradually improved every month. In time, God healed her son—just as He said.

Next, Darlene learned to see Jesus as her healer. She suffered for fifteen years with ulcerations on the inside lining of her bladder. Constant burning in her bladder, coupled with frequent trips to the bathroom, held her captive at home. Darlene held onto God's promise in 1 Peter 5:10–11: "And the God of all grace, who called you to his eternal glory in Christ, after you have suffered a little while, will himself restore you and make you strong, firm and steadfast. To him be the power for ever and ever. Amen." God led her to make dietary changes that provided some relief and freedom to venture away from the bathroom. Then she went through one year of total body cleansing. Part of the cleansing process involved fasting, which brought Darlene closer to God than she'd ever been. Her bladder was healed!

In her current season of life, Darlene has dealt with the loss of family and friends. Four girlfriends have died in the past ten years, and her husband's parents, with whom she had a close relationship, died within nineteen days of one another. The Lord has carried her through with the passage, "My grace is sufficient for you, for my power is made perfect in weakness. Therefore I will boast all the more gladly about my weaknesses, so that Christ's power may rest on me" (2 Corinthians 12:9). Weakened with grief, Darlene relied on God's strength.

One night, while sitting in bed studying for an intensive Grace Life Conference, God illuminated who she was in Christ. He revealed what was available to her as a believer through Galatians 2:20: "I have been crucified with Christ and I no longer live, but Christ lives in me. The life I live in the body, I live by faith in the Son of God, who loved me and gave himself for me." This revelation gave Darlene a sense of freedom in Christ she had never experienced. She began to think, behave, and pray differently. No longer working out of her flesh—her personality, attitude, and thoughts—she was free to grow into Christ's likeness one day at a time.

While sitting in a grocery store parking lot on January 21, 2003, God spoke to Darlene about trust by placing a poem on her heart entitled "It's All About Trust."

> Trust is the key to living in Me
> T: turning each situation completely over to Me—
> I am your keeper.
> R: readying your heart for the deep work I want to do—
> I am your digger.
> U: understanding that it is not by might or power but
> by my Spirit—

I am your Paraclete (Holy Spirit).
S: simply relying on the promises that I give you—
I am your sustainer.
T: taking everything to Him in prayer, knowing He's
My all in all,
The great I Am, and
The beginning and the
End of everything.

Today, Darlene is in a transition period. She senses God has plans for change in her life, but is unsure where He'll take her. While waiting on the Lord, Darlene rests in a deep trust that He has something good in store for her. She often sings, "'Tis so sweet to trust in Jesus, and to take Him at His word; just to rest upon His promise, and to know, 'Thus saith the Lord.'" This hymn has been close to her heart over the years because it beautifully portrays the theme of trusting God and believing in what He says.

"It is better to take refuge in the Lord than to trust in man" (Psalm 118:8).

After some research, Darlene discovered this verse lies exactly in the middle of the Bible! It's no mistake that God placed this Scripture in the center because trust is at the core of believing and knowing God. God has revealed Himself as trustworthy time and again through every trial Darlene has encountered.

Steve ~ Age 53
Beelzebub to Servant

Steve thought of himself as the devil incarnate. Intimidation was his motto. If he didn't intimidate a person right away, he found a way to make sure he did later. When only nineteen, Steve was arrested on a series of criminal charges. He pleaded insanity to avoid a harsh prison sentence, and was sent to a mental health institution for ninety days. Even though everyone thought he must have been crazy to do the things he'd done, he was not mentally ill—just bad. In fact, Steve was proud of how bad he was, and he wanted everyone to know.

He wasn't afraid of hitting anyone: his nose was broken eight times, and his face became covered with battle scars. Being arrested and placed in jail more times than he could count, Steve developed scars on his arms and wrists from repeated handcuffing. He once faced forty-three years in prison.

Steve hadn't always been bad. In fact, as a boy, he went to church, Sunday school, and attended youth camps in the summer. His dad served as a deacon in the church. He even accepted Christ as his Savior at the age of twelve. But by the time Steve was a freshman in high school, he had fallen in with the wrong crowd and turned from God. The worse his behavior became, the less he thought about God. Steve knew what he did was wrong in God's eyes, but he didn't care. The only way he could continue his behavior was to turn his back to God. So he ran away as fast as he could without looking back. His behavior became so bad in school that teachers gave Steve passing grades just to get him out of their classrooms.

By adulthood, each day began with Steve drinking a can of beer that he had placed on his headboard the night before. This made him vomit. Afterward, he went to the refrigerator and grabbed a second can of beer—and then another, and another …

In addition to being an alcoholic, Steve used drugs heavily. Every time he was invited to someone's house, he went through the medicine cabinet in their bathroom, stealing the prescription drugs. Steve owned a drug reference guide and knew what every available drug would do for him. Most Friday nights he bought an "eight ball" of cocaine. He was paranoid that someone might steal it or that the police would catch him, though, so he ran into his house and locked the door. Then he pulled the curtains and hid on the floor in a closet behind closed doors with his precious cocaine, a piece of glass, and a razor. Steve would not come out of the closet until he had inhaled every last bit of cocaine.

He would have put anything into his body if he thought it might fill the empty place in his heart. After trying just about every*thing* the world had to offer, Steve still came up empty. In fact, the emptiness had become a black pit that grew deeper day by day.

Shortly after his son's fifth birthday, Steve had an ugly argument with his wife that landed him in jail yet again. After being released, he went to stay with one of his drinking friends because his wife wanted a divorce. He remembers sitting on his friend's sofa and crying. He thought, *How much worse could things get?* Steve was only allowed to see his son for one hour every other week. By that point in his life, Steve had lost quite a bit of weight and had a grossly enlarged liver that actually protruded from his body like a pouch. Only thirty-two years old, Steve had lost everything: his marriage, countless jobs, his self-respect and the respect of his family, and his home and everything in it.

All he had left was a pickup truck and two garbage bags full of clothes.

One Sunday morning, around ten o'clock, Steve ordered a screwdriver at a local bar. After his second one, he thought he'd have one more for the road. Next thing he knew it was dark outside! He noticed that the bartender and person sitting next to him were different people than he'd seen earlier. Steve was too drunk to walk, but he somehow drove back to his friend's house. The next thing he remembered was his friend slapping and hollering at him—he was in the corner, urinating on a plant! Steve stumbled over to the sofa. He had reached rock bottom. He wondered, *What am I to do?*

Suddenly, he found himself transported to a different location. Steve was standing on a clay path in the middle of a forest. He could smell the pine needles and fallen leaves. He could hear the birds chirping and the rustling of leaves. Three tall pine trees stood in the center of the forest where the path split. From the depths of his being, Steve heard and felt a voice say, "You have come to a fork in the road. You have to decide. You can take the path you have been on, or you can take the path I have laid out for you. But if you continue on your path, you will surely die."

The next morning, February 26, 1989, was the first sober day of Steve's adult life. He hasn't had a drink since. Steve woke up feeling wonderful that day. He knew he didn't want to live like that anymore. He knew he'd had some kind of spiritual experience the night before, but wasn't totally aware of its significance or where it would lead him. Steve had no idea what lay ahead. All he did know was that he needed to talk to his mom—she would be able to help. His mom gave him the names and numbers of two men. One of the men told Steve he would meet him at the AA meeting that evening. Only a few weeks later, his liver had shrunk back to a normal size—a miracle!

Steve moved back home with his parents for a while until he could get back on his feet. For years, his parents had prayed that he would come back to God. Coming to the Lord was a process. In search of the truth, Steve even dabbled in some new age stuff. None of those things seemed authentic to him, though, and they always left him empty and searching for more. After three or four months, Steve started attending church fairly regularly. Over time, he began to understand the full significance of his spiritual experience. God had come to rescue Steve by pulling him out of the pit of despair, but he had a choice to make. He was ready to make the most important decision of his life: to follow the path of Jesus, the only path leading to life.

Everything about his life began to change: what he did, whom he spent time with, what he said, and what he thought about. He found new friends who supported his new life and walked by his side. He attended AA meetings very regularly. Later, Steve began attending an Adult Children of Alcoholics meeting that really solidified his recovery process. Six months after moving back home, Steve was awarded sole custody of his son because his ex-wife continued to drink heavily. God opened a door for Steve to go to college. He graduated five years later with a 3.67 GPA and a teaching degree. Steve taught for six years at the Rawhide Boys Ranch and several years as a teacher in the public school system.

God ended Steve's teaching career to teach him a lesson about the sinfulness of his pride. Over time, he developed the notion that because of his experiences and the blessings of God, he had some deep wisdom that others failed to recognize or possess. He became arrogant and judgmental, and some issues of anger that he had not yet dealt with came to the fore. Steve used his tongue much like he once used his fists: to bully and beat down any resistance to his ideas. Because Steve is a child of God and deeply loved by Him, God's discipline was necessary. He has since learned not to despise the Lord's discipline, and embraces humility as best he can.

Today, Steve has a passion for men's ministry. He's sharing what God has taught him about being a godly man. Steve strongly feels that men need to know their responsibilities as the spiritual leader of their home. Namely, men are to guide and direct their wives and children to follow God's ways.

In his work, he's helping to change men's lives in the local prison. Earlier in his career, Steve served as the prison chaplain. Now he works with inmates who have been diagnosed with mental disorders, including clinical syndromes (e.g., depression), developmental disorders, or personality disorders. Steve teaches men the skills they'll need to reenter society and stay out of prison. The program begins six months before an inmate's release date, and it continues one year after being released. This length of time allows Steve to build strong relationships with the men so they have an anchor of support after returning to the outside world. God has opened many doors for him to share the good news of the Bible with some of the men.

God has blessed Steve with more than he ever hoped for, and certainly more than he deserves. He has completed the hard work of raising his son into a man—a man who now works as a police officer. Steve is happily married to his third and forever wife, a godly woman who is a precious gift from God. Scars and all, Steve is now a beautiful new creation in Christ. God has changed him from a bad man to a godly man—nothing short of a miracle! The black hole in his heart has been completely filled up by God. In fact, Steve calls himself a cracked pot. God has poured so much of Himself into Steve's heart that some flows over the top and leaks out of the bottom and sides.

Steve is learning every day how to live in a way that honors God. His ears are sharply tuned to the Word of God; he doesn't want to miss anything God says to him. The most difficult lessons learned so far have been to tame his tongue and to serve others first. Being incredibly selfish at his core, it is a daily struggle to place others before himself. Steve nevertheless serves one day at a time.

"They are your servants and your people, whom you redeemed by your great strength and your mighty hand" (Nehemiah 1:10).

Here, Nehemiah is praising God for rescuing the Israelites even though they had sinned against Him by acting wickedly and not obeying His laws. Just like the Israelites, Steve turned away from God with his evil acts. Steve was too full of pride to find his way back to God so God came to Steve's rescue when he'd reached rock bottom—even though Steve didn't even ask for His help. He knew Steve needed a rude awakening that would change him completely. Having been redeemed by God's almighty hand, Steve honors Him by being a faithful servant.

Judy ~ Age 67
Renewed by God

Time and again, tears poured down her cheeks as Judy asked God, "Why me? Why do I have to go through this?" Her mom disciplined by beating, whipping, scratching, pulling hair, belittling, name calling, and depriving Judy and her sister of food. Nights of going to bed with no supper and waking up hungry without breakfast led Judy to eat junk food. The pounds began to creep on as she began using food to satisfy herself when unhappy, which was most of the time. Growing up in the shadows of a narcissistic mom—"Queen of the castle"—left Judy with low self-esteem.

Judy attended church with her mom and sister and went to parochial school; her dad only went to church sporadically. The family left God at church. Things were very dysfunctional at home, and her mom's behavior was anything but pious. Judy knew God existed, but she didn't understand much about Him or His ways.

A schoolgirl romance found Judy married and pregnant before turning eighteen. Her husband inflicted severe physical and emotional abuse on her. He became even more hostile after finding out she was pregnant. He deprived her of prenatal care, and even pushed her down the stairs. Their baby boy was stillborn. By this time, Judy weighed two hundred pounds—sixty-five more pounds than she weighed a year earlier. Her husband told her,

"I didn't marry a fat wife, and I won't live with one either." The marriage dissolved soon after.

Before long, Judy found herself dating and planning to marry again. But something told her she shouldn't marry him: he was an alcoholic, and she knew it wouldn't be a good marriage. Meanwhile, Judy found out she was pregnant. She wasn't welcome at home. Having no place to go, she found shelter at a house for unwed mothers—a cold, uncaring environment.

Judy was so depressed she wanted to die. She turned off the heat in her room in the dead of winter hoping to catch pneumonia. All the while she wondered, *Why me? Why do I have to go through this?* Chilled to the bone, she looked out of her bedroom window. Judy longed to be part of the seemingly perfect, happy family next door. All alone on Thanksgiving Day and Christmas that miserable year, Judy watched while the mother gently combed her daughter's hair and the son petted the dog. They were such a loving family. She could even feel the warmth radiating from their home. She thought, *If only my mom were so loving and sweet.* Judy made the heart-wrenching decision to give up her baby girl for adoption because she had no means of supporting herself or the baby.

A while later, Judy met a much older man who treated her well and took care of her. They married, lived in a nice house, and went to church together. Life went along pretty well for a while. She attended Bible study classes and learned how to listen to God speak to her. Before, Judy was too busy trying to do things on her own to listen.

Noticing Judy's Bible one day, her brother-in-law, who had studied to be a minister, began sharing his faith. Although she had read the Bible some, she didn't understand what she read. Judy's brother-in-law gave her Bible lessons whenever she came to visit.

Meanwhile, Judy began fainting periodically and learned she had developed heart problems. Then her husband had a heart attack and was transported to an out-of-town hospital. During his stay at the hospital, her grandma died. Not accustomed to driving out of town, Judy found herself forced to drive back and forth between several towns, visit with her husband, and help with her grandma's funeral arrangements and estate. The tears fell like rain as she again asked, "Why me? Why do I have to go through this?"

Judy's health deteriorated rapidly after her husband's recovery. She was fainting more frequently and so short of breath that she could barely walk from her car to the house. The only way she could sleep was by propping several pillows up behind her. One day, after having open-heart surgery to replace a valve, Judy knew the Lord had saved her. The doctors expected she would have a long recovery process with several uncomfortable tubes coming out of her body. Waking up after surgery, Judy felt good as new. The doctor was amazed that her heart immediately started back up without needing to be shocked. There was no pain, no difficulty breathing, and no tubes. Her cheeks were rosy, and she had an appetite. God had healed her completely as if she hadn't even had the invasive surgery!

Judy's sister and brother-in-law expressed concern about her salvation. Beginning in 1982, Judy visited them often and her brother-in-law taught her more about God and gave her books to promote a deeper understanding of the Bible. Finally, she put the pieces together: *Jesus died on the cross to save me from my sins, and He was resurrected so that I can have eternal life.* Judy wondered why she hadn't learned this in all her years of attending church.

Her husband had become emotionally abusive over the years and they divorced in 1995. Two years later, she married her third husband, a non-Christian. Judy knew it wasn't a good idea to marry a man who didn't have a heart for the Lord, but she married him anyway. She found herself, once again, in a verbally abusive relationship. Still, she came even closer to God. He was the only one whose love had always been constant and unconditional. God listened to her. Judy continued going to church, but even after attending several churches, she had still not found one that felt right to her. She longed for a supportive church family, and she often asked God, "Where do You want me to go to church?"

One Friday in 2009, Judy met a couple at the grocery store. They chatted for a while, talking about their church. The couple invited her to come sometime. Judy had no intention of going any time soon. But God had other plans. By Saturday, she couldn't stop thinking about going to their church on Sunday. Well she followed her heart and was welcomed with a warm reception. Several people even prayed with her. Judy felt the sweet warmth of God's presence that day in church. She felt at home. At last, the church she'd been searching for!

The next Sunday, she stayed after the service and asked a pastor to pray for her so she could stop smoking. Judy desperately wanted to quit, but she had failed by her own efforts. The pastor prayed with her, asking God to work in her and take away her desire to smoke. Afterward, Judy said, "Is that it?" She had expected bells to ring from Heaven! The pastor explained, "Yes, that's it. Now you need to have faith and believe God will answer your prayers."

Later that day, Judy felt God's presence in her as a tingling sensation that went from the bottom of her feet all the way up to her head. From that moment on, she never smoked another cigarette. There were no cravings, no withdrawal symptoms—nothing. It was as if she had never smoked a day in her life! After a physical exam about a week later, the doctor commented on her crisp, clear lungs (after doing a pulmonary function test).

Judy has grown in her relationship with God. As one of His children, she's comforted knowing she belongs to the most loving family that ever has or ever will exist. Bible study classes have helped her develop a greater understanding of God's Word.

She has given her stress eating and weight over to God and has lost forty-seven pounds. God is guiding her to eat a healthy diet including the full-color spectrum of fresh fruits and vegetables, nuts and seeds, and plenty of water. Eating healthy is a daily struggle because junk food still beckons her in stressful times. Judy's rosy complexion is back, and she's excited about being able to fit into clothes she hasn't been able to wear for years.

Life is still very hard. Having an unbelieving husband not only places a burden on their marriage, but on her heart as well. She prays daily that her husband will open his heart to the Lord. Judy also struggles with some serious health issues, but her strong faith in God helps keep her focus on Him, and she seeks His strength to carry her through the trials of each day. Judy has learned that God is larger than all of her troubles—and that only He can help her overcome them.

"Therefore we do not lose heart. Though outwardly we are wasting away, yet inwardly we are being renewed day by day. For our light and momentary troubles are achieving for us an eternal glory that far outweighs them all" (2 Corinthians 4:16-17).

God has renewed Judy with His strength even though she's faced repeated physical and emotional abuse along with various health issues. He's used her trials to teach her invaluable lessons, perfect her faith, and bring her closer to Him.

Gordon ~ Age 47
Wholehearted Obedience

Gordon's family moved around a lot, but his parents always found a good church to attend weekly. His parents belonged to different denominations, and he could never understand how they could switch between them. To him, denomination meant division. Even though he was a bit confused, Gordon knew that Jesus was the Son of God. What he didn't know at the time was that God wanted to have a personal relationship with him.

As a teenager and into his twenties, Gordon enjoyed partying. For almost seven years, he got high every day on pot. He enjoyed drinking a little too much, and one time a friend had to take him to the emergency room because he was so drunk.

In his mid-twenties, Gordon rented a room in a friend's house. The landlord asked if he could rent the other room to a woman. Mary, just a year younger than Gordon, needed a place to live while in culinary school. The guys offered Mary a deal: she could grocery shop for whatever she wanted, and they would split the bill. And in exchange, she would be responsible for doing the cooking. It was a delicious deal for all involved! After a while, Gordon and Mary began dating. They were married less than two years later.

Shortly after getting married, Gordon and Mary went to church one Sunday with his parents. Mary was shocked to see a drama played out and to hear drums accompanying the worship music! Nothing like this ever took place at her traditional church.

Gordon and Mary decided to find a church like his parents' after moving to a different town.

Finding a house came first. On their way to look at about the fiftieth house, Gordon stopped at railroad tracks about an eighth of a mile away from the house and said, "We're going to buy this house." Mary didn't even acknowledge what he said because she knew Gordon was a practical man who took his time to make big decisions. After walking in and seeing the orange carpet, Mary thought to herself, *We're definitely not going to buy this house!* But by the end of the evening, the papers were signed and the house was theirs! Looking back, they can see that the Holy Spirit had been at work.

Gordon and Mary expressed interest in buying a baby grand piano for sale by the owner of the house. While paying for the piano, Mary casually asked, "By the way, can you recommend a good church?" "Oh yes. I've really enjoyed my church. It's great! You should come," the lady replied.

A month or so later, Gordon and Mary had to sign some more papers related to the sale of the house, and the power of attorney happened to be the pastor of that church! He invited them to his church the following Sunday. Guess what they saw? The very same drama they'd seen at Gordon's parents' church. They felt at home right away.

Gordon and Mary decided to join the church, and they signed up for the membership class. One evening, the pastor drew a timeline on the board, filling in the steps to salvation. Neither had ever heard it explained like that before. All of a sudden, a light bulb lit up, and they glanced at each other. They finally understood what salvation really meant.

"Belief in God isn't enough. Even Satan believes in God's existence. Belief needs to be followed by action. A person can't just believe in God and go on the rest of their life completely oblivious to Him or of His ways and expect to get to heaven," the pastor explained. Gordon and Mary learned that they needed to admit they were sinners, repent and turn away from their sin and toward God, believe Jesus died for them, and receive Jesus into their hearts and lives through prayer.

Not much changed in the way they lived right away after receiving Christ. The change was inside—in their hearts. Gordon and Mary began reading the Bible, learning more and more about God and how to live for Him.

Only one year after being saved, Gordon was fired from his sales job despite the fact that sales were up 25 percent! Noticing Gordon's lack of anger and anxiety, a coworker asked, "Why aren't you freaking out?" After all, they'd just had their first baby, and Mary was down to half time. Gordon explained that he trusted that God had bigger plans for him. Within three months he found a job that led to other opportunities—eventually bringing Gordon to where he is today. God's fingerprints were obvious throughout the entire process.

After going through two years of training to become a church elder, Gordon felt compelled to turn down the position. God convicted him of waiting until his children had accepted Christ. How could he lead the congregation when his own children weren't even saved yet? Today, however, Gordon is a church elder because his children have all received Jesus.

Gordon likens the process of developing a relationship with God to marriage. At first, the excitement was overwhelming—to actually have a relationship with God Almighty! For a time, he wanted to share his experience with everyone he met so they would have the opportunity to feel the same joy. After about five years of thinking he needed to get people to understand what he knew all at once, Gordon discovered that he could only take them so far. God needed to do the rest. It's in God's time when a person comes to Him. It wasn't until years later (as a seasoned Christian) that Gordon was able to have a strong impact on nonbelievers. Any relationship is an ongoing process. Each year he's grown closer and learned more about the Lord. The deeper Gordon's love toward God grows, the more obedient he becomes. He seeks to meet God whenever and wherever he's called to do so.

When someone opens the door to talk about God, Gordon pushes his way inside. He's had several opportunities to share his faith at work. One day, a Jewish coworker said he had to leave early to observe Passover. Gordon said that he did, too. Shocked, his coworker replied, "But you're not Jewish!" Gordon said, "No. But Jesus is. The difference between Jews and Christians comes down to the lamb and lion analogy. Jews only believe in the lion part—that Jesus will be coming one day in the future as a mighty warrior to bring His children home. A Christian believes that Jesus, the lamb, Son of God, has already been here. That He came in human form as a baby and grew into a man and was crucified and rose from the dead on the third day. Christians, like Jews, believe that Jesus is coming back." Since Gordon and his family have been observing Passover, their understanding of God and the Old Testament has grown by leaps and bounds.

They've gone beyond casually reading the Bible to actively learning as much as they can. In their studying process, they've discovered God has woven intricate details into His Word that make the larger picture even more beautiful. Take the word, "Bethlehem," for example. It means "house of bread," and it was the birthplace of Jesus—the bread of life.

Gordon and Mary's deep love and reverence for God has led them to uphold His teachings. They've stopped partying and drinking—they only use alcohol for cooking purposes. Mary no longer swears like a sailor. Gordon, although still very practical, allows God to work in his life even if it means changing his routine.

The entire family plans to eventually go on a mission trip to Mexico. Their kids have never known what it means to be hungry or lack basic necessities. Gordon feels that it's important for them to see the other side to really appreciate how blessed they are to live in the United States.

"Jesus replied, 'If anyone loves me, he will obey my teaching. My Father will love him, and we will come to him and make our home with him'" (John 14:23).

After fully accepting Jesus as their Lord and Savior, Gordon and Mary dedicated their hearts and lives to Him out of love. Obedience naturally followed. Rather than obeying out of a sense of duty, they actually *wanted* to obey Him. In loving God wholeheartedly, the Holy Spirit has made His home in their hearts and helped them to follow the Lord's teachings.

Rebecca ~ Age 33
Learning to Live Each Day
As Though It Were the Last

Rebecca spent much of her childhood taking care of herself. Her father abused her at a young age, and as a result, he went to jail for a few years. After being released from jail, he returned home but seldom held a job. And he left home on several occasions. Because of the abuse Rebecca suffered at the hands of her father, she never developed any kind of relationship with him. Rebecca deeply respected her mother for doing her very best to support the family. Her mother worked a minimum of two jobs at once, and she went back to school when her father wasn't around. Rebecca's grandmother helped out a lot and played a big role in her life. Her older brother had a learning disability, and that was coupled with mental health issues that caused him to express anger and depressive symptoms. He later overcame many of the challenges he faced. Despite her chaotic childhood, Rebecca got good grades in school and always managed to have a couple close friends. For the most part, she was a good girl—but she secretly partied with friends in high school.

After graduating from high school, Rebecca went to college. She was the first person in her family to attend college. Because her parents couldn't pay for her education, Rebecca spent hours on the telephone to get financial assistance information. Her persistence paid off: she qualified for several scholarships and grants. Rebecca spent her first year of college at a state university in another town. By the end of the year, she transferred to the university in her hometown (her first choice wasn't a good fit after all). Not wanting to move back home, Rebecca moved in with her grandmother who needed help after hip surgery. Things went very well for a while.

Then a feeling of restlessness overcame her. She wanted to move far away from her family and start over. Rebecca and her boyfriend, Mike, moved to another state where she continued her education in psychology.

They married in 2002—the same year she earned her bachelor's degree and her dad died. Mike and Rebecca were married in a mainline church, but they only went on Christmas and Easter at first. Sometimes they attended a little more often out of a sense of duty, but Rebecca didn't get anything out of the services—nor did she even know what she believed. She thought God probably existed, but didn't know much about Him.

Rebecca's views were very liberal. In political, social, religious, or family related matters, she took a leftist position. She tended a bar for many years and met a lot of people with similar viewpoints. Talking with them just strengthened her convictions. Rebecca really didn't have a moral compass—she tolerated everyone and everything, except really terrible things (such as murder). From a religious standpoint, she thought people could believe in whatever they wanted and that God would be fine with that. If she was a good person and did good things, she figured God would take notice and treat her kindly. She thought, *Surely just the "bad people"—mass murderers, con men, etc.—were destined for hell.*

Rebecca's marriage deteriorated as she and Mike began to lose each other. Both were headed in different directions. Mike seemed content just getting by; he held low-paying jobs and often turned down opportunities to advance. As a result, the burden of being the primary breadwinner fell squarely on Rebecca's shoulders. They divorced in 2006. She moved back to her hometown and got a job working with high-risk sex offenders at the local prison.

That same year, Rebecca pursued her graduate degree in Clinical Psychology. During her four years in graduate school, she delved more deeply into various religious philosophies. Rebecca took an intellectual and analytical approach in her quest. Rebecca's supervisor at the prison gave her a book on Buddhism that sparked her interest, and she learned about Taoism from a Taoist boyfriend. The focus on mutability and compassion fit well with her liberal attitude of tolerance for all values and beliefs. She wasn't curious to learn about Christianity, though—she thought the "Bible thumpers" were crazy, close-minded people.

2009 was a rough year. The reality of her divorce finally hit now that she was alone again. Rebecca had gone through several relationships by that time. Although extremely busy with graduate school and work, her life seemed to be missing a purpose. This lack of direction led Rebecca to start thinking about religion. She thought, *There had to be a Creator because of how the world works, with the cycle of seasons and the cycle of life and death. The world is too complex, balanced, and perfect to have simply formed on its own.* Before this, Rebecca had never doubted the big bang theory or evolution. Her strong science background pounded these theories into her head as facts. After much reflection, though, she concluded there must be one God who created the universe and everything in it. This really contradicted her belief that all religions had credence.

Rebecca watched a show on television that featured a large Christian family. Something about the family struck her: they all exhibited a degree of peace and fulfillment that she wasn't familiar with. Wanting what they had, Rebecca did some research on Christianity. Her biggest problem was with the different denominations—many didn't seem to follow the Bible, instead developing their own rules and rituals. Several books caused her to question the validity of Christianity. Much of the information she uncovered seemed contradictory. And the Bible, to Rebecca, was just another book written by many people a very long time ago. But, because she had never read it before, she still bought a Bible.

Her next step was going into chat rooms that discussed religion. Rebecca asked people of different Christian denominations what they believed and why. She noticed that one guy—Shane—visited the chat rooms for the distinct purpose of sharing his faith in the Lord Jesus. Shane's fervor for the Lord intrigued Rebecca, and they exchanged phone numbers. Their first phone conversation happened to be on Christmas Day of 2009. They talked for hours!

The very next day, Rebecca went to a Christian bookstore and felt compelled to buy a King James Version Bible, a different version than the one she already had. She left the store wondering why she'd spent thirty dollars on a book! When she returned home, Rebecca sat down with her new Bible. She called Shane, and he led her to various passages that spoke of who God is and how people could come to Him. Tears rolled down Rebecca's cheeks. She got it: the Bible wasn't just another book written by a bunch of people many, many years ago—she knew in her heart it was the very Word of God. It was definitely a profound experience!

Rebecca went to a new church the following Sunday. The pastor gave an invitation for nonbelievers to accept Jesus as their Savior and Lord and invite Him into their hearts. Many people went up to the altar to make a public commitment, but Rebecca was too shy to walk up in front of everyone. Besides, this was a private matter between herself and Jesus—she wanted to profess her faith in private. Around nine o'clock that evening, Rebecca got down on her knees, alone in her apartment, and committed her life to Jesus. She gave up fighting her own fight, as well as her fierce independence, and she said, "Okay, God, I'm Yours." No more being alone. No more total reliance on herself.

Rebecca grew very quickly in faith. Just a few weeks later, she was publicly baptized. Rebecca's mentor in the discipleship program at church helped her through struggles often faced by new Christians, like understanding the Bible and the reality of the Holy Spirit convicting us of wrong behavior. Memorizing Bible verses came easily to her. Rebecca prayed every day—God was as real to her as any person, and she grew closer and closer to Him. She listened to recorded sermons on the drive to and from graduate school (about three hours round trip), and learned a great deal in a short amount of time.

Her liberal views gradually changed to conservative ones as she read the Bible and learned the moral values taught by Jesus. The way Rebecca looked at things changed radically. In fact, she noticed that many psychological theories she studied in graduate school were not at all consistent with Christianity. She gave less credence to what she learned in school, convinced of the Bible's truth.

Rebecca felt a great burden for people who didn't know God and were not saved. Looking back, she wondered how she made it through the divorce on her own. She wondered, *How do people deal with the struggles of life without God?* She wanted others to know that the Bible is the Word of God and can be everything to people: a rebuker, comforter, and helper.

Today, Rebecca is in the midst of a serious test of her faith. In October of 2011, she started feeling ill. Her abdomen felt uncomfortable, as if she had a bladder infection. A CT scan revealed that fluid had accumulated throughout her abdominal cavity and lungs. At first, doctors thought her right ovary might be the culprit—they suspected it was secreting fluid. Thinking Rebecca had ovarian cancer, they performed surgery on November 18, 2011. Her right ovary was removed, tested, and found to be benign. The surgeon did find tiny nodules across her whole abdomen, however, and he removed all that he could see. Then they drained the fluid from her abdomen and lungs. Everything came back benign.

On her post-op appointment, the Wednesday after Thanksgiving Day, the doctor told Rebecca that further test results revealed cancer—malignant peritoneal mesothelioma—a very rare form of cancer that develops on the protective lining that covers many internal organs. To make matters worse, the cancer had spread to her lungs and appeared to be in the advanced stage. Doctors were perplexed as to how Rebecca could have this rare cancer at such a young age and without any known exposure to asbestos. Most people have less than a year to live by the time of diagnosis, but Rebecca's doctor gave her a realistic estimate of up to five years. She's hopeful for many more. The first few days after her diagnosis are still a blur—it all happened so fast and unexpectedly.

Rebecca is receiving the best care available. God has placed the most knowledgeable surgeon and doctors in her path. Currently, experts at the nation's top medical and research centers are reviewing her case.

She has had one chemotherapy treatment so far. It went pretty well for several weeks, aside from the fact that it made her feel tired. But the third week after treatment had a rough start with severe abdominal pain. Rebecca was told that the cancer cells secrete toxins when they die, and the toxins can cause pain.

Because of adhesions in her abdominal cavity from the cancer, her digestive system largely shut down. Several medications maintain Rebecca's digestion at a low level. Nevertheless, she has to eat very small amounts of food, such as a slice of bread or a banana, every hour or two to prevent the food from coming back up again.

Rebecca has good days and bad days. On good days, she spends much of the time rejoicing in the Lord. On bad days, Rebecca might spend most of the day crying and seeking comfort from friends via the telephone. Nevertheless, God finds ways to bless her every day—even on bad days. Blessings scattered along this meandering path help keep Rebecca's spirits up.

One amazing thing about her trial with cancer is the outpouring of love and prayer. After an announcement of her diagnosis was made at church, Rebecca received over fifty cards in the mail! And so many people called to pray with her and see how she was doing that she had to charge her cell phone almost continually to prevent the battery from running low! One day, her favorite preacher, Dr. Norris Belcher, called her! It turns out that her friend, Shane, whom she met several years earlier in the chat room, contacted him, explained Rebecca's situation, and asked him to call her.

Before her cancer diagnosis, Rebecca was tight-lipped about being a Christian. She didn't openly share her faith at work. Since her diagnosis, Rebecca will talk to anyone about God. She's told several nurses about her faith, saying, "I'm not afraid to die because I know for sure where I'm going—heaven." Her coworkers have expressed surprise at her newfound boldness. Many have commented that they knew Rebecca changed in 2010, but they didn't know why. They had noticed that she declined offers to go out to bars, and she walked away from crude conversations. Now everyone at work knows Rebecca is a Christian.

Above all, Rebecca wants to bring God glory through her trial with cancer. She is thankful for the experience of having cancer, but wants it to go away. It's hard not knowing how long she will have to battle this. One thing Rebecca does know is that the Lord will never leave her side. Recently, a friend told Rebecca a quote she'd heard on the radio: "God won't protect you from what He can use to perfect you." Having cancer has definitely brought Rebecca closer to the Lord—to a state of complete dependence and trust. She says, "Even if my trial ends in death, it will have been worthwhile as long as people can say at my funeral that I loved the Lord and that my life brought Him glory."

"Trust in the Lord with all your heart and lean not on your own understanding; in all your ways acknowledge him, and he will [direct your paths]" (Proverbs 3:5-6).

Before coming to the Lord, Rebecca relied completely on herself and her intellect. Today she depends on God. She even thanks Him for her current trial with cancer because it has given her a reason to live each day as if it were her last—and it has also given her boldness to share her faith with others who are lost.

Brett ~ Age 25
From Ladies' Man to Man of God

Brett never enjoyed going to church, nor did he ever really learn
much. It seemed like the pastor gave the same sermons year after
year, only making minor changes. His parents were unable to
answer questions he had about God so, when he left for college,
Brett stopped going to church. He believed in God, but he
didn't know enough about Him to understand the importance
of learning more about His ways—or building a relationship
with Him.

Once at college, Brett quickly fell into the party scene.
Partying became more important than school, and he spent long,
four-day weekends drinking heavily. Known as a happy-go-lucky
guy, Brett got along with everyone and was always smiling.

Rather suddenly, he changed. Brett started questioning why
he was going to school at all—his grades were poor and he didn't
know what he wanted to do with his life. He stopped wanting
to hang out with friends or go to school. Secluded in his room,
Brett's restless mind reeled with concerns about the future—he
could see debt accumulating, and struggled with a career choice.
Brett started crying at night and reached a point where he couldn't
function anymore.

He met with some college supervisors, talked with a doctor,
and took a psychological test. He was medically withdrawn
from school. Brett moved back home. A doctor put him on an

antidepressant, which Brett stopped taking after a week because he didn't like how it made him feel.

After a while, his dad got him a job at the local mill. Some days Brett's dad practically had to drag him out the door. Brett didn't understand why he had so little motivation to do anything; it was very unlike him.

After seeing an advertisement on television for a book about natural cures for depression and other ailments, Brett ordered the book and discussed it with his mom. She told him about a lady friend of hers who went to a naturopathic doctor. Curious, Brett went with his mom to see Dr. Alice. With a combination of vitamins and herbal tinctures, she helped Brett through the depression.

As it turned out, Dr. Alice was a Christian who was very outspoken about her faith; she talked to him about God on nearly every visit. In fact, she asked if she could pray before every session. Her prayers intrigued Brett—they were unlike anything he'd ever heard. One day, Dr. Alice told Brett, "You have a huge purpose for God!" He thought to himself, *Cool*, and then he shrugged it off. Brett really didn't know what she meant. Another time, she asked Brett whether he was saved. He wasn't sure. Dr. Alice asked if he would like to know for sure, and then she prayed with him right then to be saved. Brett was open to the idea and halfheartedly prayed along with her, but nothing changed.

After he came out of the depression, Brett started to sleep around with girls he barely knew. If a girl got too close to him, he ran. Brett wasn't interested in dating or making any commitments—sex was his primary motive.

As time went on, Brett realized that he didn't want to work at the mill for the rest of his life. He met with a recruiter and decided to join the National Guard. In the summer of 2008, at the age of twenty-one, Brett shipped off for two months of basic training and four months of medic training in the National Guard.

He slept with two girls while in medic training. Two or three weeks after the encounter with the second girl, she called to say she was pregnant! Brett panicked. After some comparative thinking, he came up with a list of reasons why she shouldn't have the baby. He sure didn't want to marry her and wasn't interested in dating her either. Since he'd be leaving soon for Iraq, he wouldn't be able to see the baby being born. Besides, she lived in another state. To further complicate matters, the girl already had other kids with another father, not to mention that Brett didn't want to disappoint his parents, who held quite traditional views. Brett concluded that this wasn't the way he wanted to bring a child into the world or start a family.

In spite of all the reasons to not have the baby, he struggled with how wrong it was to have an abortion—a very difficult dilemma. But, in the end, Brett went with what was best for him and chose comfort. Aborting the baby would prevent his plans from being altered. After several discussions, they agreed an abortion would be the best option, and Brett gave her money for the abortion. He cried himself to sleep at night for several weeks— it was always in the back of his mind. Brett felt ashamed.

He went to Iraq in February of 2009 for a year deployment where he medically treated detainees in prison. The following February, he returned home and worked for a while before going back to college in the fall. This time he didn't have to worry about accumulating debt because the Army paid for his education. Brett still slept around but cut the partying down to two or three times per month, rather than four days a week. When he partied with friends, he drank much less than he had several years earlier.

Brett will never forget September 26, 2010. He had been invited to a friend's bachelor party. The guys had some drinks, went to a comedy club, and then they went out for more drinks. They went back to his buddy's house and ordered pizzas. The guys all planned to stay overnight because they were drunk and far from home. While innocently enjoying his pizza and talking with the guys, Brett heard a voice in his head say, "Dude, you've got to get out of here and go home." The idea seemed ridiculous! First of all, he was drunk. Second, the drive home was just short of two hours. Third, it was after two in the morning! The feeling that he needed to leave became stronger and stronger until Brett gave in, thinking, *Okay I guess I'll do this*, even though it seemed absolutely crazy.

After collecting his things and grabbing the rest of his pizza, Brett got into his car and, for some unknown reason, plugged his home address into the GPS unit. He'd made this trip countless times before and should have been able to get home with no problems, but he used his GPS anyway. Brett drove along, barely conscious, while eating his pizza. After driving for nearly an hour, he noticed his phone was on silent so he wasn't hearing directions from the GPS. How it got on silent, he didn't know.

Brett looked around and realized he was on a different highway—an unfamiliar one! In uncharted territory on a twisting road, he figured that he really shouldn't be driving home in his condition. He tried pulling over to the side of the road to sleep for a while, but he couldn't—the wheel wouldn't turn. Then Brett felt like he was going too fast and took his foot off the accelerator for a few seconds to slow down. When he placed his foot on the pedal again, it went down with great force. Before he knew what happened, he found himself going over one hundred miles per hour! Completely out of control as he went around a sharp bend in the road, the car rolled onto the driver's side, slid into a ditch and hit a culvert. Thankfully, Brett was wearing his seatbelt, but the side window had broken, causing slivers of glass to become embedded in his face.

Suddenly, two men yelled, "Hey, are you alive in there?" Brett managed to say, "Yes!" The men pushed the car over. Brett worked his way over to the passenger side and the men helped him out of the car. Somehow, Brett walked to their truck and got into the back seat. By this time, he was in a lot of pain—it felt like his right shoulder might be broken, and tiny fragments of glass were stuck in his face. Brett told the men to call the police, but they said, "No, you don't want this on your record." After some arguing, they called Brett's parents. Imagine how his parents felt when they received a phone call around four o'clock in the morning and heard a man say, "We're here with your son, he's been hurt in an accident and needs to get to the hospital." The men didn't want to take Brett to the hospital because they'd been drinking, too. They explained where his parents should pick him up, drove him to that location, dropped him off on the side of the road, and disappeared.

Brett lay on his back in the dewy grass for at least forty minutes, waiting for his parents. Since his cell phone was still in his pocket, he called his cousin. He just needed to talk to someone. Shortly after getting off the phone with his cousin, Brett's mom called and asked how they would find him. Brett said that he'd raise his hand as high as he could when he saw the car approaching. Soon, his parents came to the rescue and got him to a hospital.

The police questioned Brett at the hospital and wrote up a report. After discovering the location of his car, they said he was very fortunate the two men came along as soon as they had. The police would never have found him that night because the car was so far down in the ditch and not visible from the road—not to mention the fact that Brett hadn't followed the correct route home.

Brett's injuries were serious, but they could have been much worse considering how the car crashed. His right scapula had broken in three places, and one side of the spinal process of his sixth cervical vertebrae in his neck had broken off—plus his face needed stitching. Nevertheless, Brett was back at home four hours later. The next day, when he woke up, he could hardly move because the pain was so severe.

He went to see Dr. Alice to get some natural medicine. He walked into the office with his right shoulder hanging down about three inches lower than his left. While there, Brett met one of Alice's friends, a cranial-sacral therapist. She did a quick session with him right then. Afterward, both women suggested he have cranial-sacral therapy weekly to help heal his shoulder and neck injuries.

Also a Christian, the therapist shared her faith during the sessions and often quoted Scripture. One day, she said to Brett, "You have a big purpose!" Then she led him through the sinner's prayer to be saved, just as Dr. Alice had. But again, nothing changed.

With the help of Dr. Alice and the cranial-sacral therapist, Brett quickly recovered from the accident. He didn't even have scarring on his face from all of the stitches!

Wanting to get his finances in order, Brett met with a financial advisor and his wife—who also happened to be strong Christians. While shaking Brett's hand, the man's wife exclaimed, "Wow, your spirit is immense! You have a big purpose!" He thought, *Hmm…a third person telling me the same thing!* After talking for a time, the couple led Brett through the sinner's prayer. Again.

This time, things changed—a little. For instance, on his way to meet a girl that night, Brett felt guilty because he knew his intention was to have sex with her.

Shortly after, in December of 2010, Brett started meeting with his friend, Rob, who was involved in a small ministry group. Rob talked in depth about God's ways, backing up everything he said with Scripture. He provided Brett with answers to questions about God, His character, and marriage. Brett's mind reeled with all the revelation that came to him from Rob's teaching of the Bible. Wondering why he had never heard these things before, Brett said, "I want to know what's in the Bible."

Rob explained how the Bible's explanation of marriage differs from the way people define the word today. Brett was taken aback to learn that God considers a couple "married" and "one flesh" after they have consensual sexual intercourse for the first time!

From that point on, Brett's views on sex, dating, and marriage were forever changed. He learned that, for a Christian, dating involves focusing on the mental, emotional, and spiritual aspects of a person. Too much emphasis on the physical masks the other three. This made sense to Brett because beginning a relationship with sex always made it the primary focus.

Brett sought to "break covenants" with the seventeen girls he'd slept with. In God's eyes, he was married to the first girl he'd had sex with and committed adultery with the other sixteen! He wanted to break free from his sin, so Brett contacted the girls and told each one how God viewed marriage, according to the Bible—that it takes place after a consensual sexual union. He confessed and repented of his sin, explaining that it was for their benefit so they could have a full covenant with God and their future husband. Brett then stated that he was not in agreement with the covenant between the two of them. Finally, he asked the girls to say they were not in agreement with the covenant either.

Brett joined Rob's small ministry group that met at a couple's home. While at their home on July 24, 2011, Brett got the overwhelming feeling that he wanted to accept Jesus for real—finally all the things in the Bible made sense, and he had already started doing what God expected of him. Standing in the driveway with several other men, Brett's heart fluttered like crazy. A pastor placed his hand on Brett as he explained how the Bible says to be saved: "That if you confess with your mouth, 'Jesus is Lord,' and believe in your heart that God raised him from the dead, you will be saved. For it is with your heart that you believe and are justified, and it is with your mouth that you confess and are saved" (Romans 10:9–10). As tears rolled down his cheeks, Brett spoke to God from his heart. He cannot remember what he said, only that God gave him the words to say. This time, Brett knew without a doubt he was saved.

Right away, Brett displayed a new boldness. He even went out of his comfort zone and asked the girl he had been corresponding with in another state (via the Internet) to start dating him. She agreed even though he held nothing back; in fact, Brett was sure he would scare her off with his raw honesty. He told her how many girls he'd slept with and the fact that he had viewed pornography. To his amazement, she was fine with his past as long as he didn't sleep with any more girls.

As Christians, they made a rule not to touch one another for a year. Their focus was on getting to know one another mentally, emotionally, and spiritually by deeply sharing. After the year of "no touching" was up, they agreed to start out with hugs, then cuddling, then kissing, and so on, allowing God to direct how long they stayed in each category. The whole point of being intentional about these things was to reinstate them as effects, not causes. Both of them found the new way of dating—led by God—to be amazing! It eliminated sex as a distraction.

His fears of committing or of not knowing whether the girl was the "right one" were conquered, too. Brett says, "That fear has gone away because, by getting to know her mentally, emotionally, and spiritually, I will find out very soon if I don't like her or cannot see myself with her. We're getting right down to the most important stuff in getting to know each other for who we really are. I love it!"

Today, Brett cohosts "Man Night," a service of The Deeper Why Ministries, at a friend's home. The goal is to transform males into men, and men into spiritual fathers and leaders. Modeled after the Bible, their definition of a man in God's eyes is, "A male who is able to intentionally do the causes regardless of the effects." The measure of progress in becoming a godly man is to carry out a task, regardless of whether or not an effect is received. Men are guided through four stages to reach spiritual maturity: one, identifying their weakness and damage; two, growing in God's doctrine; three, maintaining 95 percent of their conscious brain during a sudden emotional confrontation; four, intentionally stepping into and through a stressful situation that could otherwise be avoided. One focus of the group is to get men to break their sexually immoral habits as they develop an intimate relationship with God. Once He is everything to them, there is no longer any reason to seek fulfillment elsewhere.

Brett desires to build up the body of Christ. God has given him the gift of evangelism. He recently evangelized to several people he met in a casino! A recent project involves cohosting a video series to teach and explain biblical principles. The first in the series helps Christians discern their spiritual gifts.

He seeks to better understand the Bible so he can more effectively minister. Brett knows that God will only do what he allows Him to do, according to his understanding of the Bible. Now that Jesus is in heaven, seated at the right hand of God, not only is Jesus Himself interceding for us, so is the Holy Spirit. Jesus said, "I tell you the truth, anyone who has faith in me will do what I have been doing. He will do even greater things than these, because I am going to the Father" (John 14:12). Accordingly, we can heal the sick, prophesy, and so on. Brett is in awe of the power that's available to him as a believer when he prays in Jesus' Name. It's just as Scripture says: "You may ask me for anything in my name, and I will do it" (John 14:14).

God continues to teach Brett more of His ways. Sometimes God uses dreams to show Brett His plans. He's learned that of the three potential voices in his head—God, himself, and the enemy—only God will provide the how and why. In this way, Brett can determine for sure when God speaks to him. Brett lives fully surrendered to God's will—allowing God to lead him in every area of his life.

"Put to death, therefore, whatever belongs to your earthly nature: sexual immorality, impurity, lust, evil desires and greed, which is idolatry" (Colossians 3:5).

After learning that God equates the first sexual union with marriage, Brett confessed and repented of his sin. He seeks to honor God by marrying His way.

Tami ~ Age 47
A Rebel Who Found a Worthy Cause

A rebel at heart, Tami dodged authority. Her extremist nature meant that she was either all in or not interested at all. She didn't believe most things she heard about God at church and Christian school. Actually, Tami didn't hear much of anything at church. Instead, she discreetly talked to her friend in sign language in the back pew. Her mom left God at church on Sunday. Tami's dad, on the other hand, was very involved in church.

When Tami was only six years old, her parents divorced and her mom and stepfather received full custody. Shortly thereafter, Tami's mom turned to alcohol and became a different person. Tami and her mom were physically, mentally, and emotionally abusive to one another. They didn't talk without hurling insults at each other and swearing. At times, they couldn't even watch television together without one of them pulling out a chunk of the other's hair. Tami got physical with her mom when called the "b" word. Her mom called her that name frequently, causing her to become so angry that she just couldn't control herself. In fact, for years, Tami would become verbally or physically violent with anyone who called her an offensive name.

At the age of thirteen, Tami moved in with her dad. (The state of California gives children the right to decide which parent they want to live with at that age.) Even though she and her mom didn't get along, often, when conflict arose with her dad, she'd go back to live with her mom for a while. A typical, indecisive teenager, Tami went back and forth between her parents about four times. The last time she went back to her dad's house, he said, "This is it. Either stay or go. But if you leave again, you're not coming back." Tami knew he meant business, so she stayed with him for good. Tami's father had strong faith, and she respected him for his Christian influence even though she had her own doubts about God.

In high school, Tami started dating Tom. Her whole life she'd wanted to have a baby—someone who would love her unconditionally—so she actually *tried* to get pregnant. Her wish came true at the age of seventeen, shortly after an early graduation. Tami's dad insisted they get married. They did and lived with Tom's mother and brothers. Having four sons of her own, Tami's mother-in-law loved having a baby boy in her home again.

When her son was six weeks old, Tami had her first seizure. It was a grand mal seizure, and it came out of nowhere. She continued having more mild seizures on a daily basis (but she has had at least another five grand mal seizures over the years). It wasn't uncommon to have up to twelve seizures per day. An aura preceded each one, even though Tami was usually completely unaware of the actual event. After a seizure, she felt very tired and slept for a long time. Because she was "zapping out" so frequently, Tami had to give up driving. The seizures frightened her. Tami was scared that she would have them while alone with her son. She wondered, *What if something happened to him because of me?* To make matters worse, Tom's family treated her like she had a malignant and vulgar disease.

The marriage didn't go well from the beginning. For one thing, her husband placed his mom over Tami. Not long into the marriage, Tom started going to the bar after work, and he eventually became an alcoholic. He came home drunk, and he repeatedly hit and raped Tami. One day, she left Tom with the intent of getting a divorce. Tom kept custody of their son, however, because of Tami's seizures. She had her son every other weekend.

Tami slept around a lot, searching for love. Later she returned to Tom. At the age of twenty-one, she had a daughter. Tami was afraid her kids might get hurt when she had seizures. She knew she wouldn't be able to live with herself if one of them got seriously hurt or killed while she was down. For their good, she made the heart-wrenching decision to leave them with Tom and his mom—not that Tom would be a great dad, but Tami knew his mom would take care of the kids and love them like her own. For a while, Tami continued to spend every other weekend with the kids.

Tami then met her current husband, Phil. Soon after, she became a pothead—she was stoned 24/7. Pot made her feel good. She didn't have a care in the world, and the frequency of her seizures actually decreased.

Tami and Phil married when she was twenty-five years old and moved to the Midwest from California. Less than enthused initially, Tami grew to like her new home. People were much friendlier and more accepting of her there. Her coworkers were like family; people didn't treat her any differently just because she had seizures.

At that point in her life, she had up to six or more seizures daily. Tami's doctor suggested that she see a specialist at a well-respected seizure center. The specialist said they could consider brain surgery. First, the origin of the seizures had to be determined, so Tami checked into the hospital, stopped her medications, and was monitored closely. An area of her right temporal lobe was the culprit. Tami underwent brain surgery to remove that section of her brain. The surgery helped some, but she still had many seizures—just not as many. Some years later, the center said they could do more to help, so they took Tami off her medications, opened up her head by cutting right down the center, and placed grids in her brain to monitor for seizure activity. This time they zeroed in on an area of the motor cortex. Surgery was an option, but Tami could have ended up with a motor impairment and still have had seizures. She thought, *Hmm… risk losing the ability to walk or use of some other motor skill and still possibly have seizures?* It sounded absolutely ludicrous. Tami actually asked the doctor, "What have you been smoking?"

Around fifteen years ago, the center alerted Tami to a new device: a Vagus Nerve Stimulator (VNS). They explained that the device was in the experimental stages and needed to be tested on people. If Tami was willing to be a guinea pig, they would pay for the surgery. Having nothing to lose, Tami agreed. The stimulator was surgically implanted on the left side of her chest with a wire going up through her neck to the vagus nerve in her brain. Like a pacemaker, the device is programmed to stimulate the nerve at specific intervals. Tami carries a large magnet at all times that can be rubbed over her chest to briefly activate the implant, and that usually stops the seizure. She wears a Medic-Alert bracelet on her right wrist to warn medical professionals of her seizures and the VNS. With the stimulator, Tami cannot have an MRI scan because the device could malfunction or explode. Twice, she has narrowly escaped having an MRI because hospital staff failed to check her bracelet.

The implant continues to work well. She often goes as many as eight weeks without a seizure. On the downside, Tami doesn't get auras anymore, so she never knows when one is coming. Sometimes the doctor needs to change her anticonvulsant medication when problems arise. Over the years, Tami has been on every anticonvulsant on the market. The most irritating thing to her is not being able to remember things. Every time she has a seizure, information is lost that she can never get back.

After several years of marriage, God audibly spoke to Phil one day. Previously a hardcore agnostic, he could no longer deny the existence of God. He had been having a hard time dealing with something, and God came to his rescue. He and Tami started going to church regularly. Although Tami had grown accustomed to attending church on Sunday over the years, she didn't think about God any other time. As Phil grew in faith, he felt God calling him to go to Bible College. They moved back to California where he enrolled in a well-known school. As Phil intensively studied the Bible, he couldn't help but share his newfound knowledge with Tami. In time, she had enough of his preaching and sought a divorce.

Meanwhile, Tami moved in with her dad under the stipulation that she go to church with him on Wednesday nights and Sundays. She thought, *What could it hurt?* It seemed like a simple enough request. At least she had a place to stay. One Wednesday night, the pastor spoke of how the Israelites sinned against God by worshiping idols. The pastor asked the congregation to examine themselves to see if they had any idols in their lives—anything they placed over God. Although not saved, Tami thought to herself with pride and arrogance, *I don't have any idols.* As she walked into the house later that night, Tami kept going over in her mind what the pastor had said and felt confident that she didn't worship any idols. Suddenly, she heard the voice of God audibly say, "Your music."

Tami was taken aback! She really hadn't believed that God had actually spoken out loud to Phil several years earlier. Then she pondered the words. Sure enough, she had been a hardcore Pink Floyd fan for years. Tami owned their entire collection, including a rare, very valuable, limited edition CD. When the band came to her area, she dropped everything, no matter what—even visitation with her children—to see them in concert. Realizing how much she idolized Pink Floyd, Tami walked over to the CD rack, grabbed every last one, and scratched them on the tiled kitchen floor. She made sure they were completely ruined so that no one could ever listen to them again. That night, Tami asked God for forgiveness and gave her life to Jesus.

God brought Tami and Phil back together since they were both living to serve God. Phil had always accepted her for who she was. He didn't make a big fuss about her seizures—he actually protected her. And she still loved him. Their pastor, who knew them well, refused to remarry them until they went through a year of marital counseling. With God at the center, their relationship grew stronger and closer than ever. Since Phil had completed Bible College, Tami and Phil moved back to the Midwest where they became very involved in the church.

Many years ago, Tami replaced hard rock with Christian music. Rather than being an idol, music is now a means to praise and worship God. She downloaded hundreds of her favorite songs onto her MP3 player, and she listens to them while riding her bike into town. The chorus of "Grace Like Rain," a remake of "Amazing Grace," deeply moves Tami every time. It goes like this: "Hallelujah, grace like rain falls down on me, and all my stains are washed away." The words of "Sanctuary" speak to her soul as well: "Lord, prepare me to be a sanctuary pure and holy, tried and true. With thanksgiving, I'll be a living sanctuary for you."

Psalm 27 provides comfort when Tami experiences fears, physical problems, or spiritual battles: "The Lord is my light and my salvation—whom shall I fear? The Lord is the stronghold of my life—of whom shall I be afraid?" (Psalm 27:1). Reading the Psalm is a reminder that God is in control: He will never leave her side.

A good friend (who is confined to a wheelchair) recently sent Tami a text that reads, "May God reassure you that His presence is cause for peace." The text message means so much to Tami, considering the physical struggles her friend faces each day. She has kept the message on her phone as a reminder that God's peace is always available. Tami chooses to move through every difficulty as well as she can. She looks for the positive in negative situations, and she urges others to "Let the negative things bring you closer to God."

Ecclesiastes 3:1 speaks to Tami: "There is a time for everything, and a season for every activity under heaven." No matter what life throws her way, Tami recognizes that how she responds is her responsibility. She could decide to feel sorry for herself because of her limitations (for example, not being able to drive or able to leave her home much of the year when the weather doesn't permit her to ride a bike). She never wants to become a "poor me" type of person. There is always someone worse off. Tami is thankful that her seizures are controlled. Many people suffer much more with persistent problems. Keeping her focus on God helps keep Tami from succumbing to fears or feeling sorry for herself.

Tami seeks God daily. She reads and studies the Bible, and spends time in prayer. For years, she has been part of a "prayer texting team," from her old church in California, which allows the team members to alert one another of prayer requests quickly and at a moment's notice. Being a good witness for Christ is important to Tami. God led her to use John 3:16, "For God so loved the world that he gave his one and only Son, that whoever believes in him shall not perish but have eternal life," on her voicemail greeting as a way to minister to people.

Though Tami would like to have a stronger relationship with her son and daughter, they have chosen to have little contact with her. Some of the fault may rest on her ex-husband who didn't encourage the kids to have a relationship with Tami—an all-too-common occurrence in many divorce situations. Another reason is that her son and daughter are not Christians, and they get distant when Tami talks to them about God. At this point in her life, Tami is more concerned about their salvation than anything else. Since neither is open to talking with her about God and salvation, all she can do is pray for them, and that is more than sufficient! Tami has planted the seeds and trusts in God to nurture and give them roots to grow.

"Do not turn to idols or make gods of cast metal for yourselves. I am the Lord your God" (Leviticus 19:4).

Having a baby, music, men, and marijuana were all idols in Tami's life at one time or another. Today, God comes first, and He has replaced the void she sought to fill with other things. All the glory goes to Him alone!

Jeff ~ Age 60
Saved by Grace

While high on LSD one night in 1972, Jeff wrote a song titled "Born Again." The refrain went like this:

> It was twenty-four years ago.
> I lay in my mother's lap,
> New born to life,
> Not knowing one wit of all that should hap'
> The day I was won from nothin'
> To a world of struggle and pain
> Twenty four years ago.
> And tonight I am born again,
> Jesus, for you.

He probably sang this song to over one hundred people at the time, but was unaware of its true meaning. Jeff knew the song was about God, but he overlooked the significance of one word—Jesus.

It all began with Jeff's family moving to the San Francisco Bay area in the 1960s when he was thirteen. At a very impressionable time in his life, Jeff found himself immersed in the burgeoning hippie culture. Shortly thereafter, he began using drugs. It started with marijuana, but it did not end there. He moved on to harder drugs such as LSD and cocaine. By the 1970s, Jeff found himself dabbling in the new age culture where he was introduced to occult practices. His search for spiritual meaning led him to tarot card

189

readings and reliance on a personal spirit guide. He continued these practices into adulthood, even after getting married.

Jeff's wife gave her life to Jesus in 1984, and she began attending church. But he wasn't interested. This created a big struggle in their marriage. The drugs and occult practices were the only means he knew of finding God. In a hallucinogenic state, the pains of hard times were dulled. He was managing just fine, he thought.

Several months went by, and Jeff decided to start going to church—more out of intellectual curiosity than anything. He went armed with a notebook and pen to take notes that he hoped to later refute. You see, Jeff planned on being able to talk his wife out of her faith. His diligent note taking resulted in endless questions. Jeff became interested in the Bible, and thought, *Hmm, it really says this in the Bible?* Clouds of skepticism drifted through his mind.

Much to his amazement, Jeff found himself meeting with a pastor at a local restaurant on Tuesday mornings! Pastor Warren gave Jeff a copy of the book of John as a starting point—his first introduction to the Bible. Each week they discussed passages from John and addressed Jeff's pressing questions. Pastor Warren was very gracious, and Jeff was continually confrontational. Nights found him reading and rereading the book of John. Nevertheless, Jeff failed to grasp what God was trying to tell him. He believed in Jesus, but didn't believe what He said. Jeff understood the idea of being saved from sin, but didn't think a man like himself could go to Jesus and ask for forgiveness.

One Tuesday morning, in December of 1984, Jeff handed the book back to Pastor Warren saying, "Thank you, but God won't do this for a guy like me." He left the restaurant and headed down the road to check on a jobsite (Jeff is a general contractor). It was a beautiful, crisp, sunny day without a cloud in the sky. Jeff had only driven a short way up the road when, suddenly, he saw something very unusual on the side of the road: an elevated image of light! He wondered, *What could this be?* He pulled over. Again and again, he glanced at the image of light and then looked away. *Surely the light will be gone when I look back!* Well, it wasn't; the light remained. The minutes crept by so slowly that it seemed like hours had passed. Jeff knew in his heart that God was revealing Himself. It felt like someone's hand had reached out and pulled his chest to the steering wheel. God's warm grace covered Jeff, melting his cold, dark heart. God really did love him, despite his disgraceful behavior! The tears poured out. He wept and wept until no tears were left. Jeff headed to the jobsite, awestruck by what had just happened.

After arriving at the house, Jeff walked into the kitchen to see how the work was coming along. The men took one look at him, dropped their tools, and, with their eyes wide and mouths agape, asked, "What happened to you?" Jeff grunted, "Nothing, get back to work!" Then he left. For the rest of the day, he couldn't stop thinking about what had happened along the roadside that morning. Jeff found himself singing songs of praise that he had never sung before. From that day on, the drugs and the occult were gone. Period. It was as if God had reached inside of him and pulled out all of the bad stuff!

Jeff continued going to church, only now he went for the right reason—to worship and praise God. He developed a thirst for reading and studying the Bible. Like many others with unbelief who sought to disprove the teachings of the Bible, Jeff became a strong advocate of God's Word. Jeff is now involved in his church in many ways, including being part of the worship team. God has given Jeff a heart for mission work, and he's traveled to several different countries and led others to the same hope and salvation that he found in Jesus. He and his wife went to Macedonia in November of 2010 to reach out to people who desperately needed Jesus. During their stay, Jeff formed an outreach group for abusers of drugs and alcohol. Each day, Jeff "gets up, suits up, and shows up," allowing God free reign to do the rest.

"If anyone is in Christ, he is a new creation; the old has gone, the new has come!" (2 Corinthians 5:17).

Even though Jeff didn't ask for God's help or to stop doing drugs, God came to his rescue anyway. The instant Jeff received God's grace and believed in Him, the drugs and occult practices were taken away for good.

Katy ~ Age 43
Strengthened by a Thorn
in the Flesh

While sitting on her dad's lap in a rocking chair one Sunday morning before church, Katy asked Jesus into her heart. Afterward, Katy's dad prayed with her and gave her a big hug. She was only four years old.

Her parents held leadership roles in the church, and the family was at church whenever the doors were open. They attended two services on Sunday and one on Wednesday, sang in church as a family, and went to every potluck and picnic.

Katy had a happy, fun childhood growing up with four sisters. They memorized Scripture for Bible camp. At seven o'clock each morning, the family of seven gathered for breakfast and one person shared a Bible verse from memory — a time fondly referred to as "7-up."

Early on, Katy's role became the peacemaker. She always felt most comfortable when things were even-keeled. Hating conflict, she always tried to smooth out any bumps that arose. Her older sister even called her a "goody-two-shoes." Katy just wanted everyone to get along.

Once in college, some poor choices changed her "goody-two-shoes" reputation. Katy found herself pregnant and unwed at the age of twenty. This came as a huge shock to her family and church. To this day, Katy still feels the disappointment her parents expressed as she and her boyfriend, Chris, shared the news with them. They only wanted what was best for Katy—and for her to live a righteous life.

Katy and Chris had dated since she was sixteen, and they were very much in love. They planned to marry someday, but now they had a good reason not to procrastinate any longer! A wedding was hastily put together. Their marriage was off to a rocky start. They had to adjust to adulthood, parenthood, and married life all at once—but their beautiful son was always seen as a blessing.

Two years later, Katy became pregnant again. Now she felt prepared to have another baby. Overwhelmed with excitement, she shared the good news with family and friends, and received the kinds of responses she had always hoped for. But Katy miscarried two-and-a-half months into the pregnancy. She cried for two days, and then went back to school as if nothing had happened. Dwelling on the loss didn't mesh well with her need for life to be even-keeled. Katy knew many women had miscarriages and that she could try again.

In another two years, Katy became pregnant again. This time she was more guarded about whom she told until her third month. She bought some maternity clothes and began making plans for the baby. Just after three months, Katy miscarried. Really sad for three days this time, she returned to work and put the matter behind her ... or so she thought. She knew enough about God to rationalize that He was in control of her path, and for some reason, this was the path He had given to her.

Deep down she felt hurt, sadness, guilt, and pain. She wondered, *Why had it been so easy to get pregnant the first time, but now, at an acceptable time, I can't hold onto a baby?* It didn't seem right. She felt like God was punishing her for the poor choices made in the past. Katy already had guilt, but the burden weighed more heavily on her now than ever. She just wanted to know why the miscarriages had happened. She wanted answers.

After a year or so passed, Katy longed for another child. But Chris, being a man of resolve, decided they wouldn't try again. He didn't want to see Katy go through the hurt and disappointment another time. They argued and argued, and then they sought counseling. The counselor told them he usually sides with the parent who doesn't want children because, "You don't want children in a household where one partner is unsure." Not wanting to create conflict in the marriage, she accepted Chris's decision and desperately tried to move on. Katy didn't want to blame him. Blame couldn't be part of a good marriage. She would be okay as long as everything stayed on an even keel.

About one year later, Katy started awakening each day with a heavy heart. She became more and more depressed, crying because of something happy or sad that happened, or for no reason at all. Katy cried off and on all day, every day, for several months. Everything she did seemed worthless. Somehow, Katy went about her daily routine, forcing herself to smile, talk, and work. While working, Katy shut off her emotions. She went through the day like a zombie—crying whenever she had a moment to herself. She had a constant lump in her throat.

It didn't make any sense to her. She questioned, *Why do I feel this way?* There was no reason for the depth of her sadness—she had a loving husband, parents, sisters, friends, a beautiful four-year-old boy, and a rewarding job. Katy tried hard to pin her depression on something, but she came up empty. She wanted to be happy, but she just couldn't get there. It became more and more difficult to do what she needed to do each day.

Before long, loved ones began asking questions. Thinking he'd done something to cause Katy's depression, Chris asked, "What's wrong? Do you still love me?" Friends noticed her puffy, bloodshot eyes and asked what was wrong, but she had no answer. They tried to help Katy figure out what caused her mood to fall to such depths.

Katy shared her feelings of despair with her baby sister, who happened to be struggling with postpartum depression at the time. Her sister said she needed to talk to a professional. Chris agreed. So she met with a Christian counselor and a psychiatrist who put Katy on an antidepressant. She only took the medication for a week because she hated the way it made her feel nothing; it seemed better to suffer with depression than not to feel anything at all.

By her third counseling session, it became clear that she hadn't dealt with the loss of her babies, or with the decision to not have any more children (which was sort of another death). At the time, Katy hadn't realized she'd skipped over the grief process because it hurt too much.

Katy thought her emotions needed to be in check at all times. She couldn't rock the boat. To allow herself to feel sad meant she would have to dig deep, disrupting her need to be even-keeled. She thought that the process of going through her sadness would place too much focus on her, taking it off of God. But Katy learned that "emotions lead us to a greater relationship with God." After all, God gave us emotions. There are reasons we feel what we feel. As she notes, "So I can be sad, but if in my sadness I choose to wallow and feel pity for myself without allowing God to teach me through it, it's about me, not Him. If I'm happy, but in my happiness I choose to dwell on how good I feel and what gratification and satisfaction it gives me, instead of what glory it gives God, then it's also about me, not Him."

Katy and Chris took time to work through the grief process. Now that she had something to connect her sadness to, she was at least able to cry for a reason. Instead of focusing on what she had lost, she could focus on the fact that her heavenly Father had her babies in His hands. She reflected, *What better hands could they be in?* She and Chris planted two trees in their yard, a maple and an apple blossom, to remember their babies that are already with

Jesus. This brought comfort to Katy, but there was still more to learn.

The grief process brought Katy to her knees so she could learn that joy and satisfaction come from God, not from anything she could have or want here on Earth. In the process of grieving and wishing for what she'd lost and couldn't have, Christ helped her understand that His grace is sufficient and His power made perfect in her weakness. Katy knows that God's grace and peace is perfect for her in this imperfect world. She's deeply in love with Him.

Her depression has not completely gone away. Katy still struggles with premenstrual dysphoric disorder (PMDD) every month, and she tends to easily become depressed when life gets hard. Even though God hasn't taken Katy's depression away, He equips her on a daily basis with His grace and power so she can rise above her weakness. Each day she has a choice to make: let God reign in her life or reign herself. Katy desires the Holy Spirit to guide every interaction and step she takes throughout the day.

Katy has a list of things she strives to do daily to live her life fully in God and avoid spiraling downward. Even in the midst of depression, she makes sure she's not forgetting anything. Spending time in God's Word every day is the most important. She makes time to be quiet and listen to God while praying, "Lord help me get out of the way so You can do what You need to through me." Exercise helps keep her emotions balanced, and Katy has positive, upbeat people she can call. She created a "joy list" of simple things that make her smile any time they come to mind, such as an elderly couple walking while holding hands, or having coffee with her sisters in her parents' living room. Having an accountability person who encourages her to fervently seek God's grace helps Katy change her thoughts and actions when she feels depressed.

The apostle Paul wrote: "There was given me a thorn in my flesh, a messenger of Satan, to torment me. Three times I pleaded with the Lord to take it away from me. But he said to me, 'My grace is sufficient for you, for my power is made perfect in weakness.' Therefore I will boast all the more gladly about my weaknesses, so that Christ's power may rest on me" (2 Corinthians 12:7-9).

Katy's depression has strengthened her faith in God. Before her two miscarriages and depression, life had not been difficult. When life went along even-keeled, she failed to see her need for an intimate relationship with God. Today, Christ's power allows her to walk in the fullness of His presence, even though she still struggles with depression. His grace carries her through.

Michael ~ Age 48
One Step at a Time

By the age of thirty-two, Michael had reached the pinnacle of success by the world's standards. He'd been plant manager of a large corporation for four years and earned a high salary. He lived in a three-story house with his wife and two boys. Michael owned a classic corvette, a newer car, a truck, and new snowmobiles. Being a successful businessman came with a lot of stress and responsibility, though. He drank to cope with work stress, and he became an alcoholic. Working sixty to eighty hours each week left very little time for his family. Michael's career and interests came first.

He loved the money and power that came with his position. His extreme arrogance even led him to argue with the owner of the company, a man twice his age, about how to run the business. Pride caused him to attribute the company's overwhelming success to his own efforts.

Michael was a thrill seeker, and he pushed everything to the max. His "toys" quenched his love for speed. No matter what he drove, he went fast.

Michael's life, as he knew it, came to an end on January 14, 1994. It was thirty-five degrees below zero. He and seven others were snowmobiling that morning. Michael, still drunk from the night before, stayed at the tail end of the group so he would have room to play. The last thing he remembers is coming around a blind corner at thirty-five miles per hour and seeing a woman ahead of him, stopped on the trail. He panicked and thought, *What should I do?* He couldn't stop, so he swerved to avoid her. Michael leaned as far as he could toward her sled to avoid falling off his own, which was almost sideways. *Bang!* His head struck the metal rack on the back of her sled. The force, not unlike hitting a brick wall, knocked him off his snowmobile. There he lay, unconscious in the frigid snow. The others came back once they realized the two were no longer in the pack. One woman happened to be a trauma nurse and made sure Michael's head and neck were not moved. It took a while to get help because they were deep into the North Woods.

Eventually, medics from a local hospital came on a snowmobile with a stretcher and carried him out. After arriving at the hospital, a doctor took one look at Michael and said, "We can't deal with this here," so he was transported by helicopter to a larger hospital some distance away.

Sometime during the transit, Michael died for a brief period and found himself in the presence of God. He felt ultimate joy, peace, and serenity. Michael likens the intensity of these emotions to multiplying how you felt on your best day ever by a thousand—and that still wouldn't come close. He'll never forget his conversation with an angel of the Lord. The angel proclaimed, "You cannot be here!" In his arrogance, Michael asked, "Why?" "Because it's not your time," responded the angel. Again, he asked, "Why not?"

After putting a shunt hole in Michael's head to relieve brain pressure, the doctor coldly told his family, "If he's with us tomorrow, we'll talk," and he walked away. Michael was given a rating of four on the Glasgow coma scale, which ranges from three (brain dead) to twenty-one (healthy). He was not expected to live. His family was left devastated with little hope.

Awakening from twenty-six days in a coma, Michael didn't even know who he was, much less anyone else. His right side was completely paralyzed. Doctors said he'd spend his life in a group home, and he'd never walk again. His cognitive level was never expected to surpass the fifth- or sixth-grade level, and he wouldn't be able to retain any new information.

Michael burned with anger at God for saving his life, and he began questioning why God had brought him back. Michael was so agitated that he had to be restrained. He was even diagnosed with rage syndrome by a neuropsychologist. It was presumed he would be angry and agitated for the rest of his life.

He didn't want to see or talk with anyone. The only people he even allowed to come in his room were his father, boys, and wife. Although he didn't know who they were, their faces looked familiar somehow. It would be several months before Michael warmed up to his own mother— he thought he'd disappointed her.

Michael's father sat by his bedside around the clock for days after he woke up. One night his father awakened to a strange sound coming from Michael's mouth. At first, he simply thought Michael was agitated (as usual). But, as he looked more closely, he saw blood coming from his nose and out of his mouth! The sound he heard was the gurgling of blood! If Michael's father hadn't been there, he would have choked and died before anyone would have noticed.

Then came physical, speech, and psychological rehabilitation. Every waking moment was spent in therapy—six hours per day at first. He was unable to speak, feed himself, or take care of himself. It was like being an infant again. Michael didn't remember how to do anything, nor could he recognize seemingly familiar objects. The first time a plate of food was set in front of him, he didn't know what anything was on the plate! He ate his meat, potatoes, vegetables, chocolate cake, and milk separately after receiving instruction. Even though Michael had been right-handed before the accident, his left hand took over with relative ease. The therapists were amazed how quickly he learned to care for himself. His functioning came back sooner than the doctors and nurses had seen in other patients with such a severe brain injury.

After a month or so of rehab, Michael decided he wasn't going to spend the rest of his life in a wheelchair. One day after therapy was over, he refused to get back into his wheelchair. The therapists were quite puzzled and asked, "How do you think you're going to get back to your room?" Michael boldly said, "You figure it out." Once they realized he wasn't going to cooperate and get into the wheelchair, they brought him a walker. After taking his limp right arm out of the sling, the therapists strapped it to the walker. Michael had already learned to stand, using his right leg as a peg to steady himself. With his right leg dragging behind, it took him one and a half hours to walk the sixty yards back to his room. Michael did this day after day, never using the wheelchair again.

By April, Michael was back at home, walking with a cane. He found himself drowning in a raging sea of agitation and depression. One day, when his family was away, Michael grabbed his shotgun and a slug. He went to his bedroom with his German shepherd, Roxy, following close behind. Michael sat down with his gun propped against a chair. He held a stick long enough to push the trigger. With the barrel of the gun in his mouth, he longed to be bathed once again in joy, peace, and serenity. There was only one problem, Roxy was staring him right in the eyes. He hollered for her to go away. But she wouldn't move. Michael became so angry with her that he threw down the gun. He couldn't pull the trigger with his beloved Roxy watching. When his wife and boys returned, he told his wife she'd better get rid of the gun.

Once Michael's wife knew what had happened that dark day, she admitted him to the psychiatric ward only two weeks after his return home. He was in the hospital three weeks. The doctors put Michael on several medications to settle him down. Michael did calm down, but he knew it was God, not the medication. Strangely enough, he got along with everyone in the ward! While normal people agitated him, the patients had a comforting effect. They were sincere, nonjudgmental, and kind.

Michael's stay at the hospital was a transition point in his relationship with God. Sure, he knew the basics. His family had faithfully attended church every Sunday. Michael believed Jesus was the Son of God and knew the Ten Commandments inside and out. Because his religion was so strict, he saw God as a sovereign authority figure to be feared. Michael was taught what to do and what not to do because of God's decree. There was never room for questions. His unanswered questions had prevented him from developing a relationship with God. All this soon changed. While in the hospital, he began praying and talking with God throughout the day. Michael wanted to know what God had planned for him. He wondered, *Does God want me to work with the brain injured and mentally ill?* He sure did seem to bond easily with them. Eventually, Michael learned to take one step at a time and trust God's guidance.

Shortly after returning home again, Michael suddenly developed a strong feeling his wife was having an affair. One night she was about to leave the house when he confronted her. After denying it several times, she finally confessed. Outraged, Michael threw her car keys at her. She left immediately. Mad that she had been found out, his wife called the police and stated that Michael had just beaten her. He ended up in jail that night, even though the sheriff knew he hadn't done anything wrong.

He moved back home with his parents after this because his wife didn't want him to come back. The first week with his parents, Michael was served divorce papers. Having to move back home turned out to be a blessing in disguise. Through God's grace he became reacquainted with his mother. She tirelessly worked with Michael by walking with him, talking with him, and taking care of him.

Michael attended services at his childhood church. There were icons everywhere, but one of Jesus alone caught his eye. He stared intently at the icon, and within one minute, he became fixated on it, almost losing his footing. All he could see was Jesus' face and body before him; everything else faded away. Michael came into contact with God and conversed with Him. Out of anger, he asked God, "Why do you want me to stay here?" God replied, "There are other things for you to do." "What do you have planned for me?" Michael asked. God told him not to worry about that; His plans would be revealed one step at a time.

A year after moving back home with his parents, God gave Michael the drive to push himself even more to overcome his physical and cognitive disabilities. He began working out regularly at a health club, gradually gaining strength and the ability to somewhat use his right arm.

He had resigned from his position as plant manager at the large corporation because he knew it wasn't good for him to return. The money, power, and pride didn't matter anymore.

Against all odds, Michael went back to school and earned a social work degree. Whenever he ran into difficulties at college, people offered to help. A woman came up to Michael one day at school and said, "I've been watching you for a while and can see you struggling. We're both going to school to be social workers, so I'm going to help you get through." She became his best friend, helping him through five years of school. In another instance, after failing an exam in physics, the professor called Michael up to his desk after class and asked, "How can I help?" The professor offered to tutor him after class, and he helped raise Michael's grade from an F to a B+!

While interning at a mental health institution, he was reminded of how comfortable he felt with the patients. He thoroughly enjoyed his work there. Hoping to stay at the institution, Michael asked whether any job positions were open. He was devastated to find out that no jobs were available. He thought, *Surely God wants me to work here!* But God had other plans.

Three jobs became available at the local prison; Michael was qualified for all three. Since he didn't have any experience working with prisoners—or knowledge of the criminal justice system—he was less than excited about these opportunities at first. But God changed his heart. After meeting with several social workers at the prison who happened to be Christians, Michael began to feel more at ease about working there. He went back to school, earned an AODA counseling certification, and later became certified as a brain injury specialist. Michael then accepted a position as a certified social worker and AODA counselor at the prison. Over the years, he's had opportunities to share his faith and bring some of the men to Christ. It's been so rewarding for him to see how Christ has changed their lives.

God had been at work in Michael's personal life as well. After being saved by God so many times, Michael decided it was time for him to save someone else. So he found a woman with an organic brain injury who desperately needed help. They got married and remained married for nine years. As a result of her brain injury, however, his wife was quite verbally abusive. Later, it turned into physical abuse. Ironically, the marriage ended much like his first: his wife called the police and accused him of beating her. Again, Michael found himself in jail even though he was the one who had been physically assaulted. He knew it wasn't safe to remain in the marriage. It was not his responsibility to save her; only God could do that.

Michael spent a year or so alone after ending his marriage. One day, while talking to a friend at work, Michael asked if she had any single friends who might be interested in having someone to go out to dinner with on occasion. He wasn't interested in anything serious. Her friend Mary came to mind. Michael called Mary one evening and they talked for hours. From the time he first met her, he couldn't help but stare into her eyes. This made him a bit uncomfortable—not to mention Mary.

After their second date, Michael awakened from a deep sleep around midnight with heartache. It didn't make any sense. He wondered, *Why does my heart hurt? Am I having a heart attack?* Michael assessed himself for signs of a heart attack. He had none. The pain worsened, preventing him from sleeping. So he got up at 3:00 a.m. and took a shower. The pain worsened until he cried out to God, asking what was happening. God said, "This is the one for you." Confused, Michael asked, "What do you mean?" Again God replied, "This is the one for you. She will be your wife." His eyes popped wide open, and the heartache became even more severe. Then God told him, "You will tell her you love her this morning." "You're nuts!" exclaimed Michael while shaking his head, "I don't even know this woman!" After several hours of wrestling with God, Michael gave in. The heartache lessened.

By this time, it was 5:30 a.m. so Michael decided to have some breakfast. He remembered Mary got up at 6:00 a.m. to get ready for work. So at 6:01 a.m., Michael hesitantly picked up the phone and called her. She was a bit flustered when he called her so early. She wondered what was wrong. He told her nothing was wrong. "So why did you call?" she asked. "I wanted to tell you that I love you," Michael blurted out before losing his nerve. There was dead silence on the other line for at least a minute. Feeling foolish, Michael figured he'd just ruined any chance he had with Mary. Then he heard, "What do you want me to say?" Michael replied, "I don't want anything except to let you know that I love you." Mary hung up the phone. He was certain she would never want to see him again. Later that evening, the phone rang. It was Mary! After talking for a long period, Mary and Michael decided to continue dating. Thus began a beautiful friendship that soon blossomed into love. Their marriage is a gift from God.

Today Michael walks without a cane, even though his right leg doesn't move like the left one. He's worked at the prison as an AODA counselor for ten years, and he facilitates a support group for brain-injured people. He is happily married to the love of his life. God comes first to Michael and Mary. They are involved in a home fellowship group that meets weekly. In Michael's words, he is "following God's plan." Although happier now than ever, not everything in life is enjoyable all the time. He works hard, doing what God calls him to do, and can't wait until he goes home to the Lord. The song "While I'm Waiting," by John Waller, beautifully depicts Michael's sentiments about going home.

"Your word is a lamp to my feet and a light for my path" *(Psalm 119:105).*

Michael had become so arrogant that it took being stripped of his dignity before he was able to see his need for God's guidance. He literally had to learn to talk, walk, and care for himself again. Michael's story is a beautiful example of how God guides us, step by step. The closer his relationship with God grew, the brighter his path became.

Dianne ~ Age 65
Hope in God's Word

Not long after moving into their first home came the dreaded knock at the front door. There stood two women holding Bibles! They were going door to door and sharing the message of the Gospel as part of an evangelical outreach. Before long, Dianne found herself sitting on the couch with the women as her husband watched television. After sharing the Gospel with Dianne, the women invited her to pray the sinner's prayer. She went through the motions, accepting Jesus as her Savior and asking Him to forgive her sins.

If she had fully accepted Jesus, then the Holy Spirit would have come into her heart and begun to transform her. The only thing that changed was that Dianne started taking Bible study classes a couple of months later. As she got into God's Word, she became aware that a Christian's walk involved much more than simply going to church.

Before reading the Bible, Dianne thought she'd go to heaven simply because she went to church! Surely, God noticed her faithful attendance, Sunday school teaching, and singing in the choir. But knowing about Him and serving Him wasn't enough; God desired Dianne to know Him in a deeply personal way—an intimate way that went far beyond sitting in church each Sunday and involving herself in church activities. The more Dianne studied God's Word, the closer their relationship became.

After several years, Dianne became disenchanted with her marriage. When she married, she had the idea that her husband would make her happy and be everything she needed. Her husband wasn't the man she wanted him to be, and he wasn't fulfilling her needs. Dianne had a very nice boss. She began spending more time talking with him, and their friendship soon developed into an affair. Dianne thought that if she left her husband and married her boss, then he would be able to meet her needs. She had it all figured out. But God had other plans. He stepped in, turning her plans upside down.

At the Christmas Eve service that year, the pastor highlighted Romans 8:28–29, "And we know that in all things God works for the good of those who love him, who have been called according to his purpose. For those God foreknew he also predestined to be conformed to the likeness of his Son." These verses spoke to Dianne at a deep level that night. Throughout the years, God brought good out of many bad situations in Dianne's life. He has been faithful all of the time, especially in the midst of life's storms.

Finally, Dianne was ready to surrender. She said, "Okay, Lord, I will do what You want and take care of my husband and make him happy. I trust that You will take care of me." She began looking to the Lord to meet her needs because only He could. Repairing their marriage was hard work, and it took the power of the Holy Spirit to work through her husband's anger and lack of forgiveness. God didn't let them down. Over the years, their marriage healed and grew stronger than ever.

After placing her trust in God, Dianne began to change. She even began to think differently. The Lord was on her mind all of the time. One day, God helped her to discover she was smoking out of rebellion. She had been smoking since the age of fourteen. She used to think, *No one's going to tell me what to do!* That very same day, God delivered Dianne from her addiction to cigarettes. That didn't mean she never tried to have a cigarette again. But before she could bring it up to her mouth, the Holy Spirit reminded her that to do so would be disobedient to God—the last thing she wanted was to let God down.

Then a spiritual battle raged in their home; Dianne's sixteen-year-old daughter turned rebellious. An oppressive feeling hung in the air like smog. One night, Dianne snapped and had a temper tantrum. She became very angry with God that her daughter was so defiant and peace had not come to their home. Out of desperation, she tried smoking. After one puff and a face full of smoke, she thought getting drunk might help. Of course, none of those things worked, and she asked herself, *Where else can I go or whom else can I turn to for help besides God?* She knew deep down that only God could mend her heart.

Her daughter moved out at the age of eighteen. Shortly thereafter, she left town without even telling her parents. Months went by before she called—and she only called when she needed money or got into trouble.

One day, she called—in trouble with the law and pregnant—so Dianne and her husband brought their daughter home … though it wasn't long before she left again. Two months later, Dianne received a phone call from her daughter's friend: she was in jail and needed to be bailed out. Dianne suggested her daughter should call her if she needed help. Soon after, her daughter called asking for bail money. Dianne refused to send money, but she told her that she could call them every night. Her daughter needed to learn to take responsibility for her actions.

This heart-wrenching decision ended up being a turning point for their daughter. She, along with the rest of the family, learned to have faith that God prepares and gives us insight to cope with difficult situations. After having her baby, her daughter moved back home because she wanted to raise her daughter close to the family. Now she lives only two houses away and talks to Dianne almost every day.

Today, Dianne hungers more and more for the Lord. It has been His Word and Spirit that have sustained her thus far. She's involved in women's ministries, and she teaches Bible study classes. Dianne emphasizes the importance of reading the Bible because, as she says, "If you don't know His Word, how can you claim to know Him? God reveals Himself to us in His Word." Her passion is instilling (in women) hope and faith in Jesus. Dianne wants women to be "overcomers" in Christ, knowing that He'll get them through everything they face. "Once we're new creations in Christ, there's no more shame or guilt. He doesn't want us to walk with these burdens any longer because that isn't who we are anymore. God can take our past and use it to minister mercy, grace, and truth to others," says Dianne.

"You are my refuge and my shield; I have put my hope in your word" (Psalm 119:114).

God's Word has sustained Dianne, providing her with hope. He's always worked even the most difficult situations for her good. Dianne is confident He'll continue to do so. She trusts God will use His Word to guide her through all things.

Jessica ~ Age 34
Stubbornness Transformed into Submission

Even though Jessica attended parochial school through the eighth grade, she only went to church for weddings, funerals, and religious holidays. Religion was too rigid for her. There were so many rules. Her motto was: "Don't give me rules because I'll break them!" Growing up being abused by both parents, she'd become very angry and rebellious by her teenage years.

In college, Jessica used alcohol and drugs quite heavily. She was kicked out of her house at the age of eighteen, and eventually dropped out of school. Although she was partying a lot, she somehow knew that wasn't the life for her. Jessica felt like she was being called to something more, but she was unclear what that was.

In her early twenties, Jessica started regularly meeting with a therapist who steered her toward spirituality and astrology to find meaning in life. While Jessica always knew God was there (somewhere), she was too ashamed to look any further for Him. She thought she was too bad to go to church. Scared and incredibly lost, Jessica didn't know where to turn. She thought, *If only I could get rid of the pain lurking deep in my heart.*

That was when God brought Jessica to Michelle, a new hairstylist. Because her monthly hair appointments lasted nearly three hours, the two had time to talk about everything. The friendship that soon blossomed opened Jessica's heart to talking about God. Before long, Michelle began sharing her faith. They discussed religious issues Jessica wrestled with. She argued with Michelle about everything. She used to say, "If God is this, then why does this happen?" Jessica was extremely stubborn. Although she listened to what Michelle said, she was still guarding her heart. For her, God was a harsh, authoritative ruler. You obeyed God's rules because you were supposed to, not because you wanted to obey Him. Jessica didn't feel like she could know Him personally.

After confiding in Michelle about the marital problems she was having in 2005, Michelle urged Jessica to visit her nondenominational church. But she just wasn't ready to go to church yet. Jessica wanted to go, but she still had issues about church. She had never found God amidst all the rules. The hypocrisy she saw in many "religious" people had kept her away.

By the summer of 2007, Jessica had finally built up the courage to go to church with Michelle. They had been friends for almost ten years by that time. The two met at church for a Saturday night service. It was a life-changing evening. Jessica was most impressed by the teaching. The pastor explained biblical concepts in a way she could understand. She thought, *God actually wants to have a relationship with me!* Jessica also enjoyed the worship music and felt very comfortable with the people at church; she belonged there. She left hungry for more of what she'd heard that evening.

Afterward, they went out for dinner and talked. Later that evening, Michelle encouraged Jessica to try listening to KLove, a Christian music station, to learn the songs that were sung at church. Jessica had never listened to Christian music before. As soon as she got into her car, she changed the station from heavy metal to KLove. Quite a drastic switch! Since that night, Jessica hasn't listened to anything else. God used Christian music to transform her life.

Gradually, Jessica became a different person after accepting Jesus as her Savior. Now she wanted to do the right things and live in a way that pleased God. It was as if she began to see the world through God's eyes. She felt deep compassion for those who were hurting. Jessica got a bad feeling and was repulsed when she heard people swear, saw violent messages portrayed on television, or heard similar messages in music. Suddenly, she began to think twice about things she used to say or do that were not so good. She just didn't want to behave like that anymore.

Today, Jessica and her husband attend church together. They've taken a series of "Love and Respect" classes to build a stronger marriage, and their relationship continues to grow stronger.

Jessica works on building her relationship with God and learning to trust Him. One of the hardest things for her to grasp is that God actually wants to have a relationship with her. She spends time with God in the morning reading the Bible, working on Bible studies, and praying. The Bible has come to life for her with www.Bible.is, a dramatized reading on the Internet. An application for her MP3 player, called Pocket Prayer, has really helped Jessica make prayer an integral part of each day. At the touch of a button, she can read Scripture that relates to all sorts of situations, and she can keep track of prayers for friends and family.

Recently, after months of praying for God's help to stop drinking, her desire to drink just disappeared! This was a miracle. She hasn't even thought about drinking since.

God is working hard on transforming her stubbornness into submission and flexibility. Jessica has recently responded to God's call to be baptized, and she glorified God by making a public declaration of her commitment to follow Jesus.

"Therefore go and make disciples of all nations, baptizing them in the name of the Father and of the Son and of

the Holy Spirit, and teaching them to obey everything I have commanded you. And surely I am with you always, to the very end of the age" (Matthew 28:19-20).

Jessica's story is a good example of how God often uses other Christians to bring us to Him. It took almost ten years of talking with her friend Michelle before Jessica was ready to go to church. Once she started learning about God's Word at church and from Christian music, she opened her heart to God and allowed Him to start working in her. Baptism was an important milestone for Jessica in proclaiming her commitment to follow Jesus for the rest of her life.

Jason ~ Age 39
Surrendering a Dream to Fulfill God's Purpose

Jason accepted Jesus when only four years old. One morning in Sunday school he became aware of the existence of heaven and hell and that Jesus is the only way to heaven. Since we're all sinners, we need Jesus to cleanse us of sin. He pondered the lesson all day and into the night. It bothered him that he couldn't help being naughty sometimes; it was part of his makeup. Jason understood that by accepting Jesus into his life, he wouldn't have to live the rest of his life without hope. He knew Jesus had plans for him and desperately needed Jesus to be Lord of his life.

Jason was still awake late in the evening, so he called to his twin brother in the top bunk to see whether he was awake too. He was—his brother couldn't stop thinking about what they had learned that morning either! The two decided they needed to wake up their dad to ask him some questions. So the little blond-haired boys confidently marched into their parents' bedroom and somehow pulled their burly dad out of bed. He followed them to their room and explained what it meant to accept Jesus. That night, the boys knelt on the floor by their bunk bed with their dad, and they accepted Jesus as their Lord and Savior.

Born in British Columbia, Canada, in a Mennonite Brethren culture, Jason's family was deeply involved in the church. They spent Sunday mornings and evenings, as well as Wednesday evenings, at church. And they engaged in fellowship with other believers outside of church. His parents belonged to a music group that traveled to other small churches. Mom played the piano. Dad sang and played the guitar and harmonica. Jason, his brother, and his sister all loved to sing. They have fond memories of sitting by a warm, crackling fire in the living room, singing and playing music as a family. As young children, Jason and his siblings always enjoyed the one song at each ministry event where they were allowed to come and sing with their parents on stage.

They moved to San Diego in 1980 when Jason was nine and a half so his dad could earn a master's degree in seminary. Coming from a predominantly white, German, Mennonite farm community, they were immersed in a multiethnic city during the Valley era. Culture shock! When it came time to choose a band instrument to study, Jason decided he wanted to play the trombone. Unfortunately, his arms were too short! His next choice was drums, but they were too loud for his family to handle. So he chose the trumpet because it was similar in many ways to the trombone. He took to it immediately, playing solos in church before long. In the middle of eighth grade, an awkward age for a boy, his family moved to southern Colorado. Transplanted from a big city into the boondocks, it took a while for Jason to make new friends. It was at this time he began to take more to music.

Church remained an important part of his life. He was involved in Vacation Bible School and the youth group. Jason's dad was the pastor of a Baptist church. Their family served the church in numerous ways. All of these experiences strengthened Jason's faith and trust in God. He continued his involvement in church and read the Bible—even in college, while others were partying.

An event during his high school years convicted Jason of selfishness. His dad publicly refuted an article written by Mormons, who claimed Jesus for themselves. The issue caused much unrest, and a couple came from the Mormon temple in Salt Lake City to speak with Jason's dad. They spent four nights talking with his parents in the hope that he'd retract his criticism. Each night Jason's parents asked him to pray for the couple, but Jason prayed for the safety of his family instead. He wondered, *Why should I pray for the couple when my family is being chastised?* After the couple left, his parents explained that their main concern was to share the truth about Jesus with the lost Mormons—they prayed for their salvation. The couple voiced a deep need for salvation through Jesus alone, but they were fearful of retaliation from their community. Jason realized life wasn't as much about taking care of himself as it was about taking care of others by sharing Jesus with them.

Not long after, his dad was falsely accused at church. Accusations were coming from all sides, and his dad quietly resigned as pastor to avoid further conflict. His dad tried not to argue with anyone; he simply stated that the accusations were untrue. Jason saw the footprint of Jesus in the way his dad handled the unfair situation. After this incident, Jason secretly told himself that he'd never become a pastor because he wouldn't want to put his family through that.

Jason went off to college and was very serious about becoming a professional jazz musician. He became proficient at playing the trumpet. In his fifth year, Jason went on a weeklong jazz band tour to recruit new students, but he had to drop out before the week ended. A large cyst had developed on his upper lip in the exact spot his mouthpiece rested! Within one month, Jason was nearly unable to play at all.

One day, he placed his beloved trumpet in its case and set it on the closet shelf. Then he walked out to his car, put the sunshade in the windshield, and cried and wrestled in his spirit with God for several hours. Jason wrote a letter to God saying that he could see that his pursuit of being a great trumpet player had become an idol. He had sinned against God. Jason didn't blame God for taking the trumpet away—he understood God was teaching him a valuable lesson. God would not take second place to anything or anyone. Jason promised that if, by God's grace, he could play again, he would play for God alone. After that, Jason took up playing the drums. He found he could still enjoy music in ways he hadn't previously considered. In time, the cyst on his lip healed, allowing him to play the trumpet again.

Jason was accepted into a Grammy award-nominated jazz program in graduate school. He began playing the trumpet professionally. At the end of graduate school, Jason was offered two jobs: a part-time job as a music director at church and a teaching assistant job at graduate school. Although he really wanted to work as a teaching assistant, God nudged him to take the job at church. Before long, Jason was working forty hours per week at church in the youth ministry and music program—and he was spending an additional twenty hours playing the trumpet. He just couldn't let the dream go. Not yet.

After a few years of working at the church, he accepted the opportunity to work as their full-time music pastor. Despite his position, deep in his heart Jason was still a trumpet player leading worship. Now working forty to fifty hours each week, he still practiced the trumpet for fifteen to twenty hours! And he had a wife and baby girl. Burnout was around the corner.

One day, he became overwhelmed with frustration at petty complaints from church members, as well as more serious discord. Jason wanted to be released from his position at the church to play the trumpet for God's glory. Feeling trapped in pain and conflict at church, Jason headed to his office. He taped paper over the window in his door so nobody could see in, and then he fell to his knees and cried out to God, "I don't know why You want me here, Lord, but I know that You do. I will give up the trumpet for You." This was the moment Jason became a worship pastor who happened to play the trumpet. That day he penned the song "I'm Yours."

(Verse 1)
Lord, I wait for the touch of Your hand
How I long for a taste of the Living Water's flood
I am lost in the pain of this world
Jesus, come … lift me up … I am Yours
(Verse 2)
Lord, You heal with the touch of Your hand
How You long to refresh with Your Living Water's
flood
Lord, You died for my pain with Your blood
Jesus, come … lift me up … into Your world
(Chorus)
I am Yours when the darkness comes
I am Yours when my heart's undone
I am Yours when the walls cave in
Lord, please come change my world
(Bridge)
I cry to You my King …
When sin undoes the offering
I call to You my King …
My heart and soul to You I bring.

He was crying out to Jesus to heal his emotional pain and to lift him up. Jason offered his life's pursuits to the Lord, desperate to be refreshed in His presence again.

The Lord has blessed Jason for giving up playing the trumpet professionally. He's given it back to him in bits and pieces over the years. Jason plays in church and the community once in a while. And, from time to time, he's asked to record the trumpet for various professional recording artists.

Prior to surrendering his dream, Jason spent a great deal of time longing to see God perform miracles like those he'd read about in the Bible. Since the day he gave his full obedience to God's call on him to serve in pastoral ministry, Jason has begun to see the power of God released in and through the church, witnessing many wonderful miracles that seemed so absent from his view before. The more obedient Jason becomes to God's call, the more his eyes are opened to the amazing miracles of God in and around His people.

Although described by others as humble today, Jason's peers from middle school through graduate school saw him as proud and arrogant. He still struggles—as every person does—and, in particular, he has been fighting an ongoing battle with self-deprecation, the flipside of pride. Self-deprecating thoughts sometimes rear their ugly head, especially when it comes to insecurities about his singing voice and ability to lead worship. Knowing that he can do nothing apart from the Lord, Jason relies on God's help to succeed in every area of his life, including being a worship pastor.

The Lord has proven Himself to be more and more faithful as Jason has become more faithful in the Lord. Jason tries to be faithful with whatever God brings him each day. He's having a lot more fun now than when he fought against God's will for him. Surrender has brought peace into his life. Rather than setting goals for himself, Jason leaves himself open to doing whatever God asks of him. Times when he no longer sees God at work are times when he's being tested or not being fully obedient.

Scripture has been the foundation of Jason's life. He sees the need to read, digest, test, and live God's Word. The more time he spends in Scripture, the more God does in and around his life. In fact, all amazing things that have happened in Jason's life grew out of Scripture. Only by reading the Bible—and putting it into practice—has Jason discovered the peace of God. For him, having a lack of peace is always a good indicator of not following God's will.

"Not that I have already obtained all this, or have already been made perfect, but I press on to take hold of that for which Christ Jesus took hold of me. Brothers, I do not consider myself yet to have taken hold of it. But one thing I do: Forgetting what is behind and straining toward what is ahead, I press on toward the goal to win the prize for which God has called me heavenward in Christ Jesus" (Philippians 3:12-14).

Jason's goal is Jesus. He puts his energy into being obedient to what God calls him to do each day. For Jason, that meant giving up his dream to become a professional jazz musician. By sacrificing his dream, Jason opened the door to fulfilling something even better: God's plans for him.

Sandy ~ Age 54
Forgiven, Healed, and Restored

As a child, Sandy came to see herself as the mistake that made her parents get married. She and her mom were never close. Her mom didn't show Sandy how to cook, sew, or any of the things a mother usually teaches her daughter. Rather than nurturing Sandy, her mom hurled insults at her.

As a junior in high school, Sandy learned that her mom had cheated on her dad during most of their marriage. Finally, she understood what all of the arguments had been about, and why her mom sometimes came home late or not at all. Feeling responsible for her parents' separation, Sandy wondered, *How did I cause this?*

At the end of her junior year, Sandy met her first boyfriend. She clung to him, desperate for a sense of safety and peace she never felt before. He became the center of her world. Sandy spent a lot of time at his parents' house and became part of their family. Watching his parents make meals together brought comfort to her. His mother taught Sandy how to cook and quilt—and she explained female sexuality to her. All the things Sandy's own mother had neglected.

She and her boyfriend stayed pure until the night of her sixteenth birthday. He cooked a delicious dinner for the two of them, and they ended up in bed. About two months later Sandy discovered she was pregnant! Because she was only a senior in high school, Sandy wanted to make plans for adoption. She and her boyfriend loved each other, but they were not ready to get married and start a family yet.

Sandy went to Planned Parenthood, hoping to get some information about adoption. Instead, they pushed abortion. They said she was too fragile and young to go through an entire pregnancy. And her parents would have to be notified because she was a minor. Despite being pressured to have an abortion, Sandy knew there was life inside of her—much more than "just a clump of cells in her uterus."

This decision was too big to make alone; she needed to talk to someone. Even though they weren't close, Sandy went to her mom first. She thought her mom would be less likely to judge because she had an abortion while still married. Much to Sandy's dismay, her mom said, "You need to have an abortion; otherwise your life will be ruined."

Back at home, Sandy's dad met her at the door. He saw her crying and asked what was wrong. She just couldn't tell him—not yet. Then her dad asked if she had gotten herself into trouble and she said, "Yes." He knew. "How could you do this to me?" he yelled. And then he slammed the door to Sandy's bedroom and walked away. Sandy threw herself on the bed and cried. Later, her dad came in and said, "You know, we're going to have to handle this." She couldn't believe it—he expected her to have an abortion, too! Sandy held her ground. She wanted to make an adoption plan instead. Her boyfriend's parents offered to let Sandy live with them so they could help with the baby. For them, life was the only choice.

Even though she didn't want to have an abortion, Sandy also didn't want to let her dad down. She had always tried to please her parents. Her dad made Sandy feel ashamed about being pregnant; he was concerned the courts would use that against him and take away his custody. And that would mean sending Sandy and her brother back to their mom. Eventually, her dad won out and made an appointment for an abortion. When the day came—April 15,

1975—he drove her to the hospital. She sat in a circle with other girls while being told what would happen. They had to do a saline abortion because Sandy was four and a half months pregnant. The amniotic fluid was taken out and replaced by a saline solution that killed the baby from the outside in. When the doctor inserted the large needle into her abdomen, Sandy's leg kicked, knocking everything off the table that had been sterile. Angry, the doctor swore and told her that she needed to stay very still. Sandy told him she didn't want to go through with the procedure, but he insisted, "Your dad brought you here. Your parents must think it's the right thing for you to do so I'm going to do it."

Afterward, everything inside of her was gone—her soul was empty. As a woman, a nurturer, Sandy knew life had been taken from her that day. After the procedure, she was led out into the hallway where she met her boyfriend, his parents, and her own dad. Sandy fell into her boyfriend's arms and stayed there for a long time, sobbing. Two days later, Sandy went home and her parents never spoke of the abortion again—they didn't want others to find out. Everyone stuffed it away, but Sandy couldn't forget. She couldn't forgive herself. The abortion came up periodically in discussions with her boyfriend, but she didn't work through the web of emotional trauma deep inside. Because they had already succumbed to temptation once, Sandy and her boyfriend continued to have intercourse now and then during moments of weakness.

In fall the following year, Sandy drove several hours to surprise her boyfriend at college for his birthday. As she approached his bedroom, she heard noises coming from inside and opened the door to find him in bed with another girl! Sandy ran out of the house as fast as she could and drove all the way back home. She wondered, *How could he do this to me after four and a half years of dating?*

She went straight to her friend's house for support and comfort, but she wasn't home. The friend's husband invited

Sandy in, however, seeing how upset she was. They sat down to talk, and Sandy shared what had just happened. He tried to comfort her by saying things like, "You're a beautiful young lady. He'll be sorry he did this to you." Slowly, one sweet compliment and hug at a time, he seduced Sandy. They ended up in bed. Afterward, Sandy felt awful. She asked herself, *How could I have slept with my best friend's husband?* She left feeling even worse than when she came. Afraid she might be pregnant, Sandy set up an appointment for a pregnancy test the following week. They said the pregnancy test was positive, but she knows today that it couldn't have been detected that early by a urine test. The clinic likely saw her as another opportunity to make easy money with an abortion. Harboring a deep level of shame, guilt, and resentment, Sandy agreed to a D and C abortion, figuring it couldn't be as bad as the first one because she was only about two weeks along. This time Sandy didn't tell anyone. The shame of having a second abortion was a secret she would keep to herself.

Friends of her boyfriend came and talked to her about the incident that happened on his birthday. They said he'd gotten drunk and had been set up with a girl he didn't even know. He was very sorry for his lapse of judgment and sought her forgiveness. They continued dating for several years, but the secret of her second abortion put a wall between them; she never felt as close to him as she had before. She later found out that he had been putting pinholes in condoms for months, thinking that if she got pregnant again, she would marry him for sure. He loved Sandy and would go to any length to marry her. Not being able to get past all that had happened between them, however, Sandy broke off the relationship and went to college to start a career of her own.

Two years later, in 1981, she fell into a deep depression. Sandy had recently moved to a different town to start her life over where no one would know of her past experiences. In fall of that year, her brother and ex-boyfriend both got married. It was depressing to think she might never marry. She wondered, *What man would want a marred, used woman as his wife?* All Sandy ever wanted was to be a mom and wife—and to live happily ever after. Thoughts of suicide pervaded her mind: *Maybe I could run my car off a bridge or into a wall so I wouldn't hurt anyone else.*

The following year, Sandy went on a date with a man she met at work. He took her out to dinner twice and ordered alcohol with his food. This really turned Sandy off because her mom was an alcoholic. She had many bad memories of her mom being drunk, such as finding her mom laying on the floor unconscious one day. Because of his drinking, Sandy was not interested in getting together again. Shortly after saying she didn't want to see him again, he showed up at her apartment drunk one evening, forced his way in, and raped her. The couple that lived below her was gone that night so there was no one around to hear her screaming. After he left, Sandy questioned, "Where were You God? How could You let this happen?" She felt violated and dirty. After taking a hot shower for nearly an hour, she went to the hospital due to continued bleeding (and to report what happened). The doctor did a D and C procedure to prevent a possible pregnancy. This brought her past to the forefront again—it was as if the other abortions had happened just yesterday. Her depression sank to an even darker level.

Shortly thereafter, Sandy's friend invited her on a trip to Florida during the week of Easter. Sandy went mainly because she saw it as a good opportunity to kill herself in a place where no one knew her. Early one morning, she couldn't sleep and went for a walk on the beach alone. Sandy noticed one sand sculpture after another depicting the life and death of Jesus. Each one had corresponding Scripture below. She read them all. The sculptures and Scripture really touched her soul as Sandy realized that Christ had died for her sins. God had reached down to her in a way only He could. Her thoughts of suicide pretty much ended because she thought it was an unforgiveable sin that would prevent her from going to heaven.

After returning home, Sandy attended prayer meetings on Wednesday nights with her friend. On April 13, 1983, the pastor happened to say, "There is nothing you could ever do that God wouldn't forgive." This struck a deep place in Sandy's heart, and she went forward to the altar and invited the Lord into her life after asking Jesus to forgive her sins. She reminisced about a little white Bible her parents had given her for her eighth grade confirmation. Sandy read it but didn't really understand that particular translation. As a teenager, she listened to Billy Graham and responded each time he made an altar call. This wasn't the first time she had accepted the Lord, but it was the first time she really understood the significance and experienced a change of heart. She became very involved in church. She had a hunger to learn more and more about God. For the first time in her life, Sandy realized what a relationship with Jesus actually looked like.

While attending a class called "Going Fishing" that taught how to evangelize to family and friends, Sandy talked about her abortions for the first time. The pastor told her, "God has forgiven you and will use these experiences in a different way now that you've accepted Christ." The lack of judgment from the pastor and others in the class made Sandy feel loved for who she was as a person.

After that, God began to bring girls into her life who struggled with whether or not to have an abortion (or girls consumed by anger and guilt because they had one). Sandy became involved in WEBA (Women Exploited by Abortion), and she shared her testimony in churches, high schools, and one-on-one sessions. Being open about her experiences with abortion has helped many women make the decision to keep their babies.

The ladies at work sometimes went out together. One week, they invited Sandy to go with them to a bar. Sandy declined and told them she didn't go to bars but would enjoy bowling with them some time. They said, "If you don't like bars, we know a guy you should meet." So they passed Sandy's number on to Denny who later called and asked her out on a blind date.

Their first date happened to be on April 15, 1983—the same date she'd had her first abortion eight years earlier. Denny took Sandy bowling and out to dinner. All the while she looked forward to getting back home because she didn't find him particularly attractive. The conversation was very refreshing, though; she could talk to him about things that were meaningful. They continued dating, but Sandy was ready to break it off since Denny wasn't a Christian. Her pastor said it wasn't good to be unequally yoked and that she wouldn't want to marry a non-Christian. After about four months, Sandy figured she had nothing to lose by disclosing her abortions to him. She felt like "a used woman that no one would ever want anyway." Denny's reply, "If God forgave you, who am I to judge you," came as a surprise!

Knowing that he was not a Christian still bothered Sandy. Denny then asked, "How can I accept Jesus?" She refused to tell him because it seemed as though he only wanted to become a Christian to please her, not because he genuinely had an interest. During their months of dating, Denny attended church with Sandy. One day, the pastor and his wife came to visit Sandy at her apartment when Denny happened to be over. Sandy and the pastor's wife went to the store to buy some groceries to make dinner. While they were out, Denny and the pastor talked. By the time the ladies returned, Denny had accepted Jesus! Sandy and Denny dated for nine months before getting married and remained sexually pure during that time.

After being married five months, Sandy became pregnant. When she was three and a half months pregnant, they drove home to share the exciting news with Denny's parents. But Sandy miscarried after arriving at their home. She ended up staying in the hospital for a week due to hemorrhaging.

Sandy continued getting pregnant and miscarrying—she had a total of ten miscarriages. She and Denny tried infertility treatments to no avail. After the third miscarriage, Sandy tried bargaining with God: "Okay, God, now You have three babies back. We're even. Please let me keep the rest." Deep in her heart, though, she knew God was not really punishing her.

Sandy sought counsel from her pastor, and he pointed out the real problem: "God has forgiven you, but you haven't forgiven yourself." He explained that it is sinful not to forgive yourself because you're not looking at what Jesus did on the cross as being finished. It's as if you feel the need to add something. Sandy prayed to receive Jesus' free gift of forgiveness. Then a miracle happened: the scar on her abdomen from the saline abortion disappeared! That scar had been a constant daily reminder of what she'd done. Receiving full forgiveness, plus that extra gift, made Sandy feel whole again.

After years of being unable to maintain a pregnancy, along with prayerful consideration, they decided to adopt. God led them to two different women at just the right time to adopt two precious boys only two and a half years apart. In both cases, they were able to get the boys as infants. Looking back, Sandy and Denny had prayed for twelve children shortly after getting married. With the ten miscarriages and two adopted sons, God had indeed given them a dozen children, just not quite like they had expected. Sandy learned that she needed to be careful of what she prayed for … and that God's way is always best. By adopting, they may have saved two children from being aborted.

On Sandy's birthday in December of 2004 she laughed and said, "Now that I am forty-seven, I can go to heaven." Three days later, Sandy woke up around three o'clock in the morning to find her husband not breathing—he had died in his sleep. It turns out he had a heart attack due to an enlarged heart, a condition he knew nothing about. They had been married for twenty years, and they were good years.

God prepared her heart in several ways to help her through this dreadful experience. First was the comment she made on her birthday. Second, they had a beautiful family picture taken that September to use on their Christmas cards. Third, the night Denny died he was reading *The Five People You Meet in Heaven*. Knowing Denny had accepted Jesus gave Sandy peace that he was with God.

After Denny died, Sandy feared she might lose her faith and be a poor role model for the boys, aged seven and ten. She wondered, *How will we continue on without Denny?* One day, while reading the Bible, God led Sandy to Isaiah 54. Two passages provided great comfort: "Though the mountains be shaken and the hills be removed, yet my unfailing love for you will not be shaken nor my covenant of peace be removed, says the Lord, who has compassion on you" (Isaiah 54:10). The Lord's promise of peace helped calm Sandy's fears. She knew everything would be okay—in time. "All your sons will be taught by the Lord, and great will be your children's peace" (Isaiah 54:13). What better role model for her boys than the Lord?

Sandy checked into sending the boys to a Christian school. She felt it was important to have God at the center of every aspect of their lives. She wondered, *But how can I afford to send them?* Around the time Sandy needed to make the decision, a man sent a check for the exact amount it would cost to send the boys to a Christian school for the year! The man had actually sent the money for an annual fishing trip the family always took together. Only God could have known that she had already set aside money for the trip.

Denny's death brought Sandy into closer communion with God than she ever knew possible. God is her "all in all." Reading the devotional meditations in *The Secret Place* helps Sandy set aside time each day to be alone with God. She's learned that God needs to come first in her life. God desires and deserves nothing other than her complete obedience to His will.

Today, Sandy leads a ministry called "Beyond Regrets" at church. The group is based on the twelve-week post-abortion Bible study, *Forgiven and Set Free*. It ministers God's healing grace. Based on Scripture, the study helps women deal with issues of anger, denial, and forgiveness to open the door for healing and restoration of their hearts and lives. Sandy tells women, "No matter what we've done, God is big enough to forgive and heal us completely."

She is thankful that, through God's grace and forgiveness, her pain has been turned into the blessing of helping other women heal. Sandy participates in pro-life walks, speaks in high schools, and has one-on-one meetings with women who have had abortions or are confused about what choice to make.

"In your unfailing love you will lead the people you have redeemed. In your strength you will guide them to your holy dwelling" (Exodus 15:13).

Years ago, Sandy thought she blew it and that God wouldn't love her because of what she had done. She felt used and spoiled, and she thought she would never know love. Sandy was concerned that her greatest desire to be a wife and mom would never come to fruition. God has forgiven and redeemed Sandy, and He has been using her experience with abortion for the good of other women.

Jesse ~ Age 43
Saved by a Flickering Candle
in the Dungeon

By the time he reached his senior year, Jesse didn't care about anything. His good friend, who'd grown up in a strict Christian home, rebelled and turned to Satanism. Jesse followed suit. Raised in a dysfunctional family that only attended church at Christmas out of a sense of obligation, he didn't have a religion of his own anyway. His family never prayed or talked about God—it was as if He didn't exist. Jesse dabbled in Wicca and Shamanism for a time, but he eventually settled into Satanism. He was looking for something that would fill the empty space—the cold, dead place in his heart and soul. Satanism attracted Jesse because it gave him the sense of rebelling against everything that most people considered good and just.

Jesse felt lonely. His brothers and sister moved out of the house years earlier. Since his parents' divorce, Jesse's father was out of the picture. And his mom worked long hours, leaving him home alone. Jesse always had food, clothing, and a roof over his head—just not many people to talk to.

He spent a lot of time deep within the recesses of his imagination, creating fantastical stories with a full cast of heroes and villains. The stories were so elaborate that, at night, before falling asleep, Jesse would play through a new scenario, adding depth and complexity to the previous night's sojourns. Over time, he had formed a veritable library of imaginary stories.

Everything became about him. He wondered, *How can I use people to get what I want?* Jesse and his buddy got into role-playing games, but they couldn't afford to buy the books and games. Instead, every time Jesse went into the bookstore, he'd stuff what he could under his jacket and walk out. After a while, he overflowed with burning hatred and rage that he directed at everyone, including his own family.

His breaking point came while sitting in his buddy's car at a stoplight—he pulled out a knife on a woman walking her baby across the street after the light had turned green. Seeing the terror in the young woman's face, Jesse decided to turn away from Satanism then and there.

While still a pagan, Jesse had an affair with a married woman, also a pagan, who later divorced her husband to marry Jesse. When their second daughter was just a baby, his wife left with the girls. She moved four hours away to make it almost impossible for Jesse to visit. She hardly ever let Jesse see them, yet she accused him of not wanting to see the girls.

Jesse missed his wife and daughters so much that his heartache turned into a deep depression. The inner turmoil of losing everything that meant anything to him caused him to spiral out of control. He lost his grip on his emotions. Jesse began to think dark thoughts of leaving the earthly realm. Death called to him like a sensual lover, and he had very little strength to resist. It seemed as though his legacy was meant to end like this.

At the time, Jesse lived in a dark, damp basement with his buddy (in a house belonging to the guy's friend). The stench of rot and mold made staying there horrible. Unfortunately, Jesse had no other option. With bills, child support, and gas to drive to and from work in another town, he had little money left over. There were no friends or family to turn to for support. He hadn't talked to his brothers or sister since they'd moved out of the house, and he hadn't heard from his dad since his parents' divorce. He was stuck in a dungeon when not at work, and Jesse seriously pondered suicide as an option—a way out. He even researched suicide methods. Eventually, he ran out of money, and he had no choice but to contact his sister and move in with her family.

To escape from his dim reality, Jesse played a "live game" with a group of people. One day he and a woman in the group, Rachel, just started talking. They eventually became good friends. Rachel wore her Christianity like a mantle of honor. Initially, Jesse just wanted to challenge her beliefs. She persistently talked to him about God, but Jesse wanted nothing to do with God—he said that He had never done anything for him.

Not giving up on Jesse, Rachel sent him a Bible and some James MacDonald DVDs. Pastor MacDonald has a Bible-teaching broadcast ministry called Walk in the Word. Jesse wrestled with the Bible. He threw it on the floor and stepped on it. Jesse was just plain confused. He did manage to read the book of John, but he just thought of it as a nice fantasy story. He wondered, *Why would a god love us so much to actually come live as a man and go through all the stuff we do—then suffer and die so our sins will be forgiven?* Jesse couldn't comprehend that kind of selfless love.

Having no strength left in his body, Jesse felt content to die; only he hadn't discovered an adequate method of killing himself. Then he remembered a nurse warning him not to take too many prescription pills. Jesse hadn't been diagnosed with bipolar disorder until he sought help after his divorce, even though he had suffered with the highs and lows most of his life. He speculated, *Surely I'll die if I take all of them at once!* He grabbed the bottle containing his bipolar medication. While he was crying his eyes out, something made Jesse call Rachel before taking any pills. Over the next hour or so, she counseled Jesse back to life by talking about how God had a plan for him—a plan for goodness and prosperity. After getting off the phone, Jesse put the pills down and slept for the first time in days. Never again did he pick up the bottle with any dark thoughts.

One day Rachel asked, "Do you want to come to church with me tomorrow?" Less than excited about the idea, Jesse reluctantly agreed. They went to a Harvest church to watch a James MacDonald simulcast. When it came time for communion, Jesse felt like the pastor was speaking directly to him when he invited people to let the bread and cup pass by if they hadn't yet made a commitment to Jesus. Jesse took the bread and wine against his better judgment, but he struggled with whether or not to take them. A voice in his head said not to take them, but suddenly, it seemed like God put His hand on Jesse's shoulder and said, "Take them." So he took communion for the first time.

Afterward, a flicker of a candle appeared to Jesse amidst the darkness; God had lit a little fire inside. Although only a flame at first, over time it gradually grew larger and hotter until it turned into a roaring fire—the fire of the Holy Spirit.

Jesse noticed a new sense of clarity and strength; he began to understand the Bible and to have the motivation to do things he couldn't have done before. Before this, he had always been very introverted and shy. But the Lord put on his heart the hunger and passion to help others. In fact, Jesse got a rush after helping others! On several occasions, he could almost feel his Father in heaven smiling down on him. Jesse started going to church regularly, and he even met with a pastor to learn more of God's ways.

He still had thoughts of ending his life, though. One day, Jesse noticed a pamphlet on a divorce care group offered at church. The divorce had been a hard process, and it left a gaping hole in his heart. Attending divorce care meetings helped Jesse to cope and heal. The group helped him better understand God's plan and how amazingly well His plan works. Bill took Jesse under his wing and began calling him once a week—just to make sure he was okay. The two have since become best friends.

The devil has been persistent in trying to get Jesse to leave the Lord. Whenever something goes wrong in his life, he can hear the devil jesting, "Look at what your God has done for you now!" Jesse knows that God always has his best interests at heart—even though He may allow bad things to happen, He does not make them happen. God brings good out of all situations. Jesse still gets the inclination to do the wrong things, but he is at the point where he can laugh at the devil and say, "You're not going to get me!" Whenever tempted, he calls Bill for accountability. The passage, "I can do everything through him who gives me strength" (Philippians 4:13), has been close to Jesse's heart since starting to walk with the Lord.

Jesse no longer serves himself. He now serves God, who guides him through life. Though Jesse still stumbles and scrapes his proverbial knee on occasion, God is always there to pick him up. God nurtures Jesse's strengths and reprimands him when he does wrong. He dearly loves God: his Lord and Savior.

After being gone for several years, his ex-wife returned to town with the girls. Jesse visits them every day. Although still a pagan, she's open to going for pastoral counseling to work on their relationship. God has softened her heart. After several years of nothing but arguments, now Jesse has his best friend back again. He's so grateful to have a second chance with her; he fell in love with her the first time he laid eyes on her. To him, she was an angel. Jesse has faith they'll eventually remarry and raise their daughters within a healthy, strong, Christian family.

"You did not choose me, but I chose you and appointed you to go and bear fruit—fruit that will last. Then the Father will give you whatever you ask in my name" (John 15:16).

Jesus made the choice to love and die for Jesse, but it was Jesse's choice to accept the offer of forgiveness and eternal life extended by Jesus.

Sharon ~ Age 58
Surrendering the Self

Sharon needed to look nice, act well-behaved, be the center of attention, and present herself in a righteous manner. She always tried to do the right thing, even telling on herself when she did something wrong. It all began with Sharon's relationship with her dad. She felt he favored her sister. Sharon tried pleasing him because she wanted him to like her just as much, or more. She felt that way about God, too. Sharon thought she needed to be good for Him to like her. Her need to please encompassed everyone. It defined her: she was a good girl.

Raised in a Christian home, God was an integral part of Sharon's life from the beginning. The whole family read daily devotions and studied the Bible. Her mom was a godly woman whom she's always compared to the Virgin Mary. Sharon's known and believed Jesus is the Son of God for as long as she can remember. There's never been a time when she didn't believe in God the Father, Son, and Holy Spirit. If you had asked her at any age if she thought she'd go to heaven, she would have confidently replied, "Yes. I believe Jesus died for my sins and was resurrected so I can have eternal life." Sharon even became involved in the Jesus movement of the late 1960s and early 1970s.

Sharon had always been very involved in church activities, such as youth groups and Bible studies. For ten years, she mentored other women and led Bible study classes. Sharon found that, in teaching other women about God's Word, He spoke to her as well. Always searching for more of Jesus, she talked with her pastor and others outside of her church. Sharon desperately wanted to deepen her understanding of God.

She began searching for a different church that might satisfy her craving for more spiritual "meat," and ended up meeting with a small group in someone's home for a while. But Sharon began to miss the fellowship and worship experiences of an actual church. She happened upon a nondenominational church one Sunday, which she attended sporadically for the next six months. During the church's fourth year anniversary celebration in 1989, Sharon was quite impressed with the message that morning. It was the church she'd been searching for.

One particular Sunday morning, the words of an Amy Grant song—"I Have Decided"— performed by the worship team, really hit home. Tears flooded her eyes. The song went like this: "So forget the game of being good, and your self-righteous pain, 'cause the only good inside your heart is the good that Jesus brings." She'd heard this song before, but that day God demanded her full attention. She thought, *This is exactly what God wants me to do!* Sharon knew she was saved by grace, but had still been trying to earn God's favor through good works. Pride prevented her from surrendering to the Lord and accepting His grace.

God continued working in her, once again convicting her of self-righteousness and self-importance over a decade later at a women's retreat in 2007. That four-letter word—*self*—still prevented her from having a deep relationship with God. The self had to go! Sharon's disobedience made her feel angry and embarrassed because she knew how much God hated pride.

Years earlier she had tried humbling herself by her own efforts. Sharon got the phrase, "If I humble myself, God will exalt me," printed on letterhead as a constant reminder. Her favorite acronym was JOY: Jesus first, Others second, Yourself last. She even read the book *Humility* by Andrew Murray. Sharon thought she was progressing nicely, but the only thing that changed was her head knowledge; she still behaved the same.

A mission trip to Sri Lanka in 2009 showed Sharon just how firmly she continued to grasp onto her pride. Even though some of the Sri Lankan women spoke English, they were very difficult to understand. Sharon found herself staying at a distance because she did not want to look foolish or hurt their feelings by continually asking what they had said. She had traveled across the world to share the good news of Jesus with the women, yet pride prevented her from interacting with them! On the plane ride home, Sharon read the book *Absolute Surrender*. Deep in her heart, she wanted to surrender to God. But it would be a long process!

Proverbs 3:5–6 are two verses she's gone back to repeatedly over the years: "Trust in the Lord with all your heart and lean not on your own understanding; in all your ways acknowledge him, and he will make your paths straight." Sharon has learned that she needs to get over herself—knowing and trusting that God is enough. Realizing just how great God is has made her understand just how small she is. Sharon knows every decision must be filtered through the truths in the Bible and prayer. God is in control. He knows what is best for her and wants to guide her. God is good, and He's always working for her good. She really can trust Him completely.

Sharon has always wanted to be a servant of God, but the focus had been on her and what she could do to please Him (rather than on God's will). Trying to live the perfect life had become an idol! Ever since she was a little girl, Sharon felt the need to be good so that God would love her. More recently, she has embraced the truth that God's love for her is unconditional. There is nothing she could ever do to earn His favor.

Saved by grace alone. Sharon has spouted these familiar words all her life. But is she living in the freedom of that grace in her daily life? No. As she said, "I'm a good Christian. I should know better than to do this or that." Sharon discovered that by constantly beating herself up when she fails—rather than claiming His amazing grace—she hasn't been allowing God to be in control of her life. What freedom His grace brings! Not freedom to sin more, but freedom to live for God without guilt or condemnation. His grace allows Sharon to be imperfect so that she can trust Him to bring her into His best.

Philippians 2:12–13 states, "Continue to work out your salvation with fear and trembling, for it is God who works in you to will and to act according to his good purpose." This wisdom has helped Sharon understand how He actually works in her life. God is helping her want to obey Him, and He is providing her with the power to do so. It's all His doing! She just needs to be open and vulnerable, allowing God to have His way. Sharon is working on surrendering her life to God—coming to the end of her *self* and relying completely on His power and love to work everything for her good and His glory.

"You who are trying to be justified by law have been alienated from Christ; you have fallen away from grace. But by faith we eagerly await through the Spirit the righteousness for which we hope" (Galatians 5:4-5).

Trying to be good on her own kept Sharon from having the close relationship with God that she desperately wanted. It wasn't until she accepted God's sweet grace that she became open to carrying out His will and fully experiencing His awesome love.

Gary ~ Age 59
Strengthen Your Brothers

As a young boy, Gary's grandpa told his dad, "You keep working those boys that way and they'll walk away from the farm." And they did. Growing up on a farm meant a lot of hard work for Gary and his two brothers. Dad worked on the farm seven days a week and had an angry demeanor.

Gary's parents dropped him off at Sunday school, but the family hardly ever went to church. Because he only went to Sunday school to please his parents, religion was nothing more than a game to him. He mused, *If my parents aren't serious about God, why should I be? If my parents don't need God, then neither do I.* Gary walked away from the farm and God after completing high school.

While in basic training, the Vietnam War broke out. His lottery number, 124, was called. He enlisted in the Air Force and moved to California with his wife. Before entering the Air Force, Gary drank once or twice a month—always drinking to get drunk. His drinking escalated in the Air Force—you weren't one of the boys unless you drank every night. Gary knew he shouldn't drink that much, but thought, *If only I was in a better spot in my life or had a different wife, things would change.*

He did a host of foolish things after drinking heavily with the boys that could have gotten him killed. After leaving the bar, Gary and his friends often jumped the freight trains that ran through the town at night. Drunk out of his mind one night,

Gary's feet missed the rungs of the ladder as he jumped onto the train. His legs were dangling under the bottom of the train, and he held on for dear life. In a panic, he thought, *What if I fall under the train?* By the grace of God, Gary let go and rolled away from the moving train. Even though very drunk, he knew he easily could have fallen underneath and been run over.

After leaving the Air Force, Gary said he'd only drink on weekends. That lasted a month or so, but then he had a drink in the middle of the week, too. Soon, it turned into every day. Gary told himself that his drinking didn't affect his daughter and son because he only drank after they went to bed. He mused, *How could it hurt them if they never saw it?* Well, the kids never saw him drink, but they did see his behavior: restless, irritable, and discontent. Little by little, alcoholism sank his marriage. Going to the bar after work meant years of missed birthdays and anniversaries. A wall towered between Gary and his wife. It had been slowly built, brick by brick, as drinking replaced time spent with his family.

With all of his sick days used up (due to hangovers) before May of 1982, Gary worried about losing his job. He called a treatment center for alcoholics and went into outpatient treatment. He also started going to AA meetings. Gary walked in the first night and sat down with a group of men. Before he knew it, they were talking about God—it was like walking into a religious cult! But Gary kept going to the meetings and slowly began building a spiritual relationship with God. That continued for the next four or five years until he reached a plateau.

After Gary stopped drinking, he had an empty left hand. He needed something to do with his hands. For a while he drank soda, but that soon became boring. Around that time, the day-shift supervisor at the factory began to relentlessly bug Gary about getting into woodcarving. He had toyed with woodworking in the past, but had never carved. The man showed Gary the birds he carved, and then he taught him the trade. Soon, Gary started woodcarving to keep his hands busy. It came naturally to him, and he never took any classes. He even woke up out of dead sleeps with designs in his head—he had to get up and write them down. Before long, Gary entered competitions and won several "Best Of" shows. His woodcarving abilities were clearly a gift from God, received after laying down the alcohol.

Meanwhile, Gary started talking to an attractive female coworker. They didn't have an affair, but he paid more attention to her at work than a married man should. Around that same time, Gary and his wife separated and divorced. Too much damage had been done to take down the wall between them. Shortly thereafter, he and the female coworker got married—a shotgun wedding. He had gotten her pregnant and did the right thing. His new wife was fourteen years younger and also an alcoholic. From the beginning, their relationship was tenuous at best; arguments ensued on a daily basis.

His wife developed toxemia during pregnancy and took barbiturates prescribed by her doctor to ease the symptoms. The drugs caused their son to be born prematurely, and he had to spend several weeks in the intensive care unit. He came home with a heart monitor, and Gary's wife felt overwhelmed. Unable to control her emotions or drinking, she went into a treatment center for thirty days, leaving Gary alone to care for a sickly newborn while working two jobs! With help from his mom and ex-mother-in-law, he managed to get through the month.

When his wife returned home, the turmoil and fighting continued. Again, Gary found himself restless, irritable, and discontent. His wife left with their son for days at a time without telling Gary; she would just be gone when he returned home from work.

One day, she left to look for a new car. As it turned out, she had babysat for the car dealer's children while in high school. They caught up a bit, and she told him about what was going on in her life. He said, "You don't need a car, you need the Lord," and suggested that she and Gary speak with Pastor John from his church. She immediately drove home to tell Gary what had just happened. The two went back to the car dealership and asked where they could find Pastor John. Shortly after, they were at his house. As he shared his faith and the Gospel with them, Gary felt an urge to accept Jesus into his heart right then and there. This was the best experience of his life! They began attending church services three times a week, and Gary read the entire New Testament for the first time. He kept growing closer to God, but his home life didn't change much.

While in his wife's face during a heated argument about finances one day, she shouted, "You're out of here!" This wasn't the first time she'd tried to kick him out of the house. Fed up, Gary replied, "This is the last time. If you follow through with this, I won't be back." "Leave now!" she cried. A divorce followed soon after.

For decades, Gary had been thinking about his high school sweetheart. He even had dreams in which he smelled her perfume or saw her in a store. He had never attended a class reunion, though, so he had lost touch with her. But he looked up her phone number in a book he'd been sent from one of the reunions. He gave her a call, and she said that she'd been thinking of him over the years, too! Only one problem: she was married. Although he knew it was wrong to pursue her, Gary still couldn't resist. After the affair went on for some time, she showed up at his doorstep carrying a suitcase. She said she had left her husband! Very troubled, Gary called his pastor to get some advice. The pastor told him to make her leave right away. But Gary said, "I can't." The two ended up getting married. She didn't know the Lord, but after going to church with Gary for six months, she accepted Christ and was baptized.

Since he had God in his life, Gary stopped going to AA meetings for a while. He did just fine without going. He stayed sober. But then God helped Gary realize that he failed to follow one of the twelve steps: helping others. Today, Gary is back in AA—not for himself, but to support and encourage other alcoholics. He and some others have even started a program at church called "Twelve Steps with Christ" that meets on Saturday nights. The name of the group says it all: God is in charge.

Throughout the years, Gary continued woodcarving. He became more and more skilled, and even won several awards. In 1989, a commercial wood shop subcontracted him for his first professional job: making carvings for a new Hyatt Regency Hotel on the island of Kauai. After completing the ten-month job, Gary started his own woodcarving business. He specialized in contemporary furniture and architectural carving. The business eventually grew to the point where he had a 7,500 square foot shop with twelve employees.

Gary's business went under in 2006 after an eighteen-year run. Because he was no longer able to pay his mortgage, he lost his house and property. He became very bitter. He didn't do anything wrong against God, but he didn't do the things he should have either. Gary struggled to trust God. Satan tried pulling him down, but God lifted him up.

Several things helped keep Gary afloat during this difficult time. Gatekeepers, a hardcore men's group at church, provided Gary with emotional and spiritual support. The men share their lives with one another and develop a high level of trust. They even call each other daily for accountability—making sure they're doing the things they should and not doing what they shouldn't. Today, Gary leads the group.

One particular Bible study completed in Gatekeepers, "Experiencing God" by Henry Blackaby, changed his life. It helped Gary build a relationship with God, it helped him learn that prayer was a relationship builder. He questioned, *How can I get to know God if I don't talk to Him?* Gary never prayed before that study—he thought it didn't matter because God had everything figured out anyway. Later, he learned that prayer is the way to communicate with God. He then wondered, *How can I know what*

God's plans are if I don't ask and listen for an answer? Today, Gary's walk with God is closer than ever, but still not where he wants it to be. He keeps his eyes open to "see where God moves in his life, meet Him there, and obey."

Gary continues woodcarving, blessed by the "awesome experience to be worthy of being a tool of God." In trying to carve a horse head, Gary learned that he could do nothing without God's hands guiding his. After a few days, the carving started looking like Elsie the cow rather than a horse head! One night, Gary woke up musing, *You can't do this, what are you thinking?* Panic stricken, he called his pastor the next morning. After explaining what had happened, he said, "The enemy is attacking you by putting these doubts into your head. You know you can do it." Gary prayed on his way to work, "You gave me this skill for a reason, Father. I ask You to guide my hands, my eyes, and my mind to carve a horse that would please you. Protect me from the enemy's attack, Lord. Please grant me courage and confidence as I carve today. Let me know in my heart that You are guiding my hands. In the name of Jesus, Amen." That day, chips started flying in all directions as he carved—God helped him to create a beautiful horse head better than Gary could have imagined.

Jesus said to Simon Peter, "Simon, Simon, Satan has asked to sift you as wheat. But I have prayed for you, Simon, that your faith may not fail. And when you have turned back, strengthen your brothers" (Luke 22:31-32).

Satan wanted Gary to be torn up by sin, but God wouldn't let that happen. It would have been easy for Gary to lose faith after his business collapsed and he lost everything. He did struggle with bitterness, but he chose to trust God. Today, Gary uses his experiences to strengthen other men in their walk with the Lord.

Michele ~ Age 62
Healed by the Love of Her Life

Feelings of fear and inadequacy consumed Michele from a young age. She never rested or relaxed; she was always on guard. Even though everything seemed okay on the outside, inside lurked tears, screams, and confusion. Michele thought of herself as worthless. Even the space taken up by the chair she sat on seemed to have more value. She felt like she had no right to anything good and could never be good enough for anyone.

Her family of nine was poor—financially, emotionally, and spiritually. Part of their poverty came from her father being a violent drunk. When she came home from school, Michele never knew what she would find. It could be anything from a hole in the television set because her father put his foot through the screen, to the Christmas tree laying on the living room floor with ornaments strewn all over the room. Love was never expressed in Michele's family. It was okay to love her Betsy Wetsy doll, but not other people.

As a young girl, Michele remembers peeking out from behind a chair, watching King Kong with two of her brothers. A terrible gurgling sound came from the other room as her mom yelled, "No, Jimmy, don't!" Michele and her brothers ran to see what was happening: her father was strangling her mom at the foot of the stairs! They started screaming at the top of their lungs. Hearing all of the commotion, her seventeen-year-old brother came running down the stairs, grabbed their father, and beat him up (crying the whole time).

Afterward, Michele looked at her father lying on the floor with blood coming out of his nose and running down his face. She wanted her father to die. Michele ran outside to her favorite place—a little plot of grass and trees beyond the parking lot of the apartment building—and tucked the horrendous incident into a pocket in her mind, along with all of the other bad memories. Michele was taught never to discuss anything that happened at home with anyone, and she couldn't bring it up again with her parents, siblings, or even herself.

Around the age of nine, Michele went to play with the neighbors as she often did (there were three kids). She ended up in the living room with the dad and daughters playing a game of Ghost. He hid under a blanket and tried scaring the girls as they ran past him. Suddenly, he grabbed Michele, pulled her over to him, and pressed her tightly against himself. Then he shoved his fingers inside of her. Before he could do much else, his wife called from the kitchen to say that dinner was ready, which distracted him enough to stop what he was doing. After he let go, Michele got away from him. She stood there in the living room, not knowing what to do or say. Michele felt dead on the inside. Then the man went to a nearby closet and pulled out a gun wrapped in a baby blue receiving blanket! His wife yelled, "No, Jimmy, don't!" Those words echoed in Michele's mind as she ran out of their apartment. Michele's mom yelled those exact words at her dad whenever he tried killing her!

Michele went home to tell her mom what just happened. Rather than showing concern, her mom accused her of making it all up. She warned Michele not to tell her father because it would set him off and cause him to drink. Michele felt ashamed, like she had done something wrong. She was thoroughly confused. She thought, *There must be something wrong with me for my mom to respond in that way.*

As a teenager, Michele was date-raped several times. She felt terrible after each incident, and ended up thinking she was at fault somehow—or that she made it up. Michele felt like everything bad that happened was her fault.

When Michele dressed up for dates and special occasions and asked her mom how she looked, her mom coldly replied, "You look neat and clean." She was never told that she looked pretty, so Michele learned to be tidy and clean because those behaviors were the only ones acknowledged by her mom. In fact, such comments further increased her obsessive hand washing that began after she was molested. She washed her hands thirty to fifty times every day. Michele also compulsively checked and rechecked the window and door locks every night to make sure nobody could come in and hurt her.

At the age of sixteen, Michele and her boyfriend went to a church in a nearby town for confession. A young priest asked Michele inappropriate questions about what she did with her boyfriend and where he touched her. Michele felt sick to her stomach. She ran out of the church and stood in the parking lot, noticing the brightness of the blue sky and yellow sun. Michele said, "God, if You're Catholic, I don't want anything to do with You." As she drove away from the church that day, she left God behind. For the next fifteen years, Michele became an agnostic.

By the age of twenty she married a tremendously negative man who was also an agnostic. He was a controlling alcoholic, just like her father. From the beginning, he made Michele feel like who she was would never be good enough for him. She always felt like something must be wrong with her. He lived like a single man—he ran around with other women and even went to Las Vegas by himself. Michele never knew what it was like to make love; her husband was into perverted sexuality and pornography. Anything they did had to be on his terms, for his pleasure. She didn't receive any emotional or physical security from her husband—and definitely no love. If they ever did anything she enjoyed, he made certain they never did it again. Michele became very sick physically and mentally from years of feeling like a bad person.

Even though God was the last thing on Michele's mind, He still crept in at times. Out of the blue, she had thoughts like, *Maybe there is a God.* Then, one day, she and her mom went to a discount retail store. Just inside the door was a display of green vinyl Bibles on sale for $2.97. Her mom said, "Michele, I think you should have one in your house." Michele replied, "No, I don't need that." But a strange thing happened as they walked through the store—Michele began longing for a Bible! By the time they were done shopping, Michele changed her mind and let her mom buy one before leaving. Michele had no intention of reading the Bible, so she used it as a platform for her spider plant. Each time she dusted, she questioned, *What am I keeping this for?* Countless times, Michele grabbed the Bible and walked toward the garbage can, but she couldn't throw it away. Michele reasoned with herself that, *If it's nothing, what does it hurt to have around?*

God's call on her heart became greater and greater—only Michele didn't know where to go or what to do about the call. She definitely didn't want to go back to the church she'd left. While visiting her mom in January of 1981, Michele's sister-in-law stopped by. They started chatting, and the conversation turned to God. As her sister-in-law shared what she had learned since finding God, Michele asked, "How come you never talked to me about this before?" "I just assumed you weren't interested," replied the woman. Each time Michele asked a question, her sister-in-law answered with Scripture. *That is beautiful!* Michele thought. Even though she hadn't read the Bible before, there wasn't a doubt in her mind that it was the truth of God. Michele wanted to receive what her sister-in-law said was available to her. At first, she had trouble believing that Jesus was born from a virgin, but she realized it had to happen that way to prove He was the Son of God. Michele received Jesus into her heart, and she believed that all of God's Word was true.

Immediately, colors looked brighter. Looking out of the picture window of her mom's seventh floor apartment, the dark sky lit up! Michele noticed how brightly the stars shone. She thought, *Even the stars have a purpose because God put them there one by one.* Michele relished the beauty of the midnight blue sky.

She had love in her heart for the first time. Michele felt love for her father whom she hated and feared. If he would have been standing there, Michele would have taken his face in her hands and said, "I love you and forgive you for all you've done." One of her brothers came to mind, too. And she loved him even though he was not a nice person and had done many bad things. Considering there was no love in her family growing up, this sudden outpouring of love came as quite a delightful surprise!

Before going to bed that night, Michele washed the bed sheets, blankets, and even the curtains. She wanted everything clean after being washed white as snow by Jesus. The green Bible she had been using under her plant went to bed with her. Michele was drawn to God's Word like a magnet to metal. Reading Scripture was delicious!

Soon, Michele turned into an intellectual Christian. Her faith was based on what God expected of her (the law), rather than on coming closer to Him relationally. Being a good Christian was an act more than a way of life. After seventeen years of charades, Michele hit rock bottom. She felt absolutely miserable.

One day, at the age of forty-seven, she said to God, "I can't take it anymore." Later that day, Michele listened to a message on her answering machine from a Christian acquaintance. It went as follows: "This is what the Holy Spirit told me to tell you: I love you very much and I died for *everything.*" Whew! That hit her right in the heart: *Jesus loves me?* She could see Him loving the prostitute down the street and the alcoholic swaggering home from the bar, but not her.

Michele felt compelled to get her Bible. Inside, she found a card with Ephesians 3:14–21 written on it that had been in her Bible for years. Sitting on the bed, she read those passages out loud again and again. But she kept getting stuck and tripping on verses 17 and 18 until she became quite angry with God. She asked, "What do You want? What will it cost me?" He responded, "Who wrote this?" Michele thought—the Scripture was part of a letter the apostle Paul wrote to the saints in Ephesus, but the words were really those of God. Michele reread verses 17 and 18 again, "And I pray that you, being rooted and established in love, may have power, together with all the saints, to grasp how wide and long and high and deep is the love of Christ." She thought, *I am rooted and grounded in the love of God.* Thus started a Christian walk fueled by the power of God's love.

As Michele walked out of the bedroom to get something from the kitchen, the thought, *You think you're a Christian—God doesn't love you,* popped into her head. She immediately went back to the bedroom and opened her Bible to Ephesians and started reading out loud. In the days and weeks that followed, Michele battled numerous such attacks from the enemy. Each time, she fought back with the Word of God—the most powerful weapon of all.

She wrote the message from the answering machine on Post-it notes and placed them around the house—on the fan above the stove, the kitchen cupboard, and her bathroom mirror. Her first thought in the morning and last thought before falling asleep was *God loves me.* Michele needed to continuously remind herself of that truth to make certain it sunk deep into her soul. Several times a day, Michele told God, "I love being loved by You. It's delicious!" She thought, *It's way more satisfying than chocolate!*

Many things changed. God's love burned away the constant fear that weighed heavily on Michele's heart her whole life. She gave up working late hours as a professional singer in smoke-filled nightclubs, yacht clubs, and the like. Instead, she chose to sing in more wholesome venues, especially churches. Michele felt compelled to throw out her large collection of romance novels; they disgusted her so much that she actually took them out to the dumpster. Eventually, her husband sought a divorce because he didn't like the changes he saw in Michele—she no longer allowed him to walk all over her. After her husband left, Michele's compulsive behaviors stopped. She finally felt at peace.

Over the years, Michele's blood pressure climbed higher and higher—the numbers eventually flew off the charts. The last she knew it was 256 over 180. It must have gotten much higher, though, because she became very sick. Michele routinely vomited. She often had to stop her car and open the door to throw up on the way to and from work. Eventually, she had a TIA (ministroke). Her thinking process slowed down some after the TIA. Michele had difficulty keeping things as organized and neat as she would have liked.

Then came January 1, 2004. Michele had been invited to a friend's house to watch a movie. As the evening progressed, she started feeling quite strange. She felt sick to her stomach, and her digestive system seemed ready to explode. Michele excused herself early and went home. Not long after, her right arm and leg went out to the side and stayed there. She lost control of her urine. Everything appeared upside down, making her feel dizzy and more nauseous. Because she didn't like to take medication or go to doctors, Michele decided to wait and see how she felt in the morning. On the way from the bathroom to her bedroom, Michele slammed into the walls and doorframe. She urinated and vomited uncontrollably all night. Michele lay in bed talking with God, telling Him she wasn't ready to leave this place yet. She pleaded with Him not to take away her ability to drive.

The next day Michele called her friend and managed to say, "Take me to the hospital." Her friend came right away, but getting to the car was not easy with her right limbs sticking out to the side and everything appearing upside down. But with the help of her friend, Michele eventually made it out of the house.

At the hospital, Michele was placed in a wheelchair and covered with a blanket that tucked in her arm and leg. She vomited up black stuff. Because Michele didn't mention all of her symptoms and did not have health insurance, the staff planned on sending her back home without running diagnostic tests—that is, until Michele needed to use the ladies room. A female doctor happened to notice that it took three nurses to help Michele, and she decided to investigate further. She asked, "Can we do a CAT scan?" Even though she had no money to pay for the scan, Michele said, "Yes." It revealed that Michele had a brainstem stroke. This kind of stroke is usually fatal or, at the very least, leaves a person in a vegetative state. They were amazed Michele wasn't much more seriously impaired.

The next thing she knew, someone had wrapped her in a blanket and placed her on a helicopter. After arriving at another hospital, the doctor monitored Michele carefully to watch the path of blood in her brain. If it traveled toward the cerebellum, she would need surgery. The blood did get close, but Michele never had brain surgery. She thought, *The doctor is an expert, but he doesn't get the last word; the Word gets the last word.*

Later, when a doctor told Michele that her kidneys had stopped working and there was nothing they could do, she casually replied, "Okay." You see, she knew she would win regardless: if she died, she would be with Jesus, and if she lived, she would be with Jesus. A big win either way!

Michele spent quite a while in intensive care, where her muscles atrophied. This caused extreme pain throughout her body. Each day, several nurses had to literally peel her off the sheets and make her sit up in bed for one minute—that was Michele's only exercise. Despite being incredibly weak physically, her spirit was very much alive. Surprisingly, she could still sing even though she could barely speak. Nurses commented on how they had never seen another stroke patient with such a festive spirit.

Michele began wondering how she would pay her medical bills. She thought, *I could get three jobs and pay five to ten dollars down on each bill every week.* And that was before she could even walk with a walker. Then the devil came back with, "What kind of a Christian are you? You don't even have any skills." Michele yelled out, "Jesus, look at what's happening!" She heard, "Michele, the stroke is mine. The debt is mine. The battle is mine." Michele opened her Bible to 2 Chronicles 20. A few passages really spoke to her in that moment: "For we have no power to face this vast army that is attacking us. We do not know what to do, but our eyes are upon you" (Verse 12). "Do not be afraid or discouraged because of this vast army. For the battle is not yours, but God's" (Verse 15). "You will not have to fight this battle. Take up your positions; stand firm and see the deliverance the Lord will give you" (Verse 17).

After Michele returned home, the hospital board had a meeting to discuss her outrageous medical bills and the fact that she had no health insurance. Afterward, she received a phone call and was told they unanimously agreed to forgive her bill of $47,000! Within the next eight months, the rest of Michele's bills were paid in full. She was debt free!

Michele had many adjustments to make after going back home. Even the simplest of tasks needed to be thought out, step-by-step. It took two years before she could cut an onion without it flying all over the kitchen. Everything took twice as long to do as it did before, and speaking was a chore: she spoke in broken, three- or four-word sentences.

However, there were many blessings to be grateful for. Michele could still live alone and care for herself. It was a miracle that she could walk with a walker considering the severity of the stroke. She retained her numeric memory, which many people lose. And God made it possible for Michele to drive her car after a short time.

One pleasant Saturday night in late summer, Michele went to her favorite park where she enjoyed spending time with Jesus. The colors were exquisite. The sky was blue without a cloud in sight. The trees looked like emeralds. It looked as though God had strewn diamonds all over the lake. Michele sat there thanking and praising God. Then, suddenly, darkness came in the form of, "You're nothing. You talk stupid. You don't even walk well with a walker. No one's going to hire you. You don't have a family." Michele came back with, "I'm not nothing; I'm a child of the One true living God." She kept stating who she was in Christ, and the vicious fight continued.

Michele decided to leave and go home. After returning home, she put a few things away and lay down on the couch to read. The phone rang. It was her best friend, Sue. When Michele told Sue what had happened, Sue exclaimed, "That's the enemy! There's something good right around the corner!" By the time she got off the phone, her spirit was lifted.

The next morning, on August 23, 2009, Michele woke up exhausted after only sleeping about two hours. She decided to go to her friend's church. While driving, her spirit lifted higher and higher. After arriving a good forty-five minutes late, several men ran out to help her inside as she weaved and tipped to the side with her walker. Michele sat in the back row by her friend. George Moss, a guest pastor known for his calling of healing, spoke in a deep, rich voice. She could tell that he really believed God. Something told Michele that this man was going to be attentive to her that morning. After giving his sermon, Pastor Moss began healing people.

Suddenly, he started walking contemplatively down the aisle to the back of the church toward Michele! Knowing he was coming to her, she thought, *I don't care what I feel or think—or what I've been taught. Lord, I believe You, and I receive everything You have for me.* Pointing to her walker he asked, "What do you need this for?" Michele said, "Me have stroke." Pastor Moss asked Michele to stand up and walk out into the aisle. He asked her name, when she had the stroke, and what side had been affected. Michele declared, "Lord, I receive this." Placing his hand firmly on the right side of Michele's neck, he said, "Arteries and veins, I command you to open up and allow the blood to flow through. Vocal cords, I command you to become strong and straight. And stroke, I maim you. You have no part in this woman. You no longer can stay in her body. She's healed from the top of her head down to her toes." All the while Michele repeated, "I receive it. Yes, Jesus. I believe it, Jesus." Then she fell backward and someone gently lowered her to the floor and covered her with a blanket. While lying there, she became aware of strange sensations in her diaphragm, then in her arms and legs. Her muscles came alive!

Michele felt as squirmy as a two-year-old boy. She simply had to get up and move around, so she pulled off the blanket. Several men came to help her get up. Realizing how easily she was able to stand up, Michele proclaimed, "God is good!" The only thing that hadn't improved yet was her speech. Pastor Moss came back over and said, "Do me a favor. Sit down in your chair and get up again without holding onto anything. Do this several times." And she did! Before, her legs had been too weak to get up on her own. Feeling antsy, Michele wanted to walk around the sanctuary—something she hadn't been able to do in over five years. After the service concluded, she walked down the aisle to the front of the church and walked back and forth, in circles, and even backward!

When it came time to leave, she didn't want to touch or even look at her walker. A friend offered to take it to Michele's car. They stood by her car, laughing and crying tears of joy as they discussed the indescribable goodness and love of God. Before going home, Michele walked around and even jogged in the parking lot!

Her speech returned to normal the next morning. No more three word sentences with slurred speech. She says of the healing,

"It's not about me. It's all about Jesus. You just need to believe and receive." Michele was better than she'd ever been.

Because she lived in a small town, many of the locals and business owners knew Michele. They had watched her struggling with her walker for the past five years. After the healing, people ran out of stores and restaurants when they saw Michele walk by without a walker. When they asked what happened, Michele happily proclaimed, "Jesus healed me!" They were surprised to hear her speak so clearly. Some of them looked at her quite perplexed, but they listened to her story. Michele told everyone, "He is the Lord who heals us."

Hanging on the wall in her living room is a cross positioned inside the top crook of the letter *M*. It's a lovely depiction of what she knows to be true: "Jesus in Michele." She says of the cross, "It's everything—the permanent and complete solution." Every day, Michele is reminded of Galatians 2:20, "I have been crucified with Christ and I no longer live, but Christ lives in me. The life I live in the body, I live by faith in the Son of God, who loved me and gave himself for me." Because of her intimacy with Jesus, Michele lives a restful life—free from fear and feelings of inadequacy.

Since Jesus died for everything, Michele does not accept anything that makes her feel bad. She is no longer made to feel worthless when others put her down. Instead, Michele refuses to receive statements meant to harm her. In the same way, she will not own pain anymore. Whenever she feels pain, Michele boldly states, "Pain, you have no place in my body. Get out in the name of Jesus."

Today, God is everything to Michele—her Lord, Savior, healer, Father, husband, and friend. Even though she lives alone with her precious cat, Michele knows she really isn't alone. God is with her.

"For I am convinced that neither death nor life, neither angels nor demons, neither the present nor the future, nor any powers, neither height nor depth, nor anything else in all creation, will be able to separate us from the love of God that is in Christ Jesus our Lord" (Romans 8:38–39).

Though she never received love from her parents or husband, today Michele rests in God's great love for her.

Courtney ~ Age 22
A Heart for Social Outcasts

One day, Courtney came home from high school to find her mom sitting at the kitchen table looking quite troubled. "I have something to tell you," she said, "Your dad is going to prison for second degree reckless homicide. He killed his business partner during a heated argument." Courtney burst into tears and thought, *Why do my family and I deserve something like this in our lives? I just don't understand!* An absolutely horrifying feeling came over her; it was almost surreal. As much anguish as Courtney felt, she wasn't surprised. It was just another terrible, hurtful thing her dad had done.

For as long as Courtney could remember, her dad exhibited Jekyll- and Hyde-type behavior. As an alcoholic, he vacillated between being nice and being downright mean and unreliable. When not drunk, he bought Courtney gifts and showered her with compliments. But when drinking, he said mean things and continually let her down. He said he'd pick her up from school and either not show up at all or come late. Courtney felt that her dad didn't see much worth in her because he continually chose alcohol and other things over her. Even though he'd been living with a woman since divorcing her mom when Courtney was in the third grade, it wasn't until the seventh grade that she realized he'd had an affair.

With her dad in prison, she began to see God as more than just her Savior—so much more. Previously, she had walked by her mom's faith since accepting Jesus at the age of five. Now she saw God as her Father in heaven, someone so much better than anything or anyone she could have on Earth. Courtney had to depend on God for support because He was the only One who would not let her down. He would never leave or hurt her. Only God could give her ceaseless love and comfort.

Although it was hard not having her dad around, God used the dreadful circumstance to bring her closer to Himself. Finally, her mom's faith became her own. Courtney actually wanted to go to church—rather than going out of a sense of obligation. She became more involved in youth group, and helped instill confidence in some young girls by making an extra effort to ask how they were doing or sitting with them in church. Courtney didn't want any of the girls to feel like nobody cared.

Then it came time for college. Before leaving home, Courtney decided not to get into the party scene. She felt strongly about not having sex before getting married. Unfortunately, she tried doing those things on her own without God's help. That didn't work out so well! Shortly after starting college, Courtney met a guy three years older than her. The two drank nearly every day; Courtney often went to classes hungover. She continued going to church on Sundays, though—somehow thinking that repenting for drinking would make everything okay.

Even though she really didn't want to have sex, her emotions got the best of her in the heat of the moment. Courtney felt terrible afterward: she was devastated and disappointed in herself. Then it happened a second and third time. Feeling like she couldn't turn back, she decided, *This is the person I am now.* She continued having sex and was known as the "slut of Nelson Hall." None of the girls liked her. They partied with her, but they weren't interested in being her friend.

Then, one night, her boyfriend called and said, "We need to break up; I've cheated on you." This was heart-wrenching for Courtney. Because of how her dad left, she'd developed a fear of losing other men in her life. And now it had happened again.

Sophomore year started with no boyfriend and no friends. Courtney cried every night, miserable in her loneliness. A girl she knew invited her to the university's Christian Fellowship group. She enjoyed the group and began making new friends—Christian friends. And the women's minister mentored her.

Even though Courtney's faith grew and her relationship with God deepened, she had some doubts about the drastic changes in her lifestyle: no more sex or partying. As an extrovert, she liked the excitement of a good party and asked God, "Why did I seem to have more fun before?"

Meanwhile, anxiety attacks struck randomly—usually when in close quarters with people. All of a sudden, she could hardly breathe, felt light-headed, and was sick to her stomach. It seemed like something bad was about to happen. Getting some fresh air always helped calm her down. The Lord kept softening her heart toward Himself. As Courtney let more of God in, the panic attacks gradually faded.

Forgiveness of her dad, ex-boyfriend, and herself were major issues faced in her walk with God. Courtney knew she needed to forgive so that God would forgive her. It seemed much easier to pardon others. Finally, in November of 2008, she forgave herself for drinking and having sex. Even though her burden of sin lightened, she still wasn't where she wanted to be with the Lord.

Courtney and some friends took a road trip to the International House of Prayer (IHOP) in Kansas City, a place with around-the-clock worship and prayer, seven days per week. A worship leader asked anyone who needed healing to stand up. Courtney stood up and two people prayed over her. The weight of sin completely lifted off her shoulders! How free she felt!

Courtney came back really excited about school and her new life in Christ. She just couldn't get enough of the Bible; she read it every chance she had. The campus minister asked if she would like to join the leadership team. After prayerful consideration, Courtney accepted the offer and started working with freshman girls. At first, her contribution was limited because she was too ashamed to tell anyone about her past. In her junior year, however, Courtney led a Bible study on emotional, mental, and physical purity—and she mentored some girls one-on-one, this time freely sharing her mistakes.

Then came a challenge to join a group on campus she normally wouldn't join; she would have to go outside of her comfort zone. Courtney prayed and prayed. The Rainbow Alliance of Hope, a gay and lesbian group, kept coming up during her prayer time. She questioned, *Are you sure about this, Lord? Really?* She had hoped God would lead her to join some sort of academic group. Knowing He wanted her to join this group, though, Courtney asked a friend to come along and she went. There is generally a rift between people with a homosexual orientation and Christians; the two groups rarely mix. But that was about to change! Even though she didn't agree with their lifestyle, she knew God still called her to love them. Joining the group turned out to be a blessing in disguise: Courtney made three good friends. One of the guys even went on a mission trip.

At the end of her junior year, God asked her to switch majors from education to social work! She'd planned on being a teacher her whole life! This would add another two years to her education, not to mention more expenses. But Courtney obeyed, knowing God's plans were always best.

The more she's stepped out in faith and made sacrifices for God, the more He's provided for her—His provision is not only adequate, it's incredible! An evangelistic outreach at her university provided opportunities for Courtney to see how powerfully God works. She signed up for the promotional team and worked on the media. She and two other students called over 300 radio and television stations and newspapers to secure advertising for the event. Sleep, grades, and time were sacrificed as God made it known to her that that work took priority over all else. To raise funds, students were encouraged to participate in the "Benjamin Project," which involved giving one hundred dollars. God nudged Courtney to give one hundred dollars, but she wrestled with Him about not having the money. Then her student loan money came, and God asked her to give a thousand dollars! She thought, *Really, God? Are you sure?* Faithfully, she wrote a check for a thousand dollars with a happy heart.

Not long after, Courtney went home over Easter break feeling blessed that she was able to give such a large amount of money to support the outreach. After waking up the next morning, she noticed an envelope sitting by the computer. Enclosed was a letter from her mom that expressed how proud she was of Courtney for selflessly stepping out in faith—along with a check for two thousand dollars!

A strong Christian role model, her mom is a true testament of what the body of Christ should look like. She has stood by Courtney's side no matter what. Even though it must have been difficult to see her ex-husband, she faithfully took Courtney to visit him in prison. After listening to Courtney's confession that she'd had premarital sex, her mom lovingly said, "I forgive you 110 percent; and I'm sorry you had to go through all that. I will help you get to where you want to be." Not a morsel of judgment!

Courtney's relationship with the Lord continues to grow deeper as she serves Him obediently. She worships God simply for who He is, not for what He does. She sees more of God in herself all the time.

She's learned that God makes all things work together for her good, even something as terrible as her dad going to prison. Her story has helped others in the same position. Courtney received many scholarships for college and believes they were partly due to her dad's imprisonment. After she graduates with her social work degree, she wants to work in the prison system—not something she would have wanted to do if her dad wasn't there. Today her dad has a very strong relationship with the Lord. Praise God!

Courtney has a close group of Christian friends who help keep her faith on track. They pray together and support one another. One of her girlfriends is her accountability partner. Just knowing she'll have to tell her friend if she slips up keeps Courtney from doing wrong. Sometimes she gets an urge to go to the bar and party, but then she thinks to herself, *Okay, God, I know you'll forgive me if I do this. But I don't want to have to tell my friend.* So Courtney does the right thing and stays away from the bars. She feels so incredibly blessed to have a circle of friends who care about her—some people don't even have *one* friend. Courtney has a heart for befriending those who are alone so they can experience the love and joy that comes from having good friends.

"I tell you the truth, whatever you did for one of the least of these brothers of mine, you did for me" (Matthew 25:40).

God has groomed Courtney to have compassion for social outcasts and misfits—the same people Jesus befriended. It breaks her heart to see people shunned by society; she can't bear to see someone without a friend when she has so many.

Ken ~ Age 74
Dying Is a Gain for the Believer

Rather than doing homework, Ken spent his time watching stock car races and getting into trouble with friends. He did poorly in school, mostly because of a hearing impairment—he missed much of what the teacher said.

His father died at the age of forty-four from untreated ulcers when Ken was sixteen. Shortly before he died, Ken overheard him say to his mother, "I just don't know about that boy. If he keeps messing around like this, he'll grow up to be no good." That is one of the last things he remembers his father saying.

Not long after his father died, Ken met Barb, the woman he later married. They went to church regularly because they'd learned growing up that that is what Christians did. Neither really knew what it was all about. It would be decades before he learned there was more to believing in the Lord than sitting in church every Sunday as a wallflower. Being of stronger character, Barb made him a better person. Nevertheless, Ken continued to live in a way that was anything but righteous. He wouldn't be where he is today without Barb's love, support, and forgiveness.

Over the years, Ken has done many things he's not proud of. Even though he knew better, he wasn't always faithful to Barb. Ken learned as a teenager not to commit adultery. He never forgot that lesson—nor did he ever forget his sin. At the time, he thought, *What could a little indiscretion hurt?* Well, after a time, it did hurt. It hurt badly. "It stays with you your whole life," he says.

In 1968, Ken started drinking a lot of beer after giving up smoking—one bad habit replaced another. Many years later, his grandson opened the refrigerator and, noticing the shelves full of beer, asked, "Grandpa, why do you have all this beer in here?" Ken thought about it and decided there was no reason for him to drink so much. He drank what he had and didn't buy anymore. Ken only had a beer on special occasions after that.

Ken and Barb bought a grocery store in another town in 1981. It seemed like a good way to start over, to do better. With the whole family working in the store, he would be able to spend time with them and keep out of trouble. From the beginning, the store wasn't as successful as he'd envisioned. Ken stopped going to church because he had to work seven days per week. He tried as hard as he could to make it a success—he focused on the store above all else. But the store started losing money, and he was forced to sell the business in 1996.

Gradually, he and Barb began attending church more regularly. A men's retreat in the late 1990s really opened Ken's eyes. He learned that his first commitment should be to the Lord. Prior to that, it had been to his wife and children. If he placed the Lord first, everything else in his life would improve. His faith in the Lord grew stronger. He went on to work in another grocery store. Ken did the best job he could because "when you serve your employer well, you're serving God."

They usually rented their house out during the last week of July for an international fly-in convention. At that point they would go on vacation. However, they were unable to rent it out in 2008. Ken and Barb still left town, but they had to come back early because of severe pain in his midsection that came on suddenly and worsened throughout the week. On the way home, Barb commented on what a blessing it had been that they couldn't rent the house out. Surely God had intervened, knowing their vacation would be shortened that year. After a couple of days, Ken couldn't even lie in bed; he had to sleep sitting up in a chair.

He suffered over the weekend and went to the doctor on Monday. His doctor ordered some tests and sent him to get a CAT scan. That Wednesday, Ken was told he had non-Hodgkin's lymphoma. Since there are so many types of that form of cancer, it took another week to figure out what kind he had. A PET scan revealed cancer in his lungs, midsection, and lymph nodes in his right armpit and groin. It was in stage four—the most advanced phase. Chemotherapy followed, with a total of eight treatments throughout the year.

By September 30, the cancer was already in remission! As a very thorough, straight-laced man, Ken's oncologist didn't smile much. After hearing the miraculous news, Ken said, "Not to take anything away from you, but I'm on the prayer chain of four different churches." The doctor smiled, nodding his head. By December 30, 2008, the cancer was entirely gone.

Because chemotherapy exhausted him, Ken did a lot of reading as he sat around, day after day. In addition to reading the Bible, he read several Christian books. One book, *Eternity*, by Joseph Stowell, deeply impacted him. He had difficulty putting it down. Ken learned the importance of cultivating a deeper relationship with Christ. His focus had been on what he could experience and acquire on Earth, not on the Lord. Ken highlighted several sentences in the book that were a revelation to him. One was: "Living for Christ is really not possible until we understand and embrace the fact that dying is gain." Before going into full remission, Ken had already accepted the fact that he had cancer and would either survive or perish. He believed in heaven, but he had lived much of his life for earthly gain. Faced with the possibility of early death, Ken thought more seriously about heaven. He realized that heaven was home. As his focus shifted from Earth to heaven, he was finally ready to live for Christ and place his trust in Him.

Ken and Barb discussed being baptized for months, but they didn't have the courage at first. Finally, they made their public commitment to living for Christ in June of 2009. Both had been baptized as infants, but this time it was their decision—what better way to honor the Lord! Ken wants his entire family to feel the way he does about the Lord, and he encourages his grandchildren to continue on the same road he and Barb are traveling.

"Don't worry about me. We'll meet again"—those were some of the last words spoken to Ken by his dying mother. They've been a comfort to him ever since. With the world in such turmoil, the fate of those who haven't yet accepted Christ weighs heavily on Ken's heart: "None of us knows when He's coming back or when we'll die. You could leave your house today and never come back. Many of the events the Lord said would happen in the end times in the book of Revelation are happening today. We should all have a sense of urgency to know for sure where we're going to spend eternity. If heaven is our home, we have nothing to fear."

"I want to know Christ and the power of his resurrection and the fellowship of sharing in his sufferings, becoming like him in his death, and so, somehow, to attain to the resurrection from the dead" (Philippians 3:10-11).

Being diagnosed with end-stage cancer, receiving treatment, and experiencing a miraculous full recovery in just over five months brought Ken closer to the Lord than he'd ever been. It took being faced with losing his very life to realize that dying is truly gain for the believer. Nothing on Earth is worth more than knowing Christ. By placing his trust in Christ alone, Ken experienced the same power that raised Jesus from the dead to live a morally renewed life, dead to sin.

Donele ~ Age 11
Childlike Faith

Does it Make Sense?
By Donele (2009)

Listen to God
Pray to God
Take your problems to God
He listens
He watches
He's always there
To guide you the right way
To heaven
To be there
Heaven is glorious
The angels rejoice
To heaven I come
To heaven, all done
No problems I have
No sins I make
Perfect as God
My sins as white as a flake
My sins are forgiven
Because of God
For sending His Son Jesus
Full of love

To die on the cross
For all sinners
Just like me
So it makes sense
If God would not
Have sent His Son Jesus
We would be with Satan
Not safe
Suffering in hellfire
Not safe
So believe in God
You will have eternal life
In heaven
Which is great
He loves you
He cares for you
So does it make sense?
It makes sense to me
To believe and listen to Jesus

Donele accepted Jesus while writing this poem at the age of nine. She wrote the poem alone in her bedroom without any help from her parents. Donele learned these things about Jesus while attending a Christian school from preschool through the third grade, and from her involvement in AWANA—a youth ministry outreach.

If you ask anyone who knows Donele whether or not she is a Christian, they will respond, "Yes," without hesitation. Uncommonly unselfish for her age, Donele places God and others before herself. She offers to help others without expecting anything in return. Over the years, she has repeatedly forgiven friends who have said hurtful things about her and her parents.

She carries the New Testament in her purse, and has a full-sized Bible at home that she reads daily. God speaks to Donele as she reads His Word. She has even used her Bible to teach unbelieving friends about Jesus. Donele talks to God throughout the day, thanking Him for everyday blessings and going to Him for help when she has problems. When asked who she goes to first when faced with difficulties, she quickly responded: "God."

Donele's dad died at home on September 22, 2011 around ten o'clock at night. After successfully battling lung cancer, he succumbed to chronic obstructive pulmonary disease and congestive heart failure. The night he died, Donele watched her dad get down on his knees and pray; he wanted to make everything right with God. He told Donele not to be angry with God for taking him away from her. Even though she didn't understand why her dad had to go home so soon, Donele's grief didn't turn to anger. Because he believed in Jesus, she knows her dad is in heaven—healthier and happier than he has ever been. Donele looks forward to seeing her dad again someday.

About one month after her dad died, Jesus came to her in a dream. She didn't normally remember her dreams, but she remembered this one. Donele was amazed at how vividly she could recount this very special dream. It went back to the day her dad died. The entire day replayed in her head. She saw her dad lying in the hospital bed in the middle of their living room. She heard him speak his last words to her—expressing his love for her and sharing words of wisdom. Then he gasped for air and took his final breath. Right after he died, she saw nothing but bright white light, brighter than the sun, with yellow rays coming out from the center. And then Jesus appeared. He wore a flowing white robe with a thin, gold cord around His waist. She couldn't help but notice Jesus' beautiful green eyes; they were filled with compassion and love. Jesus approached her and said, "Don't worry, everything will be okay. I'm watching over you and your mom, and I will take care of you." Just then, Donele's mom woke her up and asked why she was crying. They were tears of sadness for losing her dad, and tears of joy that Jesus had come to her. The words spoken by Jesus provided much comfort to Donele in the days and weeks to follow. This wasn't the first time Jesus revealed Himself to her. She remembers seeing Him once before when she was very little—too young to remember any details.

Losing her dad has been really hard, but Donele is still the same friendly, caring girl she has always been. She continues to laugh and enjoy playing with friends. The hardest time for her is at bedtime where she always spent an hour of quality time with her dad each night. Donele cried every night before going to bed for the first two months. Now she cries less and less. She still dearly misses her dad, but believes Jesus will care for her.

Jesus said: "I tell you the truth, unless you change and become like little children, you will never enter the kingdom of heaven. Therefore, whoever humbles himself like this child is the greatest in the kingdom of heaven" (Matthew 18:3-4).

Children have humble and sincere hearts. They are dependent on adults. In the same way, Jesus asks us to trust Him enough to humbly accept our dependence on Him. Do you have the unwavering faith of a child? Who are you most dependent upon? God? People? The things of this world?

Afterword

After reading these stories, you probably noticed several common themes. All forty people have accepted Jesus as their Savior and Lord, surrendered their lives to Him and relinquished their sinful nature, been changed by the power of the Holy Spirit, and have developed a personal relationship with God. Each person's life is much different since accepting Christ.

There is only one path that leads to God: Jesus. He said to His disciples, "I am the way and the truth and the life. No one comes to the Father except through me" (John 14:6). Jesus is very clear that He is the *only way* to God. We can receive Jesus because God calls us to come to Him. Jesus said, "No one can come to me unless the Father who sent me draws him" (John 6:44). The good news for all of us is that God, in His mercy and grace, desires everyone to come to Him: "Everyone who calls on the name of the Lord will be saved" (Romans 10:13).

Even though God has extended the free gift of salvation to us, we do have a decision to make: choosing to receive His free gift and following Jesus or declining His offer and going our own way. God has given us free will, so the choice is ours. He does not make us come to Him. However, as a loving Father, it breaks His heart when we deny Him.

If we decide to accept His gift, we need to believe in Jesus and believe that what He says is true. Praying an empty prayer to be saved will do no good—nor will doing good works, being a good person, or sitting in church every Sunday. God doesn't just listen to what comes out of our mouth or merely watch how we behave—He searches our heart. He knows whether or not we really have faith. "For it is by grace you have been saved, through faith—and this not from yourselves, it is the gift of God—not by works, so that no one can boast" (Ephesians 2:8–9). We can do nothing to earn our salvation; we simply need to receive God's gift through faith in Him.

If you die tomorrow, do you know without a doubt where you will spend eternity? If you hesitated for even a second, you may not be saved. You can be sure of your salvation. Eternity is too long not to be absolutely certain. Romans 10:9–10 states, "That if you confess with your mouth, 'Jesus is Lord,' and believe in your heart that God raised him from the dead, you will be saved. For it is with your heart that you believe and are justified, and it is with your mouth that you confess and are saved."

How will you know when you are saved? One word: *change*. You'll see God transforming you into a new creation, made in the image of Christ Himself. There will be a dramatic change in the way you think, feel, and behave. You will no longer be living for yourself, but for Jesus.

The Bible tells us we are to repent and turn from our sinful ways, choosing to walk with God from then on. This is God's Word on the matter: "No one who is born of God will continue to sin, because God's seed remains in him; he cannot go on sinning, because he has been born of God" (1 John 3:9).

If, after reading these faith-filled stories, you yearn to deepen your relationship with God, you will need to make a concerted effort to do so. Every relationship requires an intentional investment of time. The basic necessities to nurture and grow your relationship with God are daily prayer and Bible reading, along with regular church attendance. (All forty people whose stories you've read do these things regularly.) If you have difficulty understanding the Bible, you may need to find a different version. Simply ask God to give you understanding of His Word—He will gladly grant your request. Just like any relationship, we cannot expect to grow close to God without spending time alone with Him—praying and simply talking to Him about the events of our day and the things on our mind.

Having an intimate relationship with God makes life exciting. Each day is a new adventure. When we truly place our trust in God and surrender *all* to Him, He will guide us to carry out His plans. God's plans are far greater than ours, having eternal consequences for good.

I pray that you will go the right way on the path of your life when God intersects it. Don't worry: if you have taken a wrong turn or two, God will cross your path again . . . and again. He loves you too much to leave you lost and alone, traveling a winding road toward eternal destruction. I look forward to meeting you in heaven and hearing how God intersected your life.

"May the grace of the Lord Jesus Christ, and the love of God, and the fellowship of the Holy Spirit be with you all" (2 Corinthians 13:14).

To God be the glory forever and ever!

About the Author

God intersected Kelli Kossel's life many times before she finally received His free gift of salvation. Because of her intimate and rewarding relationship with God—the Father, Son, and Holy Spirit—Kelli wants others to experience the joy and satisfaction that come from really knowing God in a personal way. She strives to ignite passion for God in others by sharing all that is available to those who follow Jesus.

Intersected is Kelli's first book. Her next book will feature the remarkable story of how she came to God after many years of being pursued by Him.

For over ten years, Kelli has worked as a licensed acupuncturist in her hometown of Oshkosh, Wisconsin. She finds it very rewarding to help people improve their emotional, mental, spiritual, and physical well-being. Kelli's flexible work schedule allows ample time to pursue a Christian writing career.

CPSIA information can be obtained at www.ICGtesting.com
Printed in the USA
LVOW040858120712

289705LV00001B/3/P